ATHEISM

AND THE

CASE AGAINST CHRIST

ATHEISM

AND THE
CASE AGAINST CHRIST

MATTHEW S. McCORMICK

 **Prometheus Books**

59 John Glenn Drive
Amherst, New York 14228–2119

Published 2012 by Prometheus Books

Cover image © 2012 Media Bakery/David Chmielewski/James Mclaughlin
Cover design by Jacqueline Nasso Cook

Inquiries should be addressed to
Prometheus Books
59 John Glenn Drive
Amherst, New York 14228–2119
VOICE: 716–691–0133
FAX: 716–691–0137
WWW.PROMETHEUSBOOKS.COM

16 15 14 13 12   5 4 3 2 1

McCormick, Matthew S., 1966-
    Atheism and the case against Christ / by Matthew S. McCormick.
        p. cm.
    Includes bibliographical references and index.
    ISBN 978-1-61614-581-1 (pbk.: alk. paper)
    ISBN 978-1-61614-582-8 (ebook)
    1. Atheism. 2. Christianity—Controversial literature 3. Christianity and atheism.
I. Title.

BL2747.3.M353 2012
211'.8--dc23

2012013314

Printed in the United States of America on acid-free paper

For Kate, who made the argument from atheism.

CONTENTS

PREFACE

This book is the product of decades of thought, study, debates, lectures, arguments, research, and blogging. There is a long list of people to whom I owe thanks for helping me develop and improve my thinking about the Christian religion.

Several people engaged in careful readings of drafts and provided me with valuable comments, particularly Russell DiSilvestro, Josh May, Ricki Monnier, and Eric Sotnak. Thousands of blog readers have read and commented on early versions of my ideas at the website Atheism: Proving the Negative (provingthenegative.com). Their feedback has been very useful to me.

My Philosophy Department colleagues at California State University have been tremendously helpful. We have created a positive and constructive, yet highly critical atmosphere where we can have protracted and serious philosophical disagreements while remaining friends and collaborators. I owe the maturity of my views to their vigorous resistance. Thomas Pyne, Scott Merlino, Russell DiSilvestro, Randy Mayes, and Christina Bellon deserve special thanks for that. Richard Carrier, John Loftus, and many others are also owed thanks. I would also like to thank my family for their support, encouragement, and inspiration.

Chapter 1

SPEAKING ILL OF JESUS

INTRODUCTION

In this book, I present a case for an unpopular view: we should not believe that Jesus was resurrected from the dead. I also provide an expansion of the arguments against Christianity justifying atheism.

The argument concerning the resurrection can be put simply, although the details will be complicated: we have too little information of too poor quality to warrant our believing that Jesus returned from the dead. One problem for the Christian is internal: believing in Jesus' divinity on the basis of the Gospels in the New Testament cannot be reconciled with the standards of evidence that believers employ in other comparable cases. If we look at the sorts of claims Christians and non-Christians typically accept or reject and the evidence we take to justify those attitudes, some general principles of reasonableness emerge. If these epistemic standards are applied objectively and without bias to the Jesus case, it is clear that we should reject it. Inattention, inconsistency, desire, cultural influences, various aberrations in the human cognitive system, fallacies, and a host of other factors foster this double standard. We will consider a number of these parallel cases where it is clear by the conventions we already employ that we should not believe Jesus came back from the dead. In effect, these cases show that you already don't believe in Jesus, you just don't know it yet.

The case against Christ can also be made by considering the implications of recent research in psychology and cognitive science. Our information about Jesus is communicated to us by the early Christians. But there are good reasons for not believing these early believers. Problems concerning belief formation, human cognitive quirks, memory, social influences, and other psychological issues undermine the reliability of the ancient information we have about Jesus. And since we cannot trust the sources giving us the information, it is not justified or reasonable to accept it.

Some of the problems with believing are epistemological. That is, we have learned that a well-justified conclusion must be based upon a wide, objective aggregation of evidence followed by a balanced evaluation that adequately explores possible counterevidence, alternative hypotheses, and error checking. The process whereby the Jesus story was recorded and transmitted to us fails miserably on these criteria. The religious goal of fostering belief is at odds with the epistemological goal of believing only those conclusions that are justified by the evidence.

There are a number of philosophical reasons that fortify the case against belief. A God who performs miracles to accomplish his ends, prove his divinity, and foster belief is the foundation of the Christian religion—as well as many other religions.[1] But we will discover that miracles are incompatible with the sorts of actions a being such as God would perform. It does not make sense for God to act, accomplish his ends, or express his will by means of miracles. The notion of a violation of the natural order or interruptions of physical law cannot be reconciled with an almighty, all-knowing being. God would not do miracles.

Once the full list of issues is developed, the case against Christ is compelling. Given what we know, the case for Christ is orders of magnitude weaker than it should be to justify believing.

THE CASE FOR ATHEISM

For billions of people, the origin of their belief in God was the Christian religion. Arguably, being a Christian requires, at a minimum, that one believe that Jesus was a divine being who was resurrected from the dead. So, once the arguments for rejecting the resurrection are in place, one of the major pillars of support for modern belief in God will be removed. By extension, we will see that similar worries undermine a long list of other human religious beliefs. Our evidence for concluding that they are of supernatural rather than natural origin is poor in quality and quantity. We already routinely reject other, comparable supernatural claims, even when the evidence is far better. Various quirks of the human cognitive system suggest that neurobiology, psychology, ignorance, fallacies, and historical forces have more to do with the formation of ancient religions than bona fide encounters with the Almighty. That is, for roughly the same reasons, we should reject the authenticity of the ancient religions that claim to be founded on real encounters between God and humanity.

How then do we arrive at the conclusion that there is no God? A distinction between wide atheism and narrow atheism helps. The narrow atheist does not believe in the existence of a particular sort of god. A Christian, for example, is most likely a narrow atheist concerning the existence of Gefjun, the ancient Norwegian goddess of agriculture. A wide atheist, on the other hand, does not believe in any gods—Christian, ancient Norwegian, Islamic, or otherwise. The expanded set of arguments we will consider, then, at the very least, will justify our being narrow atheists regarding a long list of gods that have populated human religions.

The arguments of this book show that it is not reasonable to believe in the resurrection of Jesus; many of the problems undermining Christianity apply to other religions; there are a number of better, natural explanations available to explain the proliferation of human religious movements; God would not perform miracles; faith is not an acceptable justification for believing; and we must reject attempts to redefine God in some nonliteral fashion. All of these conclusions taken together then justify atheism. When it becomes reasonable to reject enough of the gods of various religions, and when we have enough legitimate doubts about other supernatural hypotheses, the conclusion that there are no gods is justified.

There will be much more to say about atheism in the final chapters of this book. For now, it is worth noting that the scope is ambitious. If I am successful, then I will have shown that it is not reasonable to believe in the resurrection or to subscribe to any of the essential supernatural claims of the most widely subscribed ancient religions in human history.

OPPOSITION

Many people will be passionately and vigorously opposed to the project of this book no matter what sort of reasons or arguments I offer. That is unfortunate, particularly because I am in agreement with many believers on a central point. If the typical claims about Jesus are true—he is the son of God, he died for our sins, his forgiveness promises eternal salvation, he was resurrected from the dead, and so on—then he is the most important person in human history. And nothing is more important for us to carefully reflect upon. If what is said about Jesus is true, then that changes everything about our lives, our plans, our fate, and our morality. As C. S. Lewis said, "Christianity, if false, is of no importance, and if true, of infinite importance. The only thing it cannot be is moderately important."[2]

The significance of Jesus is precisely why I am taking the resurrection seriously and treating it with gravity and care. But Lewis is wrong that if Christianity is false, then it is of no importance. Accepting the fundamental claims of Christianity, even if they are mistaken or unreasonable, has a broad impact on a person's life. What Christianity would require us to do, say, and believe is enormously important. Believing would require a radical shift in a person's belief structure by applying a fundamentally different perspective of the world and humanity's place in it. There is a vast difference in the life, plans, priorities, metaphysical views, and worldviews that one should have if there is a paternal, all-powerful creator who offers Christian spiritual and personal salvation. The doctrines of Christian religion would have us see our moral identities, our social structures, and our place in the universe in a deeply different form. And the Christian ideology is not without its downsides. To adopt it affects your social relationships, it may preclude certain friendships or love relationships, and it could have an adverse impact on a number of other facets of a person's life.

But even if one were to argue that believing and being a Christian would have an overall positive impact on a person's life, it would be to miss an important point about the truth. The truth and being reasonable matter. All of your goals, projects, and aspirations directly depend on the truth. Humanity's welfare depends on the extent to which we attend to the truth, among other things. We have a moral and personal responsibility to be honest and accurate with ourselves and with others. In order to have intellectual and moral integrity, we must avoid self-deception. To avoid the truth because it is unpalatable or frightening is intellectual cowardice. Humans cannot achieve fulfillment in an environment that obscures, rejects, or belittles the truth. We cannot give due respect to human rationality and moral autonomy without striving to be as reasonable as possible in all things.

The Christian—as well as many other believers—would ask us to accept something that would radically alter our lives. So a person cannot be faulted for wanting to examine the claims and the evidence for them carefully. The simple point is that people should not dedicate their lives to a mistake. The question of Jesus' resurrection, then, is vitally important because, if true, it would be perhaps the most important event in human history. If it is false, then the Christian religion is built upon a mistake. The Apostle Paul concurs, "If Christ has not been raised, our preaching is useless and so is your faith. More than that, we are then found to be false witnesses about God."[3]

CHRISTIANITY IN AMERICA

The vast majority of Americans are Christians. Recent Gallup polls showed 80 percent of Americans identifying themselves as Christian.[4] Furthermore, 70 percent of Americans polled claim to believe Jesus was resurrected from the dead.[5] Seventy-four percent of the population believes in some form of life after death, with the resurrection of Jesus playing a central role. In addition, 33 percent of Americans believe that the Bible is the literal word of God.[6]

A number of Americans also believe that miracles are quite common. Nineteen percent of the population believes that they receive direct answers to their prayers at least once a week.[7] Thirty-four percent of the population reports having witnessed or experienced a divine healing. And 9 percent report speaking or praying in tongues on a weekly basis.[8]

For millions, the belief in God and the weight of the Christian religion primarily rest upon the miracles Jesus is alleged to have performed. They believe that in first-century Palestine there was a man of Jewish origin who performed miracles, who preached a new message of love and forgiveness, and who claimed to be a divine being—the son of God. At the end of his preaching career, he was tried and executed by the Romans. Three days after his dead body was put into a tomb, Christians believe that he miraculously came back to life. He then appeared to some of his followers, communicated with them, and, finally, miraculously ascended to heaven. This is the most pivotal event in the Christian tradition. It illustrates his divinity, it indicates the eternal life that can be had by his followers, it symbolizes the power of God, and it validates the various metaphysical claims he made about his origins and God. There is very little else that unites the diverse sects of Christian practice. The resurrection of Jesus is the essential foundation upon which all of Christianity is built. If there was no resurrection, then Christianity would be groundless. And if one does not believe in the resurrection, then, arguably, one is not a Christian. This book will argue, among other things, that we should not believe the resurrection occurred, given the information we have.

FAITH

As I see it, one of our central questions is this: Do the people who are the typical believers in the United States—twenty-first-century adults with a modern education and the benefits of the knowledge at our disposal—have adequate grounds to justify their believing that Jesus was a divine being who performed supernatural acts? I find the widespread indifference to this question even more alarming than widespread belief in Jesus. It is not merely that so many people believe but that so many of them find the questions of evidence, justification, or reasonableness to be irrelevant or unimportant regarding an issue of such profound importance. At its extreme, this indifferent attitude manifests as an outright hostility among believers in response to hard questions about their reasons. Inquiries from those of us who have doubts about the grounds that favor Jesus' divinity are viewed by many as angry, intolerant, hateful, or strident. But I will discuss more on the sensitivity to criticism in a moment.

A less extreme view about religious belief invokes faith. We will address the question of faith in more detail in chapter 11, but a brief comment is relevant here. For many, the question of whether there is sufficient evidence to justify belief is beside the point. Instead, they would say they believe on faith. Their use of the term suggests that to believe by faith means believing despite insufficient or contrary evidence. Faith is invoked when there are some reasons to doubt or think that some hoped-for claim is not true. For example, I have faith that my favorite basketball team is not going to lose the championships, even though they are behind and their prospects are dim. Faith is how we describe believing when the evidence by itself, as we see it, does not provide adequate justification, but we are motivated to believe anyway by hope.

A person's faith, particularly with regard to such significant issues, is not a private or inconsequential matter. We should not be willing to ignore the fact that believers adopt ideologies that have dramatic impacts on their lives and the lives of those of us who live in society with them. We should be more troubled by the fact that when the question of justification arises, many of them admit that they cannot give sufficient evidence that would make those beliefs reasonable or warranted. They have accepted all of this on faith, and perhaps they expect us to do likewise. As social and political beings on a planet made smaller everyday by technology, our lives and our fates are deeply intertwined. Those connections place more and more responsibility on each of us for the safety, health, and education of others. The outcome cannot be left to faith if having faith implies believing on the basis of preference or hope in the face of insufficient or contrary evidence.

But the faithful Christian and I do agree about something. If someone's reaction to my argument against Jesus' resurrection is that she has faith that it happened, then it would seem that she is accepting the point. In effect, she is acknowledging that in order to believe in the resurrection, one must ignore the insufficiencies in the evidence and believe anyway. My argument will be that the evidence, all things considered, is insufficient. So we agree on the central point; what remains is to critically evaluate the prospects of believing by faith. If it also turns out that there are serious problems with taking the faith path to belief (and in chapter 11 I will argue that there are), then the foundations of Christianity have been utterly undermined. One problem with faith that will be discussed there is that if the believer decides to ignore the insufficiency of the historical evidence for her view, then the criteria she would have had to sort between acceptable and unacceptable beliefs would be lost. If the faithful believer deems the historical evidence to be irrelevant, then the floodgates would now be open for a long list of other religious and metaphysical views and the believer would have no grounds on which to decide what views would be worthy of believing. If the historical facts do not matter, then Islam, Buddhism, Judaism, Mormonism, Zoroastrianism, and thousands of other religious views would all be on the same footing. And that possible leveling of the decision field would undermine any special claim that Christianity might make on having the truth.

THE IMPLICATIONS OF THE HISTORICAL-JESUS QUESTION

For Christians to take the question of historical evidence seriously, as I am doing here, is an important and positive step. By even engaging in the discussion about whether we have sufficient evidence for the resurrection suggests a number of important points. First, and most obviously, engaging the topic indicates that one thinks that the evidence matters. This is a vast improvement over the host of arational[9] and nonevidential accounts of belief and its functions that have proliferated in the postmodern era. There are Wittgensteinian-, Fideistic-, Kierkegaardian-, Tillichian-, and Plantingan-style approaches (among many others) where, in one form or another, a straightforward appeal to the facts is not considered necessary or even important to the grounding of religious belief. Ultimately, these views are less concerned with the historical evidence than I am. As I see it, the insufficiency of the evidence for the resurrection utterly undermines the whole edifice of Christianity; as these nonevidentialist thinkers see it, the lack of evidence doesn't matter because belief is acquired through some other route, or because of the special status of religious belief in our lives. So for the Christian to take the question of evidence seriously with those views in the background represents a huge step forward. It would seem that the historical believer and I agree about the basics at least: whether we have adequate historical evidence for thinking that Jesus was real and that he returned from the dead after being executed *matters*.

Second, a willingness to consider the historical evidence also suggests that this believer is prepared, at least in principle, to change her mind if that is indicated by the inquiry. Presumably, if she thinks the historical facts support the resurrection, then she would admit that if they had been another way—if the Gospels were different, or if different archeological evidence had been found, or if the facts about how the story of the resurrection came to be known by us were different—then that would warrant our not believing that Jesus was resurrected. And if some new information changes our assessment of the reliability of these historical sources, or if some new historical information comes to light, then we should revise accordingly. The historical Christian cannot have it both ways. She cannot argue that all historical evidence, no matter what it might have turned out to be, supports the thesis or she's not really giving a historical argument at all. And on a related note, it would be a gross example of confirmation bias to only accept or employ those historical facts that support the resurrection while ignoring or rejecting relevant and legitimate information that would undermine it.

If the historical Christian is being intellectually honest, then she must be prepared to accept that the evidence could, in principle, disprove the existence or resurrection of Jesus, too. That's what gives her argument in favor of the historical resurrection its force (if it has any at all). She can say to the nonbeliever, "Look, you're not being reasonable. Here is ample evidence that shows the things I believe are true. When we consider all of the relevant facts, they show that Jesus was real, and he was resurrected. Not believing in the face of this evidence is irrational. So failing to be a Christian is irrational."

A closely related and important question for the historical Christian to consider, then, is "What sort of historical evidence (or lack thereof) would lead you to conclude that Jesus was not resurrected?" If the answer is that there is nothing that could dissuade them, even hypothetically, then there's something seriously amiss. Of course, the same goes for the nonbeliever who argues that there is insufficient historical evidence to prove the resurrection. What would convince the nonbeliever that it did happen? The point is a general one and not a requirement to outline the exact conditions of disproof. For one to believe reasonably that the evidence supports some conclusion then there must be something, at least hypothetically, that could persuade her of the contrary. In this book, I will argue that the evidence we actually have for the resurrection falls far short in terms of quantity and quality of what would generally be needed to meet the burden, and I will sketch out a number of ways in which it could have been vastly better.

Another important point is the historical Christian probably already acknowledges many cases in history where it was alleged that some supernatural event occurred but she does not think we should accept that it actually did occur. There are accounts of magic, spiritual events, witchcraft, demon possession, visions of angels, voices of gods, and miraculous events within historical episodes such as the events at the Salem witch trials, the Inquisition, the founding of many world religions, and elsewhere in religious history. But we do not take them to be real. Richard Carrier points out that in Herodotus's book on the Persian Wars, Herodotus reports without a hint of doubt "that the temple of Delphi magically defended itself with animated armaments, lightning bolts, and collapsing cliffs; the sacred olive tree of Athens though burned by the Persians, grew a new shoot an arm's length in a single day; a miraculous flood-tide wiped out an entire Persian contingent after they desecrated an image of Poseidon; a horse gave birth to a rabbit; and a whole town witnessed a mass resurrection of cooked fish."[10] Many Christians who would defend the resurrection historically would deny Herodotus's mass resurrection of cooked fish as well as the presence of real magic at Salem, black magic during the Inquisition, and Joseph Smith's confrontation with the angel Moroni. One of the theses for which I will argue is that the skeptical principles we apply to historical reports about fantastic, supernatural, and implausible events must be applied with uniformity to all historical cases—not just to those we wish to reject because of prior religious convictions.

I suspect, however, that mind changing is not likely to happen in many believers, even those who insist their belief is based on the historical evidence for Jesus. Many believers will engage in the discussion about the historical Jesus and argue vigorously for the positive conclusion. But no argument and no historical evidence could actually dissuade them in practice. If this is the case, then this discussion is actually undertaken by them in bad faith, as it were. This is a believer for whom the evidence doesn't really matter, despite what she says. Contrary to rational practice, belief comes first, and then evidence is gathered and accepted or rejected on the basis of its conformity to that belief. The interests of being reasonable will be better served by reading this book objectively and fairly and with the intent to get to the truth of the historical question, rather than with the primary intent to refuting its arguments to fortify Christian apologetics.

There is a fallacy that we are all frequently guilty of committing. Let's call it the sliding-scale fallacy. Many believers will happily concur with any pro-Jesus argument from history that they hear while treating any historically skeptical argument about Jesus with an artificially high level of criticism. Prior enthusiasm and commitment to a Christian ideology when brought to the historical question of Jesus create a de facto, non-disconfirmable position. Prohistorical arguments are accepted with less critical scrutiny while antihistorical arguments are met with inordinately high levels of skepticism and criticism.[11]

As a result, this faux-historical believer and the historical nonbeliever are actually playing two very different games, although one or both of them may not realize it. There are no scenarios, even hypothetically, where the faux-historical believer would not affirm the historical resurrection. If she's arguing for the historical evidence but, in practice, wouldn't actually accept a good historical argument against Jesus then, in effect, the only historical arguments she will accept are the ones supporting her conclusion. She believes, and she would believe no matter what the state of the historical facts. So the time and energy spent on the discussion could have been better spent by both parties.

BIAS IN THE ASSESSMENT OF EVIDENCE

We can be more specific about how the deck gets stacked for one's favored conclusions. We now have a mountain of empirical evidence confirming what everyone who has had one of these conversations already knows: humans have a strong tendency to find evidence supporting the conclusions they favor. That is, our beliefs and the evidence we find to justify them are distorted in the direction of our desires. While the bias is not confined to Christians, it often emerges when the believer comes to the historical-Jesus debate with a strong prior conviction that Jesus was real and that he really was resurrected. If a prior enthusiasm or inclination is present, then it is more likely that one will find, filter, or tilt the evidence, consciously or unconsciously, in favor of the prior conviction. Furthermore, the distortions often happen completely without our awareness. Here are two telling questions: How frequently does someone become a Christian as a result of his considering the historical evidence for Jesus' resurrection? By contrast, how often does someone adopt the Christian views held by his parents from his childhood and *then* conclude that there is a compelling historical case for the existence and resurrection of Jesus? Regarding the first question, I'm not asking about how often people are led to Christianity by reading the Bible, but rather from consulting the historical arguments that would establish the assertions in the Bible about the resurrection as being true. The strangeness or unfamiliarity of that first question should, by itself, suggest an answer. It is rare that an impartial person consults the historical evidence and comes to believe that the resurrection happened. Regarding the second question, I submit that it is much more common for belief to come first and historical evidence to be sought out second. And that suggests something else is going on other than an objective, dispassionate, and open-minded consideration of the historical facts.

So the question for all of us (including me) that is more fundamental than "What is the historical evidence for the resurrection?" is: "Did I come to the historical debate to confirm what I already believe, or am I coming to the historical debate prepared to accept the results of applying fair, uniform, and appropriately skeptical standards of reasonableness, whatever results they may indicate?" I do my best in this book to adopt the latter approach, and I ask that my readers do the same.

SCIENCE AND CHRISTIANITY

Christianity has been with us for millennia. What's changed now that bears on the reasonableness of belief? The answer is that we have vastly expanded our knowledge. We have moved into an era of enlightened self-analysis fueled by the expansion of science that affords us a perspective on ourselves and our religious beliefs, which has never been possible before. One result of billions of years of evolution is the human species' possession of a remarkable set of cognitive faculties for solving problems. And the species is unique in that it can employ those cognitive faculties to understand itself and its own history. More specifically, in the last few hundred years, many of the large pieces in the puzzle have fallen into place. For example, in 1929 Edwin Hubble published his paper "A Relation between Distance and Radial Velocity among Extra-Galactic Nebulae" in which he showed the universe is expanding. Extrapolating backward from its rate of expansion made it possible to date the explosive beginning of the universe at approximately 13.7 billion years ago. This is the simplest sort of fact and the justification for it is overwhelming, yet it has taken nearly four billion years in the history of life on this planet for us to reach the point where we are capable of learning this fact and appreciating its implications.

In 1859 Charles Darwin published *On the Origin of Species*, in which he presented a theory of natural selection whereby life on Earth evolved from early simple, self-replicating molecules into the diverse and complex organisms that we now observe three to four billion years later. Through the work of Darwin and Hubble, and countless others in the modern scientific era, a picture of what we are, our natures, our origins, and our place in the universe has begun to come into sharp focus.

As we have come to understand this picture and especially as we have filled in the details about our origins, a tension has developed with some of our earlier religious attempts to model the world. Much of what we have discovered to be true in the world has not been compatible with our ancient religious doctrines. The earth and all of its life was not created in its present form ten thousand years ago.[12] Life was present and evolving for billions of years on earth before humans came onto the scene. Disease is not the result of demon possession, as many religious sources would have had us believe. Moral sentiments and behaviors have their genesis in evolutionary history and are widespread across the animal kingdom. Many behaviors can be traced to complicated neurological and biological disorders that undermine the ancient and oversimplified views about humans' innate moral corruption. What we are learning about our genesis through the process of natural selection has profound implications for our views of human health and well-being. These discoveries are at odds with Christian views of sin, vice, weakness of will, or the magical transmission of moral guilt across centuries from Adam and Eve on to their remote descendants.

Not all of the details have been filled in, of course, but now we know more about what we are than we ever have, and what we are is not what the traditional religious doctrines would have us believe. We are also in a position to understand aspects of the human cognitive system that shed a great deal of light on the question of Jesus and the origins of Christianity. For the most part, our belief in the divinity of Jesus is based upon the information early Christians communicated to us through the Bible. Among other things, my book will show how recent psychological research on a number of our cognitive quirks should lower our estimate of the reliability of the people who originally reported the supernatural events that are the foundation of Christianity. This book will present a battery of arguments, examples, and analogies that should lead a reasonable person to conclude that there is too little evidence and there are too many doubts about the people who communicated the Jesus saga to us. My goals are to show that the biblical evidence isn't good enough to support the essential Christian doctrines about Jesus and to build a larger case for atheism, but I also hope to inspire a desire to be a better critical thinker and to outline some principles and procedures for better rational belief formation, particularly about religion claims and Christianity.

WHY DOES BELIEVING MATTER?

Some people will be indifferent to this project. Why does it matter whether people believe in God or the resurrection of Jesus? Aside from the question of reasonableness and justification, the simple answer is that Christian ideology exercises a significant effect on a person's other beliefs, his moral and political judgments, his decisions, and his activities. And those other beliefs and decisions have a substantial effect on the rest of us. Many believers read the Bible, go to church, pray, and practice Christian rituals. As a result, Christian doctrines infuse believers' worldviews. The ideology influences their votes for school board members, presidential candidates, bond measures, and legislation. It influences their views and votes on same-sex marriage, abortion, stem-cell research, healthcare, and social policies.

In a recent House of Representatives subcommittee hearing on the environment, Rep. John Shimkus assured all of those present that global warming could not be happening because the Bible says that it will not happen:

> I want to start with Genesis 8:21 and 22. "Never again will I curse the ground because of man, even though every inclination of his heart is evil from childhood, and never again will I destroy all living creatures as I have done. As long as the earth endures, seed time and harvest, cold and heat, summer and winter, day and night will never cease." I believe that is the infallible word of God, and that's the way it's going to be for his creation. The second verse comes from Matthew 24. "And he will send his angels with a loud trumpet call, and they will gather his elect from the four winds, from one end of the heavens to the other." The earth will end only when God declares its time to be over. Man will not destroy this earth. This earth will not be destroyed by a flood. . . . I do believe that God's word is infallible, unchanging, perfect.[13]

Shimkus's view about global warming is widely held, and his utter confidence in the truth of statements in the Bible as he understands them is shared by over one hundred million Americans.

Christian values affect whom Christians wage wars with, whom they will make peace with, whom they will kill, whom they will punish, whom they will boycott, whom they will protest, and whom they decide is guilty or innocent in a courtroom. Christian beliefs affect what they teach their children, who absorb those beliefs and then impart them to their children. Religious practice instills beliefs, and those beliefs develop into views about God and his relationship to us. A recent Baylor University study divided conceptions of God into the categories of authoritarian, benevolent, critical, and distant. They found that 31.4 percent of Americans subscribe to an authoritarian view of God, more than any other characterization. And that view seems to fuel views about the United States and our place in world affairs. The study found that nearly one-fifth of all Americans think that God favors the United States in worldly affairs, and that view is strongest among Evangelical Protestants who adopt the authoritarian view of God at a higher rate than other groups.[14] Christian values, for good or ill, affect almost every aspect of the public life lead by the believer in a community with the rest of us. A person's believing should not be treated merely as a personal or private matter having no broader impact. Your beliefs matter to the rest of us.

It could be, of course, that a great many people adopt Christian views that influence their lives and decisions but the net effect of those influences are positive. That view is quite prevalent. Nevertheless, it has been persuasively argued that it is mistaken.[15] But there is a confusion lurking here. Whether believing actually produces a net benefit in a person's life or makes them more inclined to be moral is irrelevant to the question of whether that would justify our taking some claim to be *true*. Prudential considerations do not justify believing, they only create incentive. Believing a claim is taking it to be true. If I believe it, I think it express an accurate state of affairs in the world beyond the belief in my mind. If I believe that Americans did not land on the moon, then I am taking one description of events in the world to be accurate and another to be false. No matter how beneficial it is to possess a belief, a person cannot take those benefits as evidential grounds for thinking the conclusion is true. Nor can having the effect of making one increasingly moral (if believing does have that effect) affect the question of truth. At best, prudential considerations will show that *if* one were to believe, then one might accrue the benefits. If I could get myself to believe that I am being observed by an alien from orbit who is going to destroy me with an atomizer in six weeks if I don't lose twenty pounds, it would be quite beneficial to me. If some peculiar billionaire offered me $500 million to genuinely believe that no Americans landed on the moon, I might find some indirect way like brainwashing or brain surgery to get myself to believe it, but the money does not make the claim true, nor does it give me *evidential* grounds to think it is true. And no one would accept those benefits as grounds for thinking it is true. Calling it true on the basis of interest, particularly when you know better, amounts to lying. The health benefits or the money create an independent set of incentives or motivations to believe, but the truth is an entirely different matter. The problem involves an equivocation between epistemic justification and prudential incentive where the former means "giving reasons to conclude that X is true," and the latter means "providing one with motivations to act or believe in order to achieve some benefit or avoid some loss."

Ironically, C. S. Lewis puts the point even more forcefully than I have:

> But still—for intellectual honour has sunk very low in our age—I hear someone whimpering on with his question, "Will it help me? Will it make me happy? Do you really think I'd be better if I became a Christian?" Well, if you must have it, my answer is "Yes." But I don't like giving an answer at all at this stage. Here is a door, behind which, according to some people, the secret of the universe is waiting for you. Either that's true or it isn't. And if it isn't, then what the door really conceals is simply the greatest fraud, the most colossal "sell" on record. Isn't it obviously the job of every man (that is a man and not a rabbit) to try to find out which, and then to devote his full energies either to serving this tremendous secret or to exposing and destroying this gigantic humbug? Faced with such an issue, can you really remain wholly absorbed in your own blessed "moral development"?[16]

My central focus here will be the question of grounds that do or could justify us in thinking it is true that Jesus came back from the dead, not the unrelated question of whether believing it is good for us. The point is that Christian belief informs and affects a great many of a person's other beliefs, decisions, and actions. If what I allege is correct and there are insufficient reasons to support Christianity, then we aren't entitled to claim or believe it is true, no matter what the benefits may be. The discussion of Jesus will give us an opportunity to develop a case for why being reasonable is important as well as an opportunity to develop some principles of reasonable belief formation. We will return to the question of what I call nonliteral belief in Jesus later, in chapter 12.

MIRACLES

This book focuses on the question of justifying miracles, particularly the alleged resurrection of Jesus. While it is common to label almost any fortuitous event a miracle, we will follow the philosophical convention and take a miracle to be a violation of the laws of nature, in other words, an event that, had the ordinary course of physical, chemical, and biological patterns continued, would not have occurred.[17] Walking on water, returning from the dead, and spontaneous healing of disease are paradigm examples.

At least since David Hume, philosophers have seen the central problem of the Christian religion as miracles.[18] Hume, in one of the most influential and widely accepted arguments in modern philosophy, gave a powerful argument that we should not accept testimony of a miracle occurring except in the most extraordinary circumstances. That is, Hume did not argue directly that miracles as such are impossible. Rather, Hume argued that when someone tells you he has witnessed a miracle it will almost always be far more likely that he is mistaken, lying, or confused. It would have to be more unlikely that the testimony is mistaken than the miracle is real for it to be reasonable to accept it. So the conclusion that no miracle occurred will be better justified in the vast majority of testimony cases.

My discussions of the miracles of Jesus do not presuppose or build directly upon Hume's arguments. Nor do my arguments presume that miracles cannot, in principle, occur. For the sake of argument, I operate with the assumption that there are no conceptual or logical contradictions with the occurrence of a miracle. And for the sake of argument, we can even accept a much lower threshold of proof for testimony that a miracle has occurred than Hume's "greater miracle that is it false" standard for evaluating testimony.[19] We don't need to go as far as Hume to see how bad the evidence for Christianity is.

I will argue that by the conventional standards of belief, evidence, and critical evaluation we already employ, the Jesus miracles, specifically Jesus' resurrection, do not pass muster. That is, for many if not most of us, given the evidence and the set of decision making practices we already implicitly or explicitly use, we have abundant grounds for rejecting the foundation of Christianity. The Christian miracles certainly do not meet Hume's standards, but *they do not even meet our own, less stringent standards for extraordinary, supernatural events.* You already reject the resurrection of Jesus. Believing in the resurrection of Jesus is inconsistent because it conflicts with our other beliefs and the standards we normally employ that lead us to reject analogous claims.

With Jesus, we are guilty of adopting a double standard. In other comparable cases we demand a relatively high standard of proof for believability, but we appear to be giving Jesus a free pass.

WHY DO WE HAVE TROUBLE ENTERTAINING HARD QUESTIONS ABOUT RELIGIOUS BELIEF?

Before we move on to the explanation of my arguments, we should reflect on why we find it so difficult to engage in critical evaluation of religious belief. One reason we are sensitive is because in American culture, and perhaps elsewhere, our religious affiliations have come to be treated as quasi-ethnic identities, and, with that, objections to the truth of religious doctrines or the questions about the evidence supporting them are frequently construed as personal attacks. We say that someone is from a Christian family or from a Jewish family. Particularly when we identify children as one or the other, as Richard Dawkins has pointed out, we are treating their religious affiliations as something inherited. She got it from her parents, like she got their blue eyes, their Italian ancestry, or a genetic condition. ("Goodness, my Lutheranism is acting up. I need to sit down for a minute.")

When someone says, "I was raised Catholic," or "My family has been Buddhist for centuries, and the views we hold are . . . ," the claim could easily be substituted with "I am from an Irish family," or "My father is Persian." And we tend to think of the resulting connection to the religion of our parents as something we are stuck with; it's in our blood. People often will offer explanations of religious beliefs by saying that So-and-So was "raised Anglican," as if his upbringing inflicted or caused him to be a certain way and nothing can change that now.

There's a mistake lurking here. Imagine if someone said, "Well, I was raised as a serial killer, and we believe that more pain is better," "I come from a long line of pedophiles, and we have always done . . . ," or, "Mom always said to hang them upside down to get all the blood out," and so on.

My point is that being raised a particular way doesn't provide us with any justification whatsoever for its being reasonable, just, sensible, or moral.

Whether the belief is reasonable is a separate question from how one was raised. The comment stems from a fundamental confusion between the causes of belief and the justifications of belief. Analyzing a belief in yourself or in others as an effect of external causes treats a person as a helpless machine—they can no more help what they are or what they believe, in this sense, than a dog can change its breed. The dangerous side, of course, is that many people feel that appealing to their families or cultural backgrounds is all the justification they could ever need for their views or behaviors. If it is used as a defense, it suggests that the fact you were raised that way effectively eliminates any further discussion of whether one should actually believe or do it. It should be clear that even if external forces played a role, finding a particular belief in yourself as a result doesn't entitle you to say or think the claim is true. Likewise, arguing that a belief is the product of environmental causes does not entitle the critic to conclude it is false. Only what philosophers call *epistemic justification* will do either for us. The question should be, "What is the evidence or the reasons indicating it is true?" and not "What were the external causes that installed the belief in him?"[20]

The conflation of religious affiliation and ethnic identity has had several unfortunate side effects. It skews our ability to think clearly about contrary positions. Personal sensitivities wound around religious views lead to perceiving doubters as angry, intolerant, spiteful, or strident. And the preoccupation with their tone eclipses the real issues. Many of the negative responses to the works of the New Atheists—Richard Dawkins, Sam Harris, Daniel Dennett, and Christopher Hitchens—have attacked them on just these grounds. Criticisms of tone and style tend to replace a concern about whether we actually have good reasons to think there actually is a God:

> But Dawkins's avowed hostility can make for scattershot reasoning as well as for rhetorical excess.[21]

> Unfortunately, Harris too often allows his anger at this continued deference to unreason to colour his tone, slipping into an incredulous sarcasm.[22]

> In his own opinion, Dennett is a hero. He is in the business of emancipation, and he reveres himself for it.[23]

A less than cheery demeanor may negatively affect one's overall rhetorical success with an audience, particularly about sensitive and personal matters, but it is irrelevant to the truth or reasonableness of what one is saying. In too many of the critical treatments of atheist works, these analyses of tone and the atheist's emotional vigor have replaced a serious contemplation of the issues and arguments. And I maintain that it is the comingling of religious ideology with our cultural or ethnic identities that is responsible for the disproportionate sensitivity to criticism in believers.

Running religious beliefs together with ethnic identity also seems to be related to some chilling quasi-ethnic prejudice in believers against atheists. In a recent study, Penny Edgell, Joseph Gerteis, and Douglass Hartman found that Americans had a worse opinion of atheists than of Muslims, immigrants, gays and lesbians, or any other minority group named in the study. Americans also were less willing to have their children marry atheists than any other group, and they see atheists as a greater threat to the American way of life. "Atheists, who account for about 3 percent of the U.S. population, offer a glaring exception to the rule of increasing social tolerance over the last 30 years," says Edgell.[24] Believers are tweaked by having people who disagree with them in their midst. At the very least, the believer ought to be concerned that his own animosity toward atheists can produce a possible bias against critically evaluating his own religious views. That social hostility stifles an important safeguard. In an atmosphere that is not open to critical inquiries about religious belief, poor thinking runs amok. For whatever reasons, enthusiasm, passionate commitment, and fervent engagement are our norms about religious matters, and when that runs to excess it can turn into a frightening zeal. Remove the stop guard of critical analysis and it becomes dangerous. Create an atmosphere of scathing rebuke, rejection, or condemnation of doubt or doubters and you stifle the only means of restraint. Sam Harris has commented that "there is no society in human history that ever suffered because its people became too reasonable."[25]

Part of our hands-off sentiment about religiousness may also arise from a concern to be respectful and honor the rights of individuals. Of course, there are good reasons to be respectful and honor individual freedoms. But we will benefit more, and ultimately we will show more respect for a person, if we take his belief seriously and try to understand why it is true (or false) or reasonable (or unreasonable), and not be satisfied merely with "I was just raised that way." We should not let the accounting of a person's beliefs and practice slide in ourselves or in others. These matters are too important to all of us to let the accidents of social conventions prevent us from examining ideas critically. Writing off someone's belief as the installed product of his environment or refusing to analyze it, no matter how outlandish, treats him with less respect than his intellect, rationality, and moral autonomy deserve. W. K. Clifford puts the point with his characteristic zeal:

> Every time we let ourselves believe for unworthy reasons, we weaken our powers of self-control, of doubting, of judicially and fairly weighing evidence. We all suffer severely enough from the maintenance and support of false beliefs and the fatally wrong actions which they lead to, and the evil born when one such belief is entertained is great and wide. But a greater and wider evil arises when the credulous character is maintained and supported, when a habit of believing for unworthy reasons is fostered and made permanent. . . . What hurts society is not that it should lose its property, but that it should become a den of thieves, for then it must cease to be society. This is why we ought not to do evil, that good may come; for at any rate this great evil has come, that we have done evil and are made wicked thereby. In like manner, if I let myself believe anything on insufficient evidence, there may be no great harm done by the mere belief; it may be true after all, or I may never have occasion to exhibit it in outward acts. . . . The danger to society is not merely that it should believe wrong things, though that is great enough; but that it should become credulous, and lose the habit of testing things and inquiring into them; for then it must sink back into savagery.[26]

People can't help which ethnicity they are, so it is unfair to criticize them or discriminate against them because they are Italian, African American, or Kurdish. But people aren't similarly just endowed with their religious views. They can (and often should) change their minds. If we treat religious affiliation with the respect due to ethnic heritage, then, in effect, we have given religious piety a blank check. Under the protective umbrella of respect for persons, religious zeal fuels ideas and behaviors; they propagate, they get fostered in children, and continue unchecked to future generations.

Without any sort of cross-checking or external reference, many of us are prone to form wilder and wilder ideas. If religious belief has a free pass from critical scrutiny, it can spiral out of control. Nearly 80 percent of the population believes in the second coming of Jesus, with 20 percent of them who think it will happen in their lifetimes.[27] For a brief period during the 2008 presidential election, John Hagee, a prominent evangelical preacher who has millions of faithful followers, publicly endorsed John McCain for president. Hagee claims that Russia and some Islamic states will invade Israel soon, precipitating the final battle of Armageddon with the anti-Christ, who will be the leader of the European Union. McCain declined Hagee's endorsement when it was revealed that Hagee had frequently identified the pope and the Roman Catholic Church as the whore of Babylon, and Hagee and his followers were seeking to accelerate Armageddon for the sake of the Second Coming. None of us can afford to let religious ideologies remain unchecked when those ideas will inform so much of the Christian's life in the community we all share.

Certainly a person's genetic background cannot be legitimate grounds for finding fault with him. And we should be tolerant of the free and open exchange of ideas. We all need to be able to get those ideas out there, including the radical, unorthodox, and antiestablishment ones, so we can have an open, intelligent, and critical discussion to sort them out. But that's the irony. In the interests of freedom of religion, religious ideologies have become insulated from the open exchange of ideas that might otherwise inject some sensibility and restraint. The result is that some believers teach their children that the earth was created six thousand years ago, angels are real, girls should not get an education, women should not leave the house uncovered or without a male family escort, or that the wine and crackers magically turn into flesh and blood.

We're confused about what religious freedom is. As many people see it, their right to freely pursue religion amounts to an entitlement to always have their religious beliefs treated as sensible or beyond criticism. Sometimes the adherent will defend a belief with the retort, "But you can't prove that my belief is false," "I'm entitled to my opinion," or "I have a right to believe what I want to." But there is a conflation of what is permissible here with what is reasonable. A right to be physically unrestrained in the exercise of religion does not give us grounds for thinking that just any religious idea is true or reasonable.

The confusion arises from an asymmetry between other physical rights we have and the so-called right to believe ("I'm entitled to my opinion" or "I have a right to believe what I want"). We have a legal and moral right to assemble, a right to free movement, a right to leave the country, and so on. And these rights preserve our ability to pursue our activities without physical obstruction from others. Nor do we have to provide any rationale to anyone else for assembling or for our movements. But the physical right to travel anywhere is not analogous to a mental right to go to any belief space we choose. Having the legal and moral right to say or do a wide range of things should not be confused with having epistemic justification for them or grounds for thinking they are true. You are entitled to pursue a much wider range of activities than is wise, reasonable, morally responsible, correct, or true. Your right to free speech entitles you to stand up in a public forum and shout that $2 + 2 = 5$, but obviously that doesn't make it true. There is no external restraint preventing you from falling down on your knees and worshipping the family dog as the all-being and master of the universe. You can burn your house down as a sign of dedication to him, get yourself tattooed from head to foot with images of him, or go wait on a mountaintop for him to come take you to the next realm of existence. But doing all of that would be foolish. Given what you know about the world, such beliefs and activities are clearly irrational, even though you are entitled to espouse them.

Furthermore, a person's freedom of religion does not impose any obligation on others to refrain from denying the tenets of her religious ideology. None of a person's rights entitle her to have the rest of us nod our heads and agree. We can point it out when we think she is mistaken, and vice versa. For all of our sakes, *we should*.

So the existence of this book and the arguments herein are not an affront or an insult to anyone's religious rights. My articulating views that are contrary to the believer's are not precluded by any duty I have to him. In fact, these arguments take religious belief seriously. This book will be a large exercise in what Sam Harris has called "conversational intolerance," or a respectful unwillingness to accept claims that do not square with the evidence.[28] We will close this chapter with another comment by Harris that echoes the sentiment:

Whether a person is religious or secular, there is nothing more sacred than the facts. Either Jesus was born of a virgin, or he wasn't; either there is a God who despises homosexuals, or there isn't. It is time that sane human beings agreed on the standards of evidence necessary to substantiate truth-claims of this sort. The issue is not, as [intelligent design] advocates allege, whether science can "rule out" the existence of the biblical God. There are an infinite number of ludicrous ideas that science could not "rule out," but which no sensible person would entertain. The issue is whether there is any good reason to believe the sorts of things that religious dogmatists believe—that God exists and takes an interest in the affairs of human beings; that the soul enters the zygote at the moment of conception (and, therefore, that blastocysts are the moral equivalents of persons); etc.[29]

I can only add that we either have good reasons for thinking that Jesus came back from the dead or we don't. If we don't, as I allege, then Christianity is based on a grand mistake.

Chapter 2

THE HISTORY OF THE JESUS STORY

D
efending any particular account of the history of the information we have about Jesus is a complicated and contentious affair. Compared to events like the Revolutionary War, the body of information on Jesus is very small and much of it is fragmented and ambiguous. The events occurred two thousand years ago and were relatively isolated in scope. But the field of research on the topic is filled with detailed disagreements about what can be inferred from this limited body of information.

I will not defend either of the extreme views that the Gospels are the inerrant records of Jesus' life inspired by God or that they are completely fabricated mythology. The best summary of what we know is much more complicated. A brief review of the current scholarly consensus will give us a framework within which we will consider our central questions in the later chapters.[1]

A consensus has developed about some aspects of the history of the manuscripts and what they report. First, Jesus (the existence of such a person is an active point of some disagreement) is thought by most to have been executed around 30–35 CE. The first four books of the Christian New Testament—Matthew, Mark, Luke, and John—and some of the letters of Paul are the primary sources of information we have about the events. By most accounts, Mark was the first Gospel to be written, and it is thought to have been authored around 65 CE. Matthew was written between 70 and 100 CE, and Luke was written around 70 CE. Matthew and Luke borrowed heavily from Mark and possibly another source or sources, now lost, commonly called "Q."

37

The existence of a single Q source is a hypothesis intended to explain the similarities in the additions Matthew and Luke make to the material they got from Mark. Most scholars believe the original Gospel of Mark ended at chapter 16, verse 8, with the women fleeing from the tomb in fear. The rest of Mark (chapter 16, verses 9–20) that details the resurrected Jesus' visits to his followers is now thought to have been added by an unknown author or authors sometime in the 100s. The Gospel of John appears to be more independent and was written around 90–110 CE, so it was written fifty-five or more years after Jesus' death. It is substantially different in tone, purpose, and detail from the other Gospels.

Up until a few hundred years ago, the traditional view was that all of the Gospels were written by the followers of Jesus for whom the books are named. But the view now, on the basis of modern work in history and Bible scholarship, is that none of the Gospels was written by the apostle to whom it is attributed. Their authors are unknown. Furthermore, it is widely agreed that none of the authors were eyewitnesses to the events themselves. They heard the stories from others and recorded them many years after the alleged events transpired.

The number of people through whom the stories passed before they were written down in the Gospels is unknown. It could have been two, twenty, or two hundred. We do not know how many different sources the authors consulted, or the degree to which they sought to corroborate the stories they heard. We do not know how much possibly disconfirming information they sought out or considered.

A great deal has been written and said about the Jewish oral tradition and its ability to codify and then transmit laws, rules, and stories from master to student with high fidelity. That is, the Jews had a verbal tradition of deliberately and carefully passing on important information, particularly religious law and its amplifications, from rabbi to student. In the intervening years between Jesus' alleged resurrection and when the stories were written down, there would have been a great deal of discussion, sharing of stories, and retelling of events among his followers. And it has been argued that at least some of what we have now bears the mark of being transmitted by means of this rabbinical method, such as Paul's brief recounting of the resurrection in First Corinthians. Some believe that the reliability of the oral-tradition method bolsters the reliability of the Gospel stories' transmission across the gap from when the events occurred to when they were written down several decades later. The full details about what parts of the stories were from the oral tradition and what parts were not, and to what extent the oral tradition contributed to the resulting Gospel stories, are unknown.

The challenge of employing the Jewish oral tradition to fortify the reliability of the Gospels is that Jesus was thought to be a radical new teacher by the majority of Jews and they would have rejected claims that he was the messiah. It was Jews who rejected Jesus and called for his execution, after all. It would be peculiar that a set of stories about a radical preacher would have been incorporated so quickly and preserved in a conservative tradition used for preserving the most time-honored elaborations on the Jewish law. And we know that a great deal of the information about Jesus spreading among early Christians was not being repeated within this tradition—it was being spread by ordinary word of mouth among converts. We will consider several issues concerning the fidelity of verbal transmission later in chapters 4 and 5.

Paul's letter that became First Corinthians is thought to have been written between 50 and 60 CE. In it, he makes a brief mention of the resurrection of Jesus. Paul does not clearly claim to be, nor is he widely thought to be, an eyewitness to the event (which would have occurred at least twenty years earlier), so we can assume that he also acquired his information about the resurrection through an unknown number of verbal sources with an unknown level of reliability. But some have argued that the best way to understand some of Paul's comments is to interpret them as though he is claiming to have seen the resurrected Jesus himself.

It is relevant to note that none of the original Gospels or other New Testament documents has survived. That is, we cannot actually consult any of the first written sources themselves. Bart Ehrman says:

> In fact we do not have the original copies of any of the books of the New Testament or of any of the other Christian writings. . . . Nor do we have copies made directly from the originals, copies made from the copies of the originals, or copies made from the copies of the first copies. Our earliest

manuscripts (i.e., handwritten copies) of Paul's letters date from around 200
C.E., that is, nearly 150 years after he wrote them. The earliest full manuscripts of the Gospels come from about the same time, although we have
some fragments of manuscripts that date earlier. One credit-card-sized frag-
ment of John discovered in a trash heap in Egypt is usually dated to the first
half of the second century. Even our relatively full manuscripts from around
the year 200 are not preserved intact, however. Pages and entire books were
lost from them before they were discovered in modern times. Indeed, it is
not until the fourth century, nearly 300 years after the New Testament was
written, that we begin to find complete manuscripts of all of its books.[2]

So to determine what is reasonable to believe about Jesus, we have a fragmented
collection of copies of copies of hearsay reports dating from the second and
third centuries and later, not the original writings from thirty to ninety years
after Jesus' death. As we will see, these details add to our doubts about the
reliability of the resurrection stories.

After the fourth or fifth century, the number of copies of these documents
and other Christian writings exploded. We have several thousand copies of
these early collected works. The proliferation of copies has led some to remark
that the New Testament is the best attested book of all ancient documents,
and more reliable as a source of truth as a result. This is a mistake, however.
What we have that is closest to the source is a tiny handful of fragments—they
would all fit in a shoebox—that are copies of copies of copies of documents
from one hundred to three hundred years after their sources were originally
written. Then we begin to find more copies in a greater state of completion in
the next few centuries until the number of surviving, complete manuscripts
of the New Testament explodes into the thousands. But any connection to the
originals is built upon the slender bottleneck of just a few of the earlier manuscript fragments. So we should not think the preponderance of copies validates
the content any more than making millions of copies of a Sherlock Holmes
book proves he was a real person, or that multiple copies of a document after
it is written somehow improves the accuracy of the original contents. The
copies are only as reliable as the few originals upon which they were based.
And those originals are only as reliable as the sources from which they were
derived. Ehrman says, "even if scholars have by and large succeeded in recon-

structing the New Testament, this, in itself, has no bearing on the truthfulness of its message. It simply means that we can be reasonably certain of what the NT authors actually said. . . . Whether or not any of these ancient authors said anything that was *true* is another question, one that we cannot answer simply by appealing to the number of surviving manuscripts that preserve their writings."[3]

The Gospels and the other books that would eventually become the New Testament were not the only Christian writings circulating and being copied in the early centuries. Early followers produced a large number of other manuscripts, letters, and documents as the movement grew. As alternating waves of persecutions and surges in popularity of Christianity swept through the region, churches would make copies of the works they considered spiritually important to share with their neighboring churches, or people would burn or destroy all their copies of some works. Manuscripts proliferated freely as they were copied and transported, and a complicated organic growth pattern unfolded. By the third and fourth centuries, many believers had begun to settle on a rough canonical collection of works that would eventually become the New Testament. Groups began to make a deliberate effort to sift through and organize the writings, separating the ones they found acceptable from the ones they did not. A variety of criteria drove this separation. Some writings were looked on favorably on ideological grounds; some were deemed heretical. Long forgotten political, social, and religious disputes also led to the propagation of some and the suppression of others. So it is significant to our discussion that the canonical New Testament, which is the cornerstone of modern Christianity, is the product of a long, contingent series of historical developments. The twenty-seven books, including the Gospels, we now have were just a few among hundreds or thousands of Christian documents that circulated among the early followers (and enemies) of Jesus. Many of these sources are now lost or destroyed. Some survive, and many offer surprisingly different accounts of the early Christian movements. In 367 CE, Athanasius, the bishop of Alexandria, was one of the first to draw a hard line between these various sources. He listed the now-familiar list of twenty-seven works as the complete teachings that should not be added to or taken from. Eventually, this list became the canonized set of sources with other early Christian works excluded as heretical, false, forgeries, or otherwise irrelevant. This means that for more than three hundred years after Jesus, a multitude of alternate Christian sources containing different accounts and doctrines circulated until one group of them was carved out of the noise and sanctioned. That these other sources existed and that they differed from the canonical group will prove relevant to our assessment of the virtues of the subset we are considering about Jesus' resurrection. We will see how, more specifically, in the next two chapters.

During the period before the New Testament was canonized, many liberties were taken with the manuscripts.

> Until the beginning of the fourth century the text of the NT developed freely. It was a "living text," unlike the text of the Hebrew Old Testament, which was subject to strict controls because (in the oriental tradition) the consonantal text was holy. And the NT text continued to be a "living text" as long as it remained a manuscript tradition, even when the Byzantine church molded it to the procrustean bed of an ecclesiastically standardized and officially prescribed text. Even for later scribes, for example, the parallel passages of the Gospels were so familiar that they would adapt the text of one Gospel to that of another. They also felt themselves free to make corrections in the text, improving it by their own standards of correctness, whether grammatically, stylistically, or more substantively. This was all the more true of the early period, when the text had not yet attained canonical status, especially in the earliest period when Christians considered themselves filled with the Spirit.[4]

The liberality involved in the reproduction and distribution of new manuscripts in early Christian writings must be considered in our assessment of the reliability of the sources. And it must be considered in our evaluation of the extent to which the Jewish oral tradition would have accurately preserved the details of the Jesus stories.

We can divide the history of the information about Jesus into periods where there are different reliability concerns. From Jesus' alleged death and resurrection until the Gospels were written, the stories appear to have been transmitted verbally from person to person until they were written down by the Gospel authors thirty to one hundred years later. These manuscripts and many more were copied and began to spread among Christian groups, and, no doubt, people continued to talk and share accounts verbally. Many copy generations and hundreds of years later, some copies of the Gospels would be made that would find their way through history, in varying states of decay, to us in the twenty-first century. Along the way, Christians would settle on a New Testament of accepted books while rejecting other books. Eventually, copies of this New Testament would proliferate and come to dominate the Christian religion and doctrine. More alterations and errors would be introduced during this labyrinthine path through the centuries. A great deal of detective work has been done on the copies of these texts:

> What is striking is that when we do [compare the 5,400 copies of the early New Testament], we find that no two of these copies (except the smallest fragments) agree in all of their wording. There can be only one reason for this: the scribes who copied the texts changed them. Nobody knows for certain how often they changed them, because no one has yet been able to count all of the differences between the surviving manuscripts.[5]

The revisions, many of which have been identified in the manuscripts, include changes in spelling; rearrangements of words; and additions of notes from the margins into the text itself. There are accidental changes in punctuation, spaces, and paragraphs. Some changes appear to be deliberate ideological and interpretative changes. Many changes are ecumenical and theological.

> One of the most common kinds of intentional changes involved the "harmonization" of one text to another, that is, changing one passage in one book to make it conform to a similar passage in another. This kind of change is particularly common in the Synoptic Gospels, since these three books tell so many of the same stories in slightly (or significantly) different ways.[6]

So, between us and the alleged resurrection, we can consider five groups of people through whom the information passed: the alleged witnesses, the people who repeated the story until the authors recorded it, the authors of the Gospels, the people who copied the Gospels, and the people who canonized the modern New Testament from a background of thousands of other documents. For the remainder of this chapter, and several of those that follow, we will consider specific problems introduced at each of these stages of transmission that undermine the reliability of the information we now have.

A SUMMARY OF THE HISTORY OF THE INFORMATION WE HAVE ABOUT JESUS

So if we are being careful about what we know and what we don't, here is a short version of what we have specifically concerning the resurrection of Jesus. Allowing that there was a person known as Jesus who was executed between 30 and 35 CE, there were some events surrounding his death. Some people are alleged to have seen some of those events. These people repeated stories about those events to an unknown number of other people who also repeated the stories over the course of several decades. Then, around 65 CE, the author of the book that is now known as the Gospel of Mark wrote down an account of those events that he heard from an unknown source (or sources). Some other unknown authors in the following decades wrote Matthew and Luke, copying their stories from Mark and another source (or sources). Some years later, another work was written that was later attributed to John. During the second century, the ending of the Gospel of Mark, containing stories about the resurrected Jesus, was added by an unknown author (or authors). Possibly as early as twenty years after Jesus' death, Paul was also writing letters to early Christians in which he described the events he had heard about from an unknown number of other sources who were removed from the actual events by an unknown number of steps.

These early documents and many others with very different stories freely circulated and multiplied for hundreds of years, during which time an unknown number of additional people corrected, "harmonized," added, subtracted, and altered their copies. After around three hundred years of this chaotic and organic growth of the writings, some Christians deliberately collected one set of stories and writings they chose to accept as official doctrine while destroying, ignoring, or rejecting a host of other writings with different teachings and accounts of the early years. Even though we believe many of these works were written down in 65 CE and later, we are reconstructing them from a number of pieces and sources from much later. The earliest actual manuscripts we have are fragmented copies of copies of copies of some of these writings from the 200s and later.

This picture is brief and rough; the discussion of the details is vast, and there are controversies among accomplished historians, anthropologists, and Bible scholars concerning every point in this sketch.

With this sketch as background, what should an ordinary person who wishes to form a reasonable opinion about Christianity's central doctrine—the resurrection of Jesus—believe is true? If it is necessary to become more knowledgeable about the labyrinthine details of contemporary biblical scholarship and to develop a defensible position about most or all of its controversies in order to draw reasonable conclusions about Jesus' resurrection, then the vast majority of Christians and others (including me) are already guilty of being unreasonable. So, if in the view of a reader, my arguments should be rejected because First Corinthians should be dated ten years earlier, or because said reader is convinced the author of Mark or Paul was an eyewitness, then the admittedly weaker biblical grounds of belief for many (most?) Christians should be rejected, too. If believing in Christian doctrine requires grounding in more or different Bible scholarship than I have given, then many, perhaps even most, self-identifying Christians have ungrounded belief. This critical reader and I will agree at least in the conclusion that it is unreasonable to believe many Christian doctrines on the grounds upon which many Christians depend.

We need not delve much deeper into biblical scholarship because many of the problems I will raise in the following chapters, or some minor variation of them, will apply equally well to a broad range of particular views about the history of the Bible. And that range extends well beyond the cluster of consensus points from above that have been accepted among respected scholars. Many of the detailed differences between views about the history of the manuscripts will not be the sort that would disarm the general applicability of my arguments to the prospects of believing basic Christian doctrines. That is, if a reader takes issue with a number of the rough details of the history of the resurrection story as I have given it, those disagreements should not derail serious consideration of the arguments that follow. As we will see, the objections to the resurrection in this book are substantial and global. They are serious enough that even if the details about the resurrection information turn out to be much more favorable to the resurrection than I have summarized them, it still will not be reasonable to accept that Jesus came back from the dead. The case for rejecting the resurrection is overdetermined by a wide margin.

Furthermore, I also argue that we can form a reasonable view about the reality of the resurrection on the basis of the information just outlined and by employing the conventional standards of evidence and belief formation we use every day. We will take this rough sketch of the Christian-manuscript history as our starting point.

WHAT DO THESE ACCOUNTS SAY ABOUT THE RESURRECTION?

What do the Christian manuscripts say more specifically about the resurrection of Jesus? A careful reading reveals that they are surprisingly conflicted. In the Gospel of Luke, Mary Magdalene, Joanna, Mary (James' mother), and other women go to the tomb. They find it open. There, they talk to two men in shining garments and then go tell what they have seen to the other disciples. In the Gospel of Mark, Mary Magdalene, Mary (James' mother), and Salome go to the tomb, find it open, and see one man sitting inside in white clothes. They talk to him, then they run away in fear and do not say "any thing to any man; for they were afraid." In the book of Matthew, Mary Magdalene and the "other" Mary go to the tomb. A great earthquake opens it by rolling the stone away. They go inside and see an angel of the Lord in white. Then they leave with fear and joy and run to bring the disciples word. In the book of John, Mary Magdalene by herself finds the tomb open. She goes and gets Simon Peter and another disciple. The two of them go to the tomb and find it empty. They leave, but Mary stays, crying. Two angels appear to her and then Jesus himself appears to her. She talks to him and goes to tell the rest of the disciples. In First Corinthians, Paul says that Cephas was the first one to see Jesus. Then five hundred people saw him, then James saw him, and finally all of the apostles.

The sources we have differ on every important detail about the resurrection. The order of events, the events themselves, the people present, and the supernatural events diverge in every account: Is the tomb empty? Does it have one person in it? Two? Are they angels? Or someone else? Was the tomb closed or open when they found it? Who found it? Who did they tell? What did they do when they found it? They even differ on the single most important question for the entire Christian religion: Was Jesus in the tomb or not? We should keep these details in mind for several discussions to come.

THE TEXAS-SHARPSHOOTER FALLACY AND THE BIBLE

Before we move on, it is appropriate to consider one form of confusion regarding the New Testament that is quite common. Philosophers and critical-thinking teachers frequently explain the Texas-sharpshooter fallacy. The Texas-sharpshooter gets his rifle and fires a round at the side of a barn. Afterward, he draws a big circle around the bullet hole, and announces proudly that he's a perfect marksman.

It has become common for some Christians to proclaim the virtues of the Bible. It has a singular, coherent narrative, they say. And there is general agreement about the events or doctrines across many books, many authors, and many centuries. Or they believe we should be struck by the consistency between the different Gospel accounts of Jesus' life. (These views persist despite the stark differences described in the previous section.) Believers urge that we should marvel at Jesus as the culmination of many Old Testament prophecies about the messiah. They ask the rhetorical question, "How else could so many people over so many centuries come to agree about so much and have such an integrated view about what God is?" The book itself is presented as evidence that the book is profoundly accurate.

Our brief sketch of the history of the manuscripts that became the Bible shows that these modern believers are part of a very long, complicated historical sharpshooter fallacy. There were hundreds of early Christian writings circulating and being copied among the early followers. These documents told a wide range of stories about Jesus, God, and the early history of Christianity, particularly those books that were excluded by canonization. In some, Jesus was not resurrected from the dead; he was only a man. In others, the course of events is very different than what is told in the four Gospels. Intense debates and analysis resulted. When the New Testament was canonized in the third and fourth centuries, the people who were including some manuscripts and excluding others had questions about consistency; plausibility; coherence with other, older texts; and unification. They were making a deliberate effort to settle on one story. This is not to mention the multitude of cases where scribes who were copying documents deliberately "harmonized" them. In short, the copyists and creators of the canon took a very large set of diverse writings and carved out of them the version of the New Testament we now have. That's why we don't usually read the Gospel of Thomas, the Gospel of the Twelve, the Gospel of Peter, the Gospel of the Basilides, the Gospel of Mathias, the Acts of Andrew, the Acts of Paul, the Acts of John, and the Epistle to the Laodiceans. And that's why most of us have not heard of Marcionism, Gnosticism, the antitactici, Montanism, and other apocryphal writings and movements, especially the ones that do not tell the same stories about Jesus. The appearance of unity, coherence, and consistency in the Jesus stories vanishes when we fold in for consideration the rest of the historical documents concerning him.

For the modern Christian to hold up that book centuries later and marvel at its coherence and unified message creates an ironic embarrassment. One obvious reason that the book has those stories with those features in it and not some others is because early Christians went through many of the early writings and sifted for the ones that would exhibit coherence and unity. In the process of copying and recopying, they actually made numerous modifications to make those books conform even more. We've been handed what may appear to be an impressive-looking bull's-eye, but what we may not have noticed is that after thousands of shots were taken at the barn, early Christians found the ones that hit the desired spot and drew a circle around them. We must keep in mind that the book was sifted and compiled from a much larger body of writings, some of which did not have those desired features. Endowing the result of the filtering process with those features was one of the deliberate goals of those who created and subsequently shepherded the canon through the centuries. It would be similarly misguided to marvel at the organization and coherence of the phone book; "What are the odds that all of these phone numbers in just this order would all come together in just this place?" They are there because people deliberately set out to gather them there. Therefore, someone is committing the Jesus-sharpshooter fallacy when he mistakes some after-the-fact improvement of the Jesus stories for a reason to think the stories are true.

THE MARK BOTTLENECK

We are now in a position to appreciate an important point about the evidence we have and to use it to draw conclusions about the resurrection of Jesus. It appears that at many points in the history of the New Testament manuscripts, the information passed through a very small conduit. The narrowness of the passageway through which our information has passed amplifies the risk of important facts being filtered, edited, distorted, or even misrepresented. Ideally, multiple independent verifications, separate corroborations, and intersubjective agreement could fortify the accounts. But we have surprisingly few of any of those.

The Gospel of Mark is the earliest written of the Gospels, and it was the principal source of information about the resurrection for the Gospels of Matthew and Luke. This means that a large part of the information we have about the resurrection passed through the narrow Mark bottleneck (keeping in mind that the author or authors of Mark's long ending dealing with the resurrected Jesus forms yet another bottleneck). Paul repeats the story briefly but in a different form. And the author of John gives yet a different account several decades later. So the genesis of those stories is not known; their information might have passed through the Mark bottleneck too, for all we know. Otherwise, the differences among these accounts emphasize why the bottleneck problem is so serious. It is also possible that the path of the stories we have now traced through history narrowed to a single person at any number of other points, given so many unknown steps in the stories' transmissions. There may have been only one person who told the first author of Mark about the resurrection. Or perhaps all of the other subsequent accounts of the story were based on Mark, making Mark's author the single line of access between the events and where we are now. Even if the bottleneck is wider than Mark, it would not appear to be wider by much. Mark, John, and possibly the Q source tell the resurrection story with Paul reiterating a somewhat similar story that he had heard. That is a disturbingly short list for the communication of what is alleged to be the single most important event in human history.[7]

At each one of those points where the transmission narrows, the edifice of modern Christian belief in God comes to rest upon whether those sources misstated, embellished, omitted, or took some artistic license. Nor is the possibility of such emendations merely speculation—we know they were common. The careful cross-referencing of thousands of the later documents has made it possible for us to identify some of the edits, revisions, and mistakes made by copyists in the centuries that followed. What we do not know, particularly because we know so little about how the stories got from Jesus' death to the people who wrote them down, is how many more alterations occurred. So there is a significant risk of error introduced by the layers of transmission the information would have gone through from the eyewitnesses (if there were any) to the authors of the Gospels. As the stories got retold and passed on, we would expect certain details to get embellished, omitted, or adjusted. That is precisely what we have seen in the later centuries. As the thirty to one hundred fifty years passed from the date of the events to their eventual recording by the authors, the risk would increase significantly.

Furthermore, it does not seem reasonable to expect that the goal of each person who served as a link in this chain would have been to preserve perfectly every bit of evidence, including the counterindications, so that future generations could decide for themselves whether the Jesus miracles happened. We would expect at a minimum that the intentions of these links in the chain would be to propagate a belief in the resurrection. That's the story they would have told and retold.

To illustrate the point, try this experiment. Find something you have written, something that came out of your own mind—a letter or an essay. Since it is entirely your own creation, you should be more familiar with it and know its details better than anyone else. Read it carefully, and then put it away. Now sit down and try to rewrite it, word for word. How successful were you at capturing every word, every important detail, every vital concept? Did the tone stay the same? Was the thesis exactly the same? Did you add anything that wasn't there before or did you leave anything out? I suspect that even with something you originally wrote that came from your own mind, noticeable and important changes occurred. I suspect that you couldn't prevent its being changed even if you had tried very hard. How much harder would it be to conduct this experiment with a story someone else told you? How much harder would it be when so many important political, social, moral, and religious issues hang in the balance? How hard would it be to keep one's most sincere hopes and passionate needs out of it? Wouldn't it be very hard to accurately retell a story after thirty years, ninety years, or one hundred fifty years?

Consider this example: the book of Mark is the only place in the New Testament where Jesus is called a carpenter. In Matthew, he's called a carpenter's son. So consider what a narrow conduit this has become. The whole culture of portraying Jesus as a carpenter has sprung from a single mention in one sentence in one book of the Bible. And the book from which this claim originates was based on hearsay evidence thirty years after Jesus died, where the earliest written copy we have is from almost three hundred years later. If the account had stated instead that Jesus was a tax collector or a magician, this would be the story and portrayal we have today. If the author had written that Jesus was a normal man with no ability to perform miracles, perhaps this would be the widespread view we have today. Or, what is more likely, given the agendas of the purveyors of the story, if a book had stated that Jesus was a normal man with no divine abilities, that particular source would have been altered or eliminated.

CONCLUSION

We now have a rough picture in place of the history of the Jesus story. There were events recounted by alleged witnesses, several decades of oral transmissions told among committed believers, and then stories written down by the authors of the Gospels. Then, after those manuscripts had been copied and recopied for two hundred or more years, some of the transferred accounts would survive the ravages of history to make it into the hands of modern scholars. Accounts of Jesus' life and death, as well as other religious communications, proliferated in the early centuries of Christianity; some of the written forms of those communications were codified into what has become the central source of Christian doctrine—the New Testament—others have survived, but many others have been lost or destroyed. The canonization of the New Testament and centuries of careful cultivation and shaping by scribes and clergy may give it the appearance of an internal coherence that was not native to the wide range of early writings. The Jesus-sharpshooter fallacy can be avoided by being cognizant of the broader history of Christian writings. Furthermore, the information about Jesus that we have passes through a narrow bottleneck in history that amplifies our concerns about placing too much weight on any of its details.

Now, with this general picture of the history of the information in hand, we can begin to build the arguments for what's wrong with believing the resurrection.

Chapter 3

YOU ALREADY DON'T BELIEVE IN JESUS: THE SALEM WITCH TRIALS

THE HISTORICAL EVIDENCE FOR THE RESURRECTION OF JESUS[1]

This chapter will present one of several arguments that believing in Jesus on the evidence we have is inconsistent with comparable supernatural cases we reject. Many people who believe in the resurrection and who think the evidence makes it reasonable already have a set of epistemic standards that would lead them to deny the resurrection, if they were to apply these standards consistently. Ironically, we typically disbelieve many supernatural claims that have far more evidence and better-quality evidence in their favor.

Before we consider one of those cases, it will be useful to summarize some of the reasons frequently given in favor of the historical-resurrection argument.[2] A vast amount has been written about the historical evidence for Jesus. There is no need to survey many of those arguments or to pursue some of the more arcane details and disputes from the literature here. The sorts of objections I have will apply to a broad class of the prohistorical arguments without our needing to delve into some of the more scholastic minutiae. The arguments focus most heavily on the accounts of Jesus' resurrection given in Matthew, Mark, Luke, and John and, to a lesser extent, on the writings of Paul.

Defenders of the historical argument have emphasized both claims made in the manuscripts and facts about the writings themselves. They say there were multiple eyewitness accounts of the miracles of Jesus, not just a few isolated people. Hundreds or even thousands of people are purported to have witnessed the resurrected Jesus healing the sick, raising the dead, and feeding the hungry. When Jesus was crucified, he wasn't buried in secret; the tomb was widely known and accessible. Given the public nature of the event, if his corpse had not actually disappeared, then a story about his resurrection would have been very difficult to fake. A number of people are reported to have found the tomb empty. On several different occasions, different groups of people are purported to have experienced Jesus resurrected from the dead. The witnesses are not a homogenous group of religious zealots. They are from diverse backgrounds with different educations and social standings. They were not a strange or fringe group. It is highly unlikely that the witnesses had any ulterior motives, it has been argued, because they stood to gain nothing from retelling what they had seen. In fact, they stood to lose a great deal. Early Christians were socially ostracized for their beliefs, persecuted, and perhaps even killed. While people will sometimes follow mistaken causes with deep passion and commitment, more often than not they are unwilling to sacrifice their lives for them. The original disciples believed that Jesus rose from the dead, despite their having every reason not to. The notion of a physical resurrection was alien to them. Such an event would have been outlandish, yet they still believed. They were so convinced that, out of their dedication, they gave up their jobs, wealth, possessions, and even families. The people closest to the eyewitnesses believed them and were impressed enough to convert. The passion and conviction of the original believers was so profound that it conquered the doubts of all those around them. A whole religious movement, which has lasted for thousands of years and spread to millions of people, sprang from these few eyewitness accounts.

Furthermore, many of the events of the New Testament have been historically corroborated, say the historical-resurrection defenders. Archeologists, historians, and other scholars have been able to find a great deal of independent evidence confirming many of the historical claims in the Bible, such as the reign of Herod, the destruction of the Jewish temple, and the growth of the early Christian church.

The Gospels focus on a real, historical person. They are not comparable to a book of mythology or fairy tales like Paul Bunyan. They present their accounts as factual records of events in history, not as allegory or fiction. Furthermore, the Jewish tradition of orally transmitting information accurately and reliably was highly developed and successful.

Paul, who previously was an ardent persecutor of Christians, claims to have seen the resurrected Jesus on several occasions. In fact, since he wrote many books of the Bible, his account *must* be an immediate one given by someone claiming to have seen Jesus. He must have been utterly convinced to have so radically changed his mind about Christianity.

Once we consider all these factors, say the defenders of the historical resurrection, no other hypothesis can explain the story of Jesus as well.

Gary Habermas has presented a popular, recent version of the argument. In addition to making many of the points above, he argues that many people who were enemies of the early Christian movement, such as the Jewish leaders, failed to contest the empty tomb in the stories we have about the resurrection. The absence of their denials in the historical sources is relevant, Habermas says, because if they had rejected the story, their protests would be evident. Furthermore, when Jesus' followers are alleged to have seen him after his death, it created a radical transformation in these followers' lives. The followers were utterly convinced, and many critical scholars concur that they were convinced.[3]

Furthermore, as Habermas sees it, the failure of naturalistic explanations fortifies the case for the supernatural answer—a real resurrection. For example, he offers this list of objections to the hallucination explanation, a commonly proposed naturalistic alternative to Jesus' actually returning from the dead:

> For example, (1) hallucinations are private experiences, while clearly we have strong reasons to assert that groups of people claimed to have seen Jesus. (2) The disciples' despair indicates that they were not in the proper frame of mind to see hallucinations. (3) Perhaps the most serious problem is that

there were far too many different times, places and personalities involved in the appearances. To believe that with each of these varying persons and circumstances a separate hallucination occurred borders on credulity. (4) Further, on this view, Jesus' body should still have been located safely in the tomb! (5) Hallucinations very rarely transform lives, but we have no records of any of the eyewitnesses recanting their faith. Two huge problems are the conversions of both (6) Paul and (7) James, neither of whom had a desire to see Jesus. These are just a very few of the serious questions for this alternative view. All other proposed natural hypotheses have similarly been disproven.[4]

Problems with the naturalistic alternatives, such as these with the hallucination explanation, point to Jesus' actual return from the dead:

> The more thoroughly the natural hypotheses fail, the more likely are the historical resurrection appearances. To state this principle more briefly as a mock mathematical equation: given a reasonable explanation, the disciples' experiences plus the failure of alternatives equals the historical resurrection appearances of Jesus.[5]

So the summary above and some of the details from Habermas give us an abbreviated picture of common historical arguments for Jesus. The authors focus on some of the inclusions and omissions in the texts; they triangulate with common sense about human nature; they reason that when the full list of the considerations they emphasize are taken into account, the competing naturalistic hypotheses fail, leaving the miraculous resurrection of Jesus as the last, best explanation.

In the next chapter, we will consider some psychological research concerning hallucinations, the neurological effects of bereavement, and aspects of eyewitness testimony and memory that undermine the type of argument Habermas is making here. But for now let us consider the broader question of accepting miraculous, supernatural, or magical events on the basis of historical evidence. What can we learn from other historical cases like the story of Jesus' resurrection?

THE SALEM WITCH TRIALS

Between 1692 and 1693, dozens of people were accused, were arrested, stood trial, and were tortured or hanged for various acts of witchcraft, possession by devils, and other supernatural ill deeds in Salem, Massachusetts. The events began with the strange behavior of some little girls, which fed suspicions. The girls had been seen running about and freezing in grotesque postures, complaining about biting and pinching sensations, and having violent seizures. As suspicions grew, people claimed to have witnessed a number of miraculous occurrences such as acts of witchcraft, inflictions of blindness and sickness through the use of spells, and human flight.

Ultimately, over 150 people were accused. William Phips, the governor of Massachusetts at the time, got involved. A court was established with judges, prosecutors, defenders, and a large number of respected members of the community. Thorough investigations were conducted. Witnesses were carefully cross examined. A large body of evidence was meticulously gathered. Many people confessed. The entire proceedings were carefully documented with thousands of sworn affidavits, court documents, interviews, and related papers. In the end, nineteen people—including Bridget Bishop, Sarah Goode, Rebecca Nurse, and Giles Corey—were tried, sentenced, and executed.

In most people's minds, the Salem witch trials are a frightening example of how enthusiasm, hysteria, social pressure, anxiety, and religious fervor can be powerful enough to lead ordinary people to do extraordinary and mistaken things. The term *witch hunt* has become synonymous with an irrational and emotionally heated persecution.

EVIDENCE FOR WITCHCRAFT?

Suppose we were to consider the hypothesis that the women accused of performing magic at Salem really were witches. That is, suppose they possessed some supernatural powers or the ability to harness forces beyond the natural realm to make magical events happen. The interesting and crucial questions for us are:

What is the state of our evidence when taken as support for this hypothesis? Does our evidence justify concluding that there was real magic at Salem?

Much can be said for the supernatural explanation. First, hundreds of people were involved in concluding that some of the accused were witches. Eyewitnesses testified in court, signed sworn affidavits, and demonstrated their utter conviction that those on trial were witches. Furthermore, the accusers came from diverse backgrounds and social strata, including magistrates, judges, the governor of Massachusetts, respected members of the community, husbands of the accused, and so on. They all became passionately convinced the charges were true on the basis of what they had seen. The witnesses, accusers, and investigators had a great deal to lose by being correct—men would lose their wives, children would lose their mothers, community members would lose friends they cared about. It seems very unlikely that such accusers could have had ulterior motives leading them to such a dramatic and profound conclusion. Accusing a friend or a wife of being a witch very likely would have the horrible outcome of getting her executed.

How good was the evidence-gathering process at the time? The trials were part of a thorough, careful, and exhaustive investigation. The investigators deliberately gathered evidence and made a substantial attempt to view it objectively and separate truths from falsehoods, mistakes, and lies. In the court trials, they took great care to discern the facts. The accusers must have become convinced by their evidence; why else would so many people agree and act so decisively and with such conviction? It strains credibility to suggest there was a conspiracy or a mass hallucination shared by the hundreds of people involved. The same hallucination cannot be had by large groups of people. Or, according to Habermas, one doesn't hallucinate something one doesn't wish to see.

What about the state of the evidence as it was passed to us, centuries later? That there were witch trials in Salem and that many people were put to death has been thoroughly corroborated with a range of other historical sources. The witch trials were historically recent, so we have hundreds of the actual documents that were part of the evidence. We have the signed, sworn testimonies of the eyewitnesses claiming to have seen the magic performed—not as it was repeated and relayed for decades to others, but immediately after it occurred.[6] We have whole volumes written by witnesses to the trials, such as those by Cotton Mather and John Hale.

How much evidence do we have? Enough to fill a truck. Modern archives at the University of Virginia and elsewhere have thousands of documents, books, records, transcripts, affidavits, testimonials, and other works detailing the events. That there were witch trials convicting the accused women is beyond a shadow of historical doubt.

BUT THEY WEREN'T WITCHES

Of course, I am not making a serious case for real witchcraft at Salem. I do not think you should conclude that the accused were really witches. Real witchcraft is *one* of the possible hypotheses that could explain the events in Salem, but it is not the best or most probable one. The point is they were not witches, and you (probably) do not believe that they were based on this substantial body of historical evidence.

If we take seriously the attempts to prove the resurrection of Jesus on historical grounds, then in order to be consistent we must also accept that the Salem witches actually performed acts of black magic. In fact, the Salem comparison (there are many others we can make) has an ironic result. When it is put up against the case for the resurrection, in the important respects, the historical evidence for witchcraft is *better* than the historical argument for the resurrection. In the case of Salem, the trials were a mere three hundred years ago, not two thousand. For Salem, we have thousands of actual documents surrounding the incidences, including the sworn testimonies from people claiming to have seen the magic performed. In contrast, we do not have any of the original Gospels, only copies from centuries later. The events in Salem were actively investigated by thoughtful, educated, (relatively) modern people. The supposedly possessed girls were repeatedly examined and interviewed. A large number of people devoted a great deal of time and energy to carefully examine the cases, and they concluded that whatever was going on must be of supernatural origin. As we saw in chapter 2, the Gospel stories are only a few anecdotal, hearsay stories from passionate and committed religious adherents passed by word of mouth for decades through an unknown number of people before being written down. All that remains of those stories are copies of copies from decades or even centuries later that were actively culled and patched together from a wider range of more varied writings.

By reasonable measures of *quantity* and *quality*, the evidence we have for witchcraft at Salem is vastly better than the evidence we have for the magical return from the dead by Jesus. But despite the better evidence, it is simply not reasonable to believe that the women in Salem were really witches or that they really performed magic. No reasonable person with a typical, twenty-first-century education should believe, even though some of the accused were tried, convicted, and executed for witchcraft, that they were *really* witches.

The comparison between the historical resurrection of Jesus and the Salem witch trials should produce a great deal of cognitive dissonance for the historically-minded Christian. You cannot consistently accept Jesus' returning from the dead while rejecting the magical powers of the Salem witches. Something's got to give.

There are at least three ways someone might respond in an attempt to reconcile the cases.

Response 1: Bite the Bullet

First, he might achieve consistency by lowering his threshold of required evidence for extraordinary supernatural events to the point that he accepts *both* the resurrection of Jesus and the magical powers of the Salem witches. Indeed, there will be some who believe that supernatural forces, magic, and spiritual phenomena are quite common, so acknowledging real witchcraft at Salem may not seem that troubling. The bite-the-bullet response resolves the incongruity between Salem and Jerusalem by accepting magic in both.

When I first conceived of the Salem witch trials argument and began discussing it with believers, I confess, I did not take this response very seriously. The possibility of real witchcraft at Salem struck me as obviously mistaken, and I expected that the majority of believers would argue that the Jesus and Salem cases are disanalogous (the second of the three responses). But after interacting with thousands of people in public lectures, in classes, on my blog, and in interviews and podcasts, I have been greatly surprised to find that this is one of the more common responses for the dedicated Christian. I've been forced to conclude that either these believers' dedication to the Christian ideology is deep enough to push them to bite the bullet, or there is far more belief in real magic out there than I once imagined.

Why shouldn't we accept the presence of real magic at Salem? There are a number of problems with the bite-the-bullet response. The biggest problem is that it resolves the incongruity between Salem and Jerusalem by accepting magic at Salem, but the best explanation of the Salem case does not involve real magic. First, the magic thesis would somehow have to fit with the views of historians and scholars arguing for various naturalistic explanations. Of course, there are experts and there are experts. It is almost always possible to find someone with some credentials arguing for an outrageous position—consider what I am doing in *this* book. And disagreeing with experts may not be very troubling. They make mistakes like everyone else, and even the consensus view is wrong sometimes. But consider the widespread acceptance of the general claim among the people who are best qualified to evaluate the quality of historical evidence that something natural—not supernatural—happened at Salem. Accepting magic at Salem puts one at odds with the experts' considerable brain power, credentials, and knowledge. And it raises this question: Are my reasons for thinking the resurrection was real better than all the reasons for thinking magic at Salem was not? That is, which is better: my reasons for thinking that Jesus was supernatural or my reasons for thinking that what happened at Salem was not supernatural.

And accepting witchcraft in this case doesn't just run afoul of the consensus historical view about the events at Salem, it also wreaks havoc with a whole approach to history. Lowering the standards here requires lowering them across the board. If magic was real at Salem, then, by extension, so was demon possession during the Plague years and the Inquisition in Medieval Europe. Werewolf and vampire stories in history must also be treated as facts. Hexes, the evil eye, and spectral beings must be treated as real, historical phenomena. Kings, emperors, and religious leaders must also have magical powers.

A second problem with the bite-the-bullet response is that acknowledging magic at Salem requires lowering our evidential thresholds to unacceptable levels in too many other cases where it is unlikely. If both cases were real magic, then you must draw a similar conclusion in the thousands or even millions of other comparable cases. In Saudi Arabia, for example, investigations into and public trials involving charges of witchcraft or sorcery are quite routine and frequently result in guilty verdicts that are punished by execution. On YouTube® there are countless *videos*—a powerful form of evidence not available in the Jesus or Salem cases—of allegedly magical, spiritual, supernatural, and miraculous events occurring. In 1988 the African publication the *Kenya Times* reported thousands of people to have witnessed the second coming of Jesus.[7] If magic was real in both Salem and Jerusalem, then it is incredibly common. If we are gullible enough to accept it in Salem, then we open the floodgates for cases that are surely not real.

There are several problems with accepting this volume of magic in the world. To begin, in the vast majority of these cases, people make mistakes. We know that people get confused, they are easily swayed by sleight-of-hand tricks, they make mistakes, they are carried away by their enthusiasm, they are hopeful, and they are often just poor critical thinkers. For vivid debunkings and examples of common mistakes and deceptions, see the works of Michael Shermer, James Randi, Theodore Schick and Lewis Vaughn, Stephen Law, Jonathan Baron, Carl Sagan, and Elizabeth Loftus, just to name a few.[8]

But the problems get worse for the Christian who bites the bullet. If the believer's response is that magic was real in Salem and miracles were real in Jerusalem, and it is reasonable to believe it on the basis of the historical evidence, then they open the door to thousands of other religious movements that present comparably poor historical proof for *their incompatible magic*. Unless we cheat, there's no way to custom tailor the threshold for acceptable historical supernatural beliefs so that Christianity ends up as the only reasonable movement. You either get Christianity and a whole bunch of other religious movements, or you get none of them. The Christian won't want to accept all the other movements because so many of them, like Christianity, claim exclusivity. Lots of them, on the basis of *their* historical miracles, claim that theirs is the "one true religion" and the "one true God," and all the others must be rejected as false. The Christian has a problem if the miraculous events authenticating another religious movement corroborate a religious ideology that is incompatible with Christianity. What can she say if that god is not the Christian God, or if that doctrine denies the truth of essential Christian claims?

There is a comparable internal problem, too. Many advocates of some particular Christian sect's doctrines are suspicious that various miracle claims from other Christian sects are unfounded; for example, a Jehovah's Witness, given his doctrinal commitments, will want to reject the authenticity of alleged Catholic miracles at Lourdes. If some Catholic miracles are real, then it would appear some of what the Jehovah's Witness has to say about the exclusivity of his religion's interpretation of the Bible or their privileged connection to God would be mistaken. Baptists would want to reject Mormon miracles. How does the evangelical Christian, who explicitly denies the doctrines of other Christian denominations, explain the widespread occurrence of miracles in those churches that seem to legitimate their doctrines? Lowering one's criteria to allow the supernatural events at both Salem and Jerusalem brings along all the others. If we let them all in, then we have a hopeless mess of conflicting doctrines; theological incompatibilities; and a supernatural realm overrun with competing gods, saints, spirits, and forces. A reasonable person should not lower her threshold of acceptance to the point where all these demonstratively false or incompatible cases flood through the gates. The cost of doing so would result in being too gullible, too wrong, or too conflicted.

It is difficult to avoid the conclusion that someone who would bite this bullet must be deep in the grip of an ideology. Accepting the ideas of Jesus' resurrection and magic at Salem forces one to accept a world teeming with spiritual and supernatural forces. On the believers' account, we inhabit a world that is filled with cell phones, rapid genetic analyses, sophisticated biochemical cancer treatments, handheld computers with fifty-nanometer silicon-etched chips, planes flying at seven thousand miles per hour, and spacecraft capable of leaving the solar system, but it is also teeming with ghosts, demons, magical spells, miracles, fairies, elves, and psychic powers. Ultimately, this spooky worldview in response to the Salem case will be disproved by its own peculiar and false accounts of natural and ordinary phenomena. If these supernatural things are so real and so common, then where are they and why can't we find better evidence in their favor than the passionate testimonials of converts? Do they only manifest themselves when there are no credible witnesses or skeptics present? These questions should weigh heavily on someone who makes the bite-the-bullet response.

We now have a staggering assemblage of evidence for causal closure, or the view that physical events or effects are fixed by a fully physical prior history. The physical realm, as far as we can ascertain, is causally complete— "all physical effects can be accounted for by basic physical causes."[9] Across the spectrum of scientific fields, we find no exceptions to causal closure.

If the bite-the-bullet response is correct, then it seems we must deny causal closure on a massive scale. We must accept widespread instances of physical events being brought about by some nonphysical entity or force. And if that is correct, then one of the central pillars of the natural sciences has been undermined. Now, one must ask: Are my reasons for resurrection better than all of the reasons we have for thinking that the entire scientific enterprise's naturalistic worldview is correct? If a decently educated, twenty-first-century adult is willing to say, "Yes, it is reasonable to believe on the basis of the witch-trial evidence that Sarah Goode, Rebecca Nurse, and the rest were actually witches," then I think we must take said admission to be a *reductio* of his view about the authenticity of the Jesus-miracle stories.

To be fair, there could be situations where believing in real witchcraft is reasonable. For at least some in Salem at the time, it may have been a fair conclusion to draw given what else they knew, the context, their levels of education, the culture, and the beliefs of those around them. But the question is not about what was reasonable for the citizens of Salem to have believed, it is about what is reasonable to believe for the ordinary person of today.

Response 2: Deny the Analogy

Alternately, the response to the Salem witch trials argument may be to deny the analogy. One may argue that the cases are different in some respects that justify denying witchcraft at Salem while accepting Jesus' resurrection. One might say there are important details in the case of Salem that are not present in the Jesus case, or there are powerful points in favor of Jesus that are not shared by the Salem example. So on this view, accepting Jesus and rejecting Salem is not inconsistent because there is a principled separation of the cases.

Denying the analogy is doomed to fail, however, by ad hoc rationalizing and special pleading. One problem is that any such approach will have to be reconciled with the fact that we have so much more information about the events in Salem. If someone wishes to argue that we are justified in concluding that there were naturalistic causes in Salem on the basis of the evidence, he faces a challenge when it comes to defending Jesus. He needs to argue that no similar naturalistic explanation can be true about Jesus on the basis of a much smaller, more fragmented, older, and less corroborated body of information. Attempts to rule out some alternative naturalistic explanation of the resurrection story will be undone by the fact that we have only a few stories (which conflict on many important details) recorded on the basis of unknown hearsay testimony decades after the fact. We just don't have enough good information about the events to rule out anything definitively. In contrast, since there is so much evidence available concerning Salem, there remains a better possibility of justifying some naturalistic explanation there. The lack of evidence in the Jesus case and the extent to which the accounts of Jesus have been cultivated, altered, and canonized will make it very difficult to rule out with any confidence some comparable naturalistic explanation.

Denying the analogy runs into another problem. We don't need to be deeply committed to the Salem case in order to make the point. There are many other examples where we can find a body of information as good as or better than the Jesus evidence supporting the conclusion that some supernatural event occurred, but it is not reasonable to draw such a conclusion. Hundreds of thousands of Hindus claim to have witnessed statues of the Lord Ganesh drinking milk. Millions of thoughtful, educated, fairly reasonable people have left the shrine at Lourdes, France, utterly convinced they witnessed a miraculous healing. Gurus, New-Age spiritualists, and other quasi-religious leaders gather millions of devoted followers who become deeply convinced their spiritual advisor possesses otherworldly powers. The original accounts of Islam, Mormonism, Buddhism, and Hinduism are filled with supernatural claims, and the circumstances surrounding their advents resemble Christianity in too many relevant respects. Whatever particular virtues may strike us about the historical-resurrection case, there is a multitude of non-Jesus cases where the evidence is just as good or better by those criteria, but the reasonable view is to reject the magical conclusion.

The general form of prohistorical arguments is something like this:

A) The sources of historical evidence concerning event E (e.g., the resurrection) have virtues X, Y, and Z.

B) Virtues X, Y, and Z are adequate to warrant our believing the sources of historical evidence concerning event E.

C) Therefore, we are warranted in believing that event E (the resurrection) occurred.

Earlier in the chapter I noted that my set of arguments against the resurrection is broad enough to make it unnecessary for us to delve too deeply into many of the details of the prohistorical arguments. Now we can see why. Generally stated, my argument is that it is possible for us to substitute a wide range of details into the first premise for virtues X, Y, and Z. We can model a variety of pro-resurrection arguments with very different emphases and details in this general form. But what the cases of Salem, Lourdes, Mormonism, Islam, and the like show is that the presence of those virtues is not generally sufficient to warrant the supernatural conclusion.

A defender of the historical case for Jesus' supernatural powers may emphasize this feature of the evidence or that one. He may present us with a selective list of what he takes to be the virtues of the Jesus evidence justifying his conclusion that Jesus really had supernatural powers. Whatever those general features are, we must ask this question: In general, when the evidence has these features, is the best explanation the supernatural one? If the prohistorical defender approaches this question objectively, without any ad hoc qualifications in favor of the Christian conclusion, he will be disappointed. He will find numerous other cases where (1) we have a body of evidence as good as or better than the evidence for Jesus, (2) it is possible to tout the same virtues (e.g., numerous witnesses of high character, devotees with no apparent ulterior motive, utter conviction among the followers, the beginning of a worldwide movement, and so on), and yet, (3) it is not reasonable to accept the supernatural conclusion in that other case.

Advocates of the historical resurrection have sometimes argued that unless some naturalistic explanation can be successfully defended, then we must accept the supernatural conclusion. If the naturalistic explanations we can come up with are all doubtful, then the resurrection must be real. There's a mistake concealed in this seemingly reasonable approach. The Salem example illustrates the point that one need not believe or defend any *particular* alternative naturalistic explanation. Some scholars have argued that many of the residents of Salem had eaten rotten rye grain that caused them to hallucinate. But it can be reasonable to think there were no real witches at Salem even without knowing exactly what happened. In fact, in historical matters, there is always much we do not know. The Salem case shows that we don't need to have a fully articulated naturalistic explanation in place with the supporting evidence to believe reasonably that there is such an explanation. Even if it turns out that a number of proposed naturalistic hypotheses do not readily fit with what we believe are the facts about the case, it would not follow from those failures alone that we should default to the supernatural explanation as the best hypothesis. At this point in history, we have seen countless examples of allegedly strange or remarkable phenomena that resisted our attempts at explanation. We have also seen countless cases of events where it was alleged something miraculous occurred. Then later, when we continued to pursue it or after we learned more about ourselves and the world, the answers became clear to us. The real source of the bubonic plague (not demon possession or God's wrath for our sinfulness) wouldn't become clear to us for *several centuries*, until the plague bacillus was discovered. Likewise, no one in Salem or in Europe during the Inquisition years could have known about Sydenham's chorea, a disease caused by streptococcus infections and rheumatic fever. Many months after initial infection, its victims, usually young girls, would have been seized by rapid, uncoordinated jerking movements in their feet, hands, and faces.

The evidence in favor of causal closure is vast. This is not to rule out a magical explanation a priori—it remains a possibility, I suppose. But clearly the threshold of proof for reasonable people is and should be very high before magic becomes the best among all competing hypotheses. History has taught us that there is a very strong presumption in favor of naturalistic causes. And not even the copious body of evidence for real witchcraft at Salem is enough to exceed that threshold. A fortiori, the paltry body of evidence we have in favor of Jesus' resurrection certainly does not achieve the threshold. Among other things, the Salem witch trials show it is possible to meet an even heavier burden of proof than what we have for the resurrection of Jesus, and it remains unreasonable to believe anything magical happened. No clear-headed person should accept that doubts about the naturalistic explanations imply Jesus coming back from the dead is the only reasonable conclusion. We don't know a priori that only natural events occurred in 35 CE. Surely there must be some threshold of evidence that could, in principle, make it reasonable to believe Jesus was resurrected, but the evidence we have falls far short.

Response 3: Evidence Doesn't Matter

When confronted by the Salem case, the believer may simply refuse to accept arguments that do not corroborate the resurrection of Jesus. As it turns out, once we scratch the surface, some of the allegedly historical arguments for Jesus are more like exercises in confirmation bias than objective historical investigations. For many, the possibility that Jesus was not resurrected is simply a nonstarter.

Noted advocate of the historical resurrection N. T. Wright suggests this is the view of history held by Luke T. Johnson, Christopher Seitz, H. Frei, and others. According to this view, the problems with the historical evidence show not that there was no resurrection but that our approach to history is wrong:

> If we attempt to argue for the historical truth of the resurrection on standard historical grounds, have we not allowed historical method, perhaps including its hidden Enlightenment roots, to become lord, to set the bounds of what we know, rather than allowing God himself, Jesus himself, and indeed the resurrection itself, to establish not only what we know but how we can know it?[10]

In *Reason within the Bounds of Religion*, Nicholas Wolterstorff says,

> The religious beliefs of the Christian scholar ought to function as control beliefs within his devising and weighing of theories. . . . Since his funda-

mental commitment to following Christ ought to be decisively ultimate in
his life, the rest of his life ought to be brought into harmony with it. As
control, the belief-content of his authentic commitment ought to function
both negatively and positively. Negatively, the Christian scholar ought to
reject certain theories on the ground that they conflict or do not comport
well with the belief-content of his authentic commitment.[11]

That is, since Jesus must come first, the only acceptable historical methods
for proving Jesus was real must be ones proving he was real. If our historical
methods do not produce the correct conclusion, then it must be the methods,
not the conclusion that are wrong.

Once this pernicious circularity is exposed, it casts the historical question
in an entirely new light. It turns out these believers aren't really playing by the
same rules. If the believer simply refuses to take seriously the Salem argument,
the causal-closure problem, or the long list of other problems with the historical
case, then I think we must conclude she is more committed to believing in
the resurrection than accepting that which is best supported by the evidence.
Indeed, some believers have openly announced this as their intention. She is
thereby rejecting the basic presumption of the inquiry in this book. In that case,
she and I aren't disagreeing about the historical evidence for the resurrection
anymore. Perhaps she is someone who, like William Lane Craig, has resolved to
subordinate reason to faith: "The way in which I know that Christianity is true
is first and foremost on the basis of the witness of the Holy Spirit in my heart
and this gives me a self-authenticating means of knowing that Christianity
is true wholly apart from the evidence." According to Craig, faith must be
held immune from the doubts induced by the shifting sands of evidence and
reason.[12] Craig, who has also extensively argued for the resurrection on historical
grounds,[13] insists this special sense gives him indefeasible, inerrant knowledge
no historical contingencies could possibly refute. If we are to take seriously this
view about subordinating reason to his religious commitment, then we have to
conclude that his *historical* arguments for the resurrection are disingenuous. We
would all be better served by believers being this forthright about where their
priorities ultimately lie between Christian ideology and historical methodology.
The historical facts are irrelevant. This sort of believer has resolved to doubt

everything else before doubting the authenticity of the Jesus story. This illuminates what I meant by the comment earlier in the chapter of one being "deep in the grip of an ideology." There really can be no useful discussion about what is reasonable or even what is true with such a person. They have left the rationality playing field. Craig is correct, however, in concluding that the only way to sustain one's belief in the resurrection is to disregard the evidence.

CONCLUSION: NO WITCHCRAFT IN SALEM, NO RETURN FROM THE DEAD IN JERUSALEM

We've seen that the only plausible response to the Salem argument is to reject the reality of the resurrection in parallel with our rejection of magic. It is internally inconsistent, at odds with the evidence, and unjustified to think Jesus returned from the dead. All things considered, and by the standards of evidence we already employ elsewhere, one should believe that the overall likelihood of some naturalistic explanation is greater than the resurrection.

But many questions remain unanswered. Why exactly should the threshold for historical supernatural claims be so high? Why should there be a prima facie preference for a naturalistic explanation over a supernatural one? Why have so many people been convinced by the resurrection? Why are so many people disposed to believe in miracles? What do we know about the psychological makeup of the early Christians that would bear on our accepting their stories? In chapter 4 we will consider evidence that has come to light in modern psychology and our studies of human cognition that answer some of these questions. In particular, what do we know about the way people think now that could shed light on the beliefs of the early Christians and their reliability in transmitting the resurrection story to us?

Chapter 4

BELIEVING THE BELIEVERS

In the previous chapter, we saw that accepting the resurrection would force us to abandon a set of standards for evidence gathering and belief formation that serve us perfectly well in other cases, like the Salem witch trials. Believing in the resurrection is at odds with our reasonable rejection of real magic at Salem. The consistent and correct answer is to reject both. We may still wonder, however, about the details of what makes it unreasonable to believe in magic at Salem and in miracles at Jerusalem.

The central question can be put this way: Given the quality and quantity of information we have, what conclusion should a reasonable, educated, twenty-first-century person draw about Jesus and the allegations that he returned from the dead? The specific problem we must consider in this chapter is the reliability of first-century people from whom the information about the resurrection originated.

SOME LINKS IN THE CHAIN

The information about Jesus is transmitted to us through a series of people, their words, and their writings. The events themselves are first in the chain. Then, from those, we can distinguish five kinds of links in the chain:

- *The alleged witnesses:* the people who originally claimed to witness the events and then reported them.

- *The repeaters:* the intermediate group who repeated that story until it was written down decades later.
- *The authors:* the writers of the Bible books.
- *The copyists:* the people who copied and recopied the works until some of those copies survived to reach us.
- *The canonizers:* the people who culled the books of the modern Bible out of the many Christian writings that proliferated in the early centuries of the religious movement.

We can look at the oldest surviving documents from these people and see for ourselves what they say, so in effect, surviving copies make it possible for us to jump over centuries and avoid some questions about transmission fidelity, copying errors, or manipulation that might have occurred since those copies were made. An actual document from the fourth century instead of from the eighth century, for example, is that much closer to the events, reducing some of our concerns about what may have intervened between the fourth and eighth centuries.

Let's consider some clusters of problems relevant to each of the links in the chain. And if there are real doubts undermining our confidence in each of these stages of transmission, then the net effect will be the accumulation of all the doubts that intervene between us and the alleged events. In chapter 5 we will consider how doubts amplify when they accumulate and are considered together.

THE ALLEGED EYEWITNESSES

How reliable are eyewitnesses to miracles? It varies with the type of information in question. My reliability for information about NFL football is much poorer than my reliability for information about the history of philosophy (I hope). People are pretty good at making trajectory estimates for thrown objects, but they are quite bad at making compound estimates of probability that involve more than a few variables. We might trust a medieval source to inform us about the starting and ending dates for a significant battle, but if the same source recommends trepanation as a cure for the bubonic plague because a hole drilled in the skull releases the evil demons, we would be more reluctant to take his claim to be true no matter how authentic or well-corroborated the claim is.

The cases in which we are interested are the cases where people have encounters leading them to claim that some miraculous, supernatural, or spiritually and physically extraordinary event has occurred. How reliable are people at relaying this sort of information? At first glance, it may seem like a very difficult question to answer. It's hard to know how many real miracles there are or how many reports there are. Our habit is to trust people as sources of information about their own reliability. That is, not only do we believe many of the things people say, we also take a person's claims about her own reliability as a useful indicator of her reliability, especially when there is no other way to corroborate. When I see something and become certain that it happened, it is very difficult for me to imagine that I am mistaken about it. My own feelings of certainty are compelling to me. And when we imagine being in a position like the first Christians are alleged to have been in, it's similarly difficult to imagine they could be wrong when they seem to have been so utterly convinced.

In general, people give high marks to their own abilities, including the ability to judge the truth about events they have seen. When you ask people how good they are at judging character, for example, they are quite confident. It the question were put to you, you might recall believing someone was a certain way, for example, that your friend's husband was trustworthy, or suspicious, or foolish. Then you will recall instances where that judgment seemed to apply accurately and, thus, your initial judgment was validated.

Question: How good are you at judging character?

Answer: I'm pretty good. When I met Maria's husband for the first time, I could just tell that something was not right with that guy. And look how that turned out. I can't believe he buried so many bodies in that basement."

Some of the problems here should be obvious. To get an accurate judgment of your reliability, we would need to know your failure rate, too, and the success/failure rate of others at a similar task. Then we could compare your real rate with a baseline for other people.

Consider a clearer example: suppose Mr. Munchausen claims he is very good at predicting the outcome of college basketball games. To figure out how good he actually is, we would need a reliable, objective method for gathering several pieces of information. We can't simply take his word for it or his memories about his successes. We would need an accurate record of all his predictions, not just the ones he remembers or the ones he got right. Then we would need an accurate record of the actual outcomes of all the basketball games for which he made a prediction. When we compare these two, we might discover that he correctly predicts the outcome 65 percent of the time. That is, he is only mistaken about the winner in thirty-five out of one hundred cases. Would that confirm his special skill? Not quite. It may be that other fans are just as good at making these predictions. Or it could be worse; it could be that other fans typically outperform his predictions. Their average success rate might be 75 percent, in which case he appears to be bad at the task. The point is that the data about his success rate alone doesn't tell us much; for all we know, other people can accurately predict the games 90 percent of the time. Suppose Munchausen's success rate is 45 percent. That means he's actually doing worse than random chance or simply guessing. We need his numerator (the number of games he correctly predicted) and his denominator (the number of games he predicted rightly or wrongly) in order to attach a value to his reliability. He may claim to have a special method for determining the winner, but the method actually makes him do worse than he would otherwise, and we wouldn't know that until we looked at both ratios.

If one person's ability is better than others, then we should find some evidence of it in objective, blind testing. If we compared Munchausen's prediction rate to the rates of other fans and nonfans and found that his rating was, on average, much better than both groups, then we might conclude that he's good at predicting games. But no matter how well he compares to other people, if his rate is not above 50 percent, then his predictions will actually be a better indicator of who will *not* win the game. That is, we could do better by just guessing. Or we could do even better than that by choosing the opposite of his pick.

It is possible to do something similar for people's reliability with regard to miracle reports. For miracle-testimony reliability, first, it would be valuable to know how often people claim to have witnessed a miracle. Second, in those cases where they report one, we need to know how often a miracle *really happened*. And third, we need to know how often they witness a real miracle but do not claim to have seen one. Most of us think that reporting a miracle is a relatively or exceedingly rare thing. People don't just claim such a thing very often. And most of us probably think that real miracles are exceedingly rare, too, although this estimate will vary significantly from person to person. Your rough subjective estimate of miracle-report reliability for people will be a function of how frequently you think people make miracle claims and how often you think they are correct. There will be a real, objective rate depending on the real number of reports and the real number of occurrences, but perhaps only an omniscient God will know those numbers. We have to do the best with what we've got. It would be valuable, then, to consider these first two values. Fortunately, we can do better than mere, subjective best guessing on the basis of personal experience by considering some cases like Lourdes, France, where miracle reports and miracles appear to be common.

Since 1858, when Bernadette Soubirous claimed to have seen an apparition of the Virgin Mary in Lourdes, France, people have sought the waters from a nearby spring in a rocky cliff. By some estimates, there have been at least eighty thousand pilgrims a year for over one century, totaling over eight million people who have gone there. Other estimates put the total number of visitors at two hundred million.

Out of those millions of visitors, many have had what they thought was a miraculous experience, a special spiritual event or healing. And a number of those experiences have been submitted to an official investigating body of the Roman Catholic Church to determine if they were really miracles. As of now, out of the thousands of cases they have considered, sixty-seven miracles have been declared to be real by the Lourdes Medical Bureau, which is made up of church-appointed clergy and doctors who select themselves to serve. For now, let's treat those sixty-seven as real.[1]

What the numbers suggest is that for every officially recognized miracle, there are hundreds of thousands, or even millions, of cases where someone thinks a miracle has occurred, but that claim would not pass muster, even with the favorably inclined, church-appointed investigating board. Now we must engage in some educated guesswork: out of the eight million to two hundred million visitors to Lourdes over the decades, how many of them had an experience of something that they took to be a miraculous or supernatural event? Surely there have been many people who have gone and did not notice or feel anything special. But no doubt there have been far more who went with high expectations, after having heard about the special, miraculous occurrences that are common there, and who saw, felt, heard, or experienced something they took to be of a divine origin. Let us make the conservative conjecture that one-half of the low estimate of total visitors, or four million people, thought that something miraculous from a spiritual source happened to them. If there are good reasons to revise the number up or down, then we can do so.[2] Unless this estimate is off by whole orders of magnitude, the conclusion of this argument will be similar.[3] If there are sixty-seven real miracles and four million alleged miracles (out of eight million to two hundred million visits), then the general miracle reliability rating for visitors to Lourdes is 0.0000167 or 0.0016 percent. That is, without any other information, if someone from Lourdes claims to have witnessed a miracle, then there is a 99.99833 percent probability that it did not happen. Recalling our previous point about Mr. Munchausen, the result here means that, in general, when someone claims a miracle has occurred, his claim is a far stronger indicator that it did not happen than that it did.

We need not be strongly committed to the 0.0016 percent rating, however. There is much we don't know. But what the rating does make clear is that the error rate is enormous, even if we are charitable and grant that a number of dubious miracles are real. People make many miracle and supernatural claims. Nearly one in five Americans believe that he receives direct answers to his prayers once a week.[4] But we now have numerous well-designed studies showing that prayer has no effect.[5] So that amounts to about sixty million new false miracle claims a week. In addition to Lourdes and unanswered prayers, there are alleged sightings of ghosts, psychic contact with

the dead, clairvoyance, supernatural interventions, and countless other supernatural events on the planet every day. Millions of people in India claim to
have witnessed statues drinking milk from saucers, or others see tears fall from
the eyes of statues of the Virgin Mary or images of her face in their food. In
the United States over one hundred million people believe that houses can be
haunted; thirty-five to forty million people believe that astrology works; and
over sixty million (20 percent) believe in communicating mentally with the
dead.[6]

The point is that mistaken supernatural claims are exceedingly common,
but any real supernatural events are orders of magnitude more rare. In informal
discussions with students in my classes over the years, a majority claim to have
seen at some point something spooky, supernatural, or that defied the ordinary
natural course of things. But it is very rare to hear of an example where there
is not an obvious and better natural explanation. On any given day in the
United States there are thousands, or possibly hundreds of thousands, of faith
healers who are holding faith-healing revivals. Some of these revivals take
place in huge stadiums where ten, twenty, or thirty thousand seats are filled.
During the events, hundreds or even thousands of people will stream down
to the front to be healed by the preacher, hundreds or thousands more will
have what they take to be intense spiritual and physical healing experiences
in their seats. None of these appears to be real or to be able to stand up to any
significant critical examination. In other cases, people watching prayer and
healing sessions conducted by televangelists on cable television stations will
experience what they take to be miraculous healings. Evangelist preachers like
Pat Robertson, Robert Tilton, Benny Hinn, and countless others sustain their
multimillion-dollar ministries on the donations of these hopeful watchers.
The vast majority of these alleged miracles go unreported except perhaps to
family and friends.

So across the country, every day there will be millions of people who are
experiencing what they take to be miracles. A tiny fraction of these will get
reported. Even fewer will be investigated with any serious scrutiny. James
"The Amazing" Randi, a renowned skeptic, has been conducting a $1 million
paranormal challenge for many years for anyone who "can show under proper
observing conditions, evidence of any paranormal, supernatural, or occult

power or event." To date, hundreds of people, including many claiming to have healing powers, have attempted to demonstrate their abilities and to satisfy some rudimentary observation requirements in Randi's test. All have been resounding failures.[7]

Of the millions of daily cases where someone thinks he or she has experienced a miracle, how many of them are real? We can't know for sure, but we should not be optimistic. It should be obvious to any reasonable and mildly skeptical person that the vast majority of them are not real. Cases of known fraud, mistakes, enthusiasm, confusion, delusion, placebo effect, confirmation bias, urban mythology, hoaxes, and failures of scientific protocols such as double blind controls should lead us to be very skeptical. Even if you believe that miracles are real and happen often, the examples above show that vastly more of the reports are wrong than right.

If someone is dissatisfied with the 0.0016 percent estimate from the Lourdes case, then we have to ask: What is a better estimate justified by the empirical evidence? We must keep in mind that this percentage is not the rate of miracles, but the comparison of the number of times someone thinks or claims something supernatural has occurred contrasted to the number of times it really did. How reliable are people about these sorts of events? One in one million? One in one thousand? One in ten? The evidence above suggests that at the very least, the rate is millions to one, probably worse. If the critic believes that human testimony about miracles is generally more reliable, then the obvious challenge will be to produce those real cases of miracles or other supernatural events that will push the numerator up and change the low estimate justified by the examples above. Consider the evidence you have for the numerator and the denominator, and keep this rate in mind for our next step.

BELIEVING IN THE SUPERNATURAL

What other factors should inform our assessment of the reliability of the alleged eyewitnesses to the miracles of Jesus? Here's an important question: Would the early followers of Jesus have been more or less reliable about reporting miraculous events than the people at Lourdes or the people in recent

American polls? The answer: they would have been much less reliable because of who they were and when they lived.

Let's consider how disposed a person is, in general, to accept or reject claims about supernatural entities, forces, or events. We can call this her supernatural-belief threshold (SBT). If her threshold is low, she is more readily disposed to believe supernatural claims are true. For whatever reasons, she is inclined to accept claims about events that transcend or violate the natural order more readily, with less evidence, or with less skepticism. Let's imagine that Gloria has a low SBT. In the course of her life, just like the rest of us, she encounters claims about supernatural events. Gloria sees a headline on the cover of a magazine at the supermarket about the psychic powers of Sylvia Browne (who claims to be able to talk to the dead), she has a friend who says he saw what he thought was a ghost one night when he was alone in an old house, she had a lucid dream of a conversation with her grandfather the night after he died, she sees a news story about reports of a statue at a nearby church that appears to be crying. Gloria is more disposed to accept these stories at face value whereas someone with a high SBT would consider alternative explanations, think of objections, or otherwise be skeptical.[8]

As a result, there will be a group of these claims Gloria believes are true that we can contrast to the ones that really are true. As with other matters, there are lots of false claims circulating out there. Even if there are many supernatural events occurring out there, not all of the reports about them will be accurate; rumors, urban myths, mistakes, and sensationalism have their effect. Even Gloria will acknowledge that not everything she hears is true. But since her SBT is low, Gloria's error rate with regard to supernatural claims would be high; she will conclude that miracles, ghosts, or strange happenings are more common than they really are, for example.[9] If there were supernatural ideas circulating about that were false or unfounded, a person like Gloria would be more likely to believe them anyway and repeat them. That is, if you were to take her word for it, a person with a low SBT would mislead you (perhaps not intentionally) in the direction of accepting more of those claims than are actually true. If you have a friend who is utterly dedicated to the Detroit Lions and who believes they will win every game in the coming season, he is likely to be right for at least some of the games. But he believes those truths at the cost of many more false beliefs. As they say, even a broken clock gets the time right twice a day. And if you believed all of his testimony, his errors would become your own.

We can also put the point in terms of a person's skepticism, doubtfulness, or disposition toward critical scrutiny. If a person habitually reflects on the evidence with care, makes a conscious and careful effort to gather the broadest body of relevant evidence, and actively seeks out disconfirming grounds for a claim, *that (all other things being equal) is favorable with regard to their trustworthiness as a source of information*. If a person whose skepticism is high becomes satisfied that it is true, then you could be more confident that it is true (all other things being equal) than you would be if your source for the same claim was someone whose skepticism is generally low.

Of course, skepticism can go too far. If someone has the opposite problem from Gloria's, and there are some supernatural claims that are true, this person would misrepresent reality in the direction of concurring with too few claims of the type that are in fact true. If someone's threshold for believing certain kinds of claims is out of whack with reality, then she becomes an unreliable source of information about these claims in either direction. Ideally, a source's SBT would produce a set of supernatural beliefs that match reality as closely as possible.

With respect to my main thesis, the lesson here for the Jesus case (and many others) is that there are many influences that push our thresholds for believing certain kinds of claims away from where they should be for maximum accuracy. Enthusiasm, desire, ideological commitments, emotional attachments, poor critical-thinking skills, misinformation, and a host of other factors lead us to accept or reject different types of claims on the basis of faulty or inconsistent standards. When he makes a good roll, the gambler is highly inclined to think that his secret method for winning at the craps table works. He's inclined to take any win (that would have happened anyway), and even some near misses at winning as confirmation that his system works.[10] When she finds some incriminating evidence, the worried wife grasps for reasons to think that her husband is not cheating on her and clings to that account long after his infidelity has become clear to those who are not so invested. If the arguments of this book thus far had been undermining the legitimacy of some non-Christian religious miracles, a Christian might be much more sympathetic. If you are Protestant, consider parallel arguments against Catholic or Mormon miracles (and vice versa). If I were a visiting preacher in a Christian church presenting the very same arguments from this book against the historical foundations of Islam, chances are the skepticism about the reliability of the Koran would be warmly received.

There are several points to make here about first- and second-century Christians. Generally, people living in an agrarian, Iron Age society with very low levels of scientific knowledge, education, and literacy will have a low of level of skepticism for what we would identify as supernatural, miraculous, or paranormal claims. We have good empirical evidence that as a person's education level increases, her belief in survival of the soul, miracles, heaven, the resurrection, the virgin birth, hell, the devil, ghosts, astrology, and reincarnation drops off dramatically.[11] *Religiousness, superstition, and supernaturalism are positively correlated with ignorance; when people have more education, they are less likely to believe.*

We can make the same sort of projection back across time. Consider the difference between your level of education (or the general level of knowledge of the average American with a K–12 education) and the level of ignorance of a fisherman or a beggar living in first-century Palestine. Almost all of the information you take for granted—the education, the science, the technology, and our methods for acquiring information—was unavailable to them. A tiny fraction of the population would have been literate. For most of them, their mathematical abilities would have been worse than today's average third grader. They would not know that the earth moves or what the sun is. They would not know what electricity or hydrogen is. They did not know what caused disease, or pregnancy, or death. If religiousness, superstition, and supernaturalism rise as education goes down, then they must have been rampant among those who had contact with Jesus (if he was real at all).

The characteristic we are considering in them is not gullibility, per se, although that may be a factor. We should separate gullibility, which can be thought of as a generally low threshold of evidence, from ignorance. For many important phenomena, the correct explanation would not have been available even to the most discerning and informed person. In the first century, given their expectations, background information, general level of knowledge, and culture, there simply would not have been as many nonsupernatural explanations available to ordinary people for all sorts of ordinary and many extraordinary events. Overall, their supernatural-belief threshold would have been much lower than ours. Another way to put the point is that they would assign supernatural explanations to a much broader range of events than could be correct. Bart Ehrman has a useful perspective:

> In the ancient world miracles were not understood in the quasi-scientific terms that we use today [as a supernatural violation of the laws of nature]. . . . Everyone knew, for example, that iron ax-heads would sink in water, and that people would too, if they tried to walk on water. . . . But in the ancient world, almost no one thought that this was because of some inviolable "laws" of nature, or even because of highly consistent workings of nature whose chances of being violated were infinitesimally remote. The question was not whether things happened in relatively fixed ways; the question was who had the power to do the things that happened. . . . For someone like [Jesus] to heal the sick or raise the dead was not a miracle in the sense that it violated the natural order; rather, it was "spectacular" in the sense that such things did not happen very often, since few people had the requisite power.
>
> This means that for most ancients the question was thus not whether miracles were possible. Spectacular events happened all the time. It was spectacular when the sun came up or the lightning struck or the crops put forth their fruit. . . . For ancient people there *was* no closed system of cause and effect, a natural world set apart from a supernatural realm. Thus, when spectacular events (which people today might call miracles) occurred, the only questions for most ancient persons were (a) who was able to perform these deeds and (b) what was the source of their power?[12]

In this cultural context, mistaken beliefs about supernatural events would have been ubiquitous.

Interestingly, even though naturalistic explanations are much more readily available for us now for a wider range of phenomena, the appeal of the other side persists. Magical, supernatural, paranormal beliefs are common, even among relatively highly educated, twenty-first-century Americans. Even with our scientific, educational, and cultural advantages, our supernatural-belief threshold remains low. The Baylor Religion Survey says,

> Paranormal beliefs are rampant in American culture: 41% believe in the lost city of Atlantis, 78% believe in alternative medicine, 28% believe in tele-kinesis, 32% believe in haunted houses, 49% believe in prescient dreams, 29% in UFOs. 28% of the population has consulted a horoscope to get an idea about the course of their lives.[13]

Another issue relevant to evaluating the reliability of first-century Christians is that passionately invested and dedicated religious followers are disposed to believe their leaders are capable of supernatural acts. Millions of people believe that Tupac Shakur, Elvis Presley, Michael Jackson, and Osama bin Laden are still alive. Many North Koreans believed that Kim Jung Il had the magical power to change the weather with his moods and had other extraordinary powers. It was also reported on Korean news that he made multiple hole-in-one shots on his first attempt at playing golf, finishing thirty-eight under par for the course.[14] If modern humans who know what we know are so strongly disposed to accept magical claims about the people they admire, and if they are so strongly inclined to accept paranormal, spiritual, and supernatural claims when they should know better, then how much more readily would people two thousand years ago have accepted them? Oddly, given the context, it would be more remarkable for a popular and influential religious leader to die in such a culture and for multiple reports of magic surrounding his death *not* to surface. From our perspective we can see it is quite common for people to believe that a dearly loved and exalted spiritual or social leader has returned from the dead, or is still alive after his alleged death, and it would be even more common for people in the first century to do it.

So the question is not whether his early followers would have reported having unusual experiences. If the followers were normal people and if Jesus was real and they were as emotionally committed to him as has been alleged, then we would expect magical stories to spring up around the execution. The question will be, given that so many normal people report mistaken super-natural, miraculous, or magical events, what reasons do we have to think that the reports from the followers of Jesus are not like the mistaken beliefs we see so frequently around us?

IGNORANCE

For the sake of argument, let's allow that some of Jesus' followers actually did see something they found inexplicable—some of them heard voices; saw what appeared to be Jesus back from the grave; or experienced a strange disassociated state, a seizure, or a vision. What would an ordinary person in the first century be led to think if he had a hallucination, heard something strange, had a remarkable dream, or had some other notable experience? The explanations I cited in the previous section wouldn't have been available to them. They had scarcely any conception of what a brain is or what role it plays in fabricating, falsifying, or altering experiences in special circumstances. Such an experience would have been utterly mystifying. We can imagine it would have seemed to them that the only obvious and reasonable explanation of what they saw was that they were being visited by a ghost or the resurrected person they loved.

Failure to appreciate the nature and capacities of the human brain have no doubt played a huge role in the fact that 70–80 percent of modern Americans still believe in ghosts, after all. If modern humans are having these experiences and concluding that there are real ghosts, then surely the devoted first-century religious followers of Jesus would have been no more insightful or informed. It may even have been reasonable for them to think Jesus was resurrected, given that they just wouldn't have known any better. But we have substantial reasons to think his followers were wrong. Clearly, what might be reasonable for someone two thousand years ago without the benefits of science and the vast body of knowledge we have today should not be accepted as reasonable for us. What remains is the baffling puzzle of why so many people are willing simply to accept what the early believers claimed without question while being so much better informed about so many other things.[15]

When people undergo an emotionally traumatic event, it has dramatic effects on the brain. When people lose someone they love, it is quite common for them to have hallucinations of the person (or even a pet) shortly after the loss. The phenomenon is now well documented and is known as a *bereavement hallucination*. In one study, a remarkable 80 percent of elderly widows reported having hallucinations—either visual or auditory—up to one month after the spouse had died. It appears that the neurochemistry of grief is playing an active role on systems in the brain that contribute to visual and auditory representation. And these are not just fleeting glimpses or vague feelings that these widows and widowers are experiencing. They report seeing or hearing the lost person in some familiar environment, being visited in their dreams, or having complete conversations with them while being wide awake.[16]

These phenomena suggest several interesting points about religious beliefs. First, if Jesus was a real person and he was executed in the alleged public and dramatic fashion, then the emotional impact on his devoted followers would have been devastating. Suppose there were twenty people in Jesus' immediate circle of committed followers. If the studies we discussed can be taken as indicators of the likelihood of some sort of postdeath hallucination in which Jesus would revisit the followers, we can actually generate some probabilities. If we attach a conservatively low probability of 0.5 for each person that he or she will experience a hallucination of some sort (the widows in the study were 0.8) after Jesus' death, then we would expect roughly one-half of them to have one. The odds that none of the followers would have a hallucination are vanishingly small. What are the odds that you could flip a coin twenty times and get all heads? (It's $\frac{1}{2}^{20}$ = 1/1,048,576.) If the probability of each follower's having a bereavement hallucination was comparable to the 80 percent in the studies we discussed, then the odds that none of them would have had a hallucination are one in hundreds of millions. That is to say, knowing that bereavement hallucinations are so common, we would predict with high probability that many of Jesus' followers, like any other normal human beings, would have had them. It would be far more surprising and unlikely for his followers *not* to have reported seeing Jesus return from the dead; it would be vastly more unlikely, verging on the *miraculous*, for none of them to hallucinate Jesus.

The obvious objection here will be: "But whole groups of people don't have the same hallucination at the same time." To this there are several responses. First, the information we have are hearsay reports from the authors of the

Gospels, which were created decades after it is alleged that Jesus appeared to the disciples. (Recall that the ending of Mark was added in the second century, making the connection to direct, eyewitness reports even more remote.) It is easy to imagine how some of the followers could have seen or felt something, and then as they recalled and discussed it, the details of their stories began to converge.[17] Then rumors spread, stories were repeated, memories were embellished (see the next section of this chapter), and by the time the stories had been transmitted across thirty years, to the author of Mark, perhaps it appeared to that author that Jesus appeared jointly to all of the disciples. We can imagine many other scenarios whereby the accounts would develop until they were written. It is quite possible that the author of Mark was the first one to put together some of the disparate accounts into the form his narrative takes. The late, long ending of Mark could have been taken from several different stories circulating at that time. And it bears repeating that this central source of information about the resurrected Jesus did not surface until one hundred to two hundred years after the alleged events.

So the objection that all of the apostles couldn't have had the same hallucination is not as strong as we might have thought. What we have are some reports from decades and centuries later that a group of apostles had an experience. And we should keep in mind that the different Gospel accounts vary on every important detail. Perhaps the Apostles did see Jesus, but we have other much more probable hypotheses and a long list of unknowns about the fidelity of the information that has reached us. We can readily imagine several likely natural explanations for why a consolidated story would develop in the decades after Jesus' death. We will see in the next sections more details about how the claim that Jesus returned from the dead could have developed naturally.

EMBELLISHING MEMORIES AND CONSCIOUSNESS

Recognizing that many of Jesus' followers most certainly would have had bereavement hallucinations, we can be sure that they would have talked with each other, encouraged each other, adjusted their stories, and filled in or altered the details just as normal people do when they talk to each other about important events. (They would have conferred and compared notes, as it were, even if Jesus really did appear to them.) What would have happened next? The simple answer is that people's stories change with time.

A pervasive view is that the human memory functions more or less like a video camera recording a single, unified, accurate film of events that can be consulted later.[18] In fact, when we encode memories, we extract important elements, associate the events with other things we know, and omit or de-emphasize details. Later, when we recall the events, those highlights are embellished, altered, or substituted with new, often-fabricated details. During this process, many alterations are made and the events continue to get edited as time passes and we repeat the recollections. We change a memory every time we access it. But, importantly, many of these edits are invisible to us. We do not realize that we are doing it; in fact, we often have the powerful intuition that our story has remained exactly the same.

One well-documented human memory flaw is *source amnesia*. Memories about some event or piece of information are first stored in the hippocampus. But as the idea is recalled, reconsidered, or repeated, it is broadcast across the brain and becomes embedded without a strong connection to the context in which it was first learned. Even if someone makes a claim and precedes it with a disclaimer such as "I don't know if there's anything to this but . . ." or "I heard that . . ." or, even stronger, "It's not true that . . .", we are prone to register what follows and, if it is repeated often enough, we forget the disclaimer and take it as true. That's why the claims that Barack Obama is not an American citizen, or that the Americans didn't land on the moon, seem to have such longevity in the public mind. We store the idea but not the source. Once the idea is out there in the popular consciousness, it does not die. Repetition endows it with the luster of truth.[19] Ironically, repeating claims like the one about the president's citizenship or that a female cannot get pregnant the first time she has sex (a common view among high-school students) can serve to embed it as an even more vivid memory and propagate it.

We might think the extent of the problem is just that when we recall, we often do not recall where or how we heard some claim. But the problem is much worse. We are actually prone to completely co-opt memories of events as if they had happened to us when in fact someone else experienced the events and told us about them. Someone tells me a story about meeting a famous person or about a funny event, for example, then I repeat the story, and as time passes I begin to remember the event as happening to me. I unknowingly annex the events into my own history. Psychologist Elizabeth Loftus and her colleagues have demonstrated this effect simply by having a test subject imagine some event that did not happen, such as taking a ride in a hot air balloon or getting lost in a mall as a child, and then asking the subject about it later, people can readily be made to believe that the event actually happened to them. They go on to recall a high level of detail, and the false memory comes to feel completely real to them, so much so that when the subjects are debriefed and shown that it did not happen to them, many are incredulous.[20]

We are all familiar with the phenomena of urban mythology. It has become quite common for certain memes to spread and reproduce in the population—stories about a guy on a date who is drugged and then wakes up with a kidney missing, or a vengeful woman who wins her ex-husband's cherished sports car in a divorce settlement and sells it for $250. But the incredible attendant phenomena is that even though the story has little or no basis in fact and is being repeated across the culture, many individuals will vociferously insist, "No, really! It happened to this guy I know." That is, we co-opt these fantastic and appealing—but false—stories ourselves, often without even realizing what we have done. It is not uncommon for an individual to co-opt the story entirely and insist that it happened to her personally.

The proliferation and widespread acceptance of the Jesus story can lead believers to be incredulous about the suggestion that mere urban mythology could have seeded all or part of the Jesus story. How could a global movement of such profound influence and significance and of millions of followers have sprung from a mistake? With so many people accepting the resurrection, then and now, and with Jesus' return being a matter of such fame and public importance, it seems utterly implausible that it was all a mistake.

While researching material for this book, I came across two useful quotes about faith: Martin Luther King Jr. is alleged to have said, "Faith is taking the first step even when you don't see the whole staircase." And Benjamin Franklin is alleged to have said, "To follow by faith alone is to follow blindly." Both of these quotes have proliferated across the Internet in thousands of sources. The poignant and inspiring MLK quote has been taken up, repeated, and expounded upon in self-help books, pop-psychology books, websites, essays, forum discussions, sermons, and inspirational guides. The Franklin quote has proliferated among skeptics, freethinkers, atheists, secular humanists, naturalists, and countless others who are critical of faith. That King and Franklin made these comments fits comfortably with our cultural conceptions of them; the vivid metaphor and optimism of the King quote dovetails with our larger-than-life image of him as a visionary spiritual leader. The Franklin quote fortifies our portrait of him as a shrewd, skeptical, scientific rationalist. Given the way the Zeitgeist has developed around these two historical figures, the attributions make perfect sense. Even I, when searching for the sources, had the distinct feeling that King and Franklin *must* have made these comments; they are just the sorts of things that they would say.

But despite the fact that the attributions have proliferated across thousands of sources, it appears that neither King nor Franklin made the claims. At some point, someone attributed the claims to them. And the attribution—having the ring of authenticity—caught on. As the popular conception of some character in history develops, our image of them morphs and grows into something distinct from the facts. Memes take on lives of their own, and movements of global import that span centuries are spawned on the basis of mistakes. Is it such a stretch of the imagination to suggest that something similar happened with stories about Jesus coming back from the dead?[21]

The implication for the Gospel accounts is that when the authors of the Gospels spoke to others who claimed to have heard about the resurrected Jesus or even to have seen it themselves, there would have been decades of these sorts of embellishments, annexations, and edits. The authors, if they spoke to any other sources at all, may well have encountered people who claimed to have seen the resurrected Jesus themselves but had in fact co-opted the memories just as we do with urban myths and false memories. In the course of thirty to ninety years, hundreds or thousands of people could have heard about an event concerning Jesus and then, as they retold it, many of them came to think that they had actually seen it themselves. The authors, not knowing the first thing about modern memory research, may well have been struck by the passion, detail, and earnestness of the alleged witnesses' testimonials. The authors could have even co-opted the stories and come to think they had witnessed the events firsthand themselves.

One might think, however, that with important, momentous, or unusual events, the tendencies to embellish, co-opt, or fabricate might diminish. Perhaps we can imagine how people might come to believe that an urban myth had happened to them but not how they could believe they had actually seen a divine being return from the dead. In defense of the validity of the Gospel accounts of Jesus' life, it is frequently claimed that despite the years that passed between the events and their recording, matters of such profound significance as witnessing miracles or hearing Jesus' words would not have slipped easily from the minds of his followers. Our memories may be less reliable with trivial and ordinary matters, but with events of vast implications, such as the resurrection of the son of God, memories can be trusted. Many believers are unimpressed by appeals to normal human error rates because it seems to them that for a claim about an event as extraordinary as seeing someone *returned from the dead*, the testifiers would be less likely to be mistaken. They might be bad at other sorts of observations, but for something as unusual and significant as a resurrection, they would take great care and their accuracy would improve. A mere feeling that something special has happened at Lourdes, for instance, is not the same as looking at the animated, talking body of someone who was dead just a few days ago.

For an older generation, the assassination of President Kennedy was one such "flash bulb" moment. People believe they can recall with great detail and accuracy where they were and what they were doing when they heard the news. Likewise, when the news went out about the first plane crashing into the World Trade Center on 9/11, and then the second, a vivid picture of where you were, what you were doing, and how you felt was likely burned into your memory.

There are several problems with this objection, however. First, resurrection reports are not uncommon. Televangelist Oral Roberts reports them in his autobiography.[22] Pat Robertson has reported them to millions of his watchers on his television show and even produced video.[23] Worldwide there are many more, particularly in primitive societies more closely resembling the Iron Age culture that produced Christianity. In 1988, the *Kenya Times* published a report stating that Jesus had returned to a village in Africa and performed miracles witnessed by thousands.[24]

Second, the objection suggests that as the event gets more extraordinary, or as conviction and passionate avowal increase, the reliability of testimony increases. That relationship is not borne out by empirical research, however. Reports about important events taken right after the event vary significantly with our recollections of the event months or years later.[25] But our sensation that the memories are accurate remains just as strong. Shortly after the news of the space shuttle *Challenger* disaster went out, Ulric Neisser and Nicole Harsch had students in a psychology class write an account of where they were and what they were doing when they found out. Then, two and a half years later, they had those students write another record of what they were doing when they heard the news. Before they reread the earlier record, the students predicted their memories were accurate. But when Neisser and Harsch compared, the details matched in fewer than 10 percent of the paired accounts. More than 75 percent of the accounts had significant errors, some of them dramatic. Yet, even when confronted with this clear evidence to the contrary, many students refused to believe that their later memories were inaccurate.[26]

So our memories of important events get more inaccurate as time passes, even though our subjective estimates of our accuracy remain high. And contrary to the intuition many people have about these flashbulb memories, they become more inaccurate as time passes, just like our memories of ordinary events. But, ironically, while our confidence about ordinary memories goes down as time passes and their accuracy diminishes, as the accuracy of important memories goes down, our confidence in them does not.[27] To make matters worse, our own lack of competence is positively correlated with confidence. That is, for many tasks, the worse we are at it, the more confidence we express.[28] This Dunning-Kruger effect, named after the researchers who identified it, is one of the most frightening sorts of mistakes. Not only are we demonstrably bad at something, but our capacity to even recognize or rectify our poor performance is diminished. In other studies, people disregard information from an external source that conflicts with their strong, subjective sense that something is true or that they have a certain ability.[29]

So the intuitions driving the historical argument for the resurrection—

the importance and uniqueness of the resurrection and the deep, heartfelt convictions of the early Christians bolster the reliability of their resurrection stories—cannot be trusted. In fact, the empirical research shows that people are *less* reliable under these circumstances.

There are several implications for the question of religious belief. First, we forget the sources of claims we hear, true or false. Second, we are demonstrably bad at remembering events, even occurrences of enormous personal, emotional, and social importance. Third, the degree of confidence about our ability to remember important events is often grossly out of synch with the facts. That it *feels* to me like I can remember with great clarity isn't a reliable indicator that I can. And the disparity between my confidence and the real accuracy of my memories is even worse for important events. Fourth, we are prone to annex into our own memories stories we hear. As a result, events in our personal lives having profound religious significance that we recall later as the foundation of our beliefs can't be trusted to be what we remember and aren't more trustworthy because they have a great deal of poignancy. We also know that when confronted with evidence demonstrating how poor we are at remembering and judging, people are prone to reject that evidence in favor of their highly unreliable gut feelings. Therefore, taking heed of these lessons about ourselves will take some substantial effort to overcome our own resistant natures.

CONSTRUCTIVE CONSCIOUSNESS

In general, the line between what is consciously experienced and what is imagined is murky, at best. Consciousness itself and our memories of what we were conscious of undergo constant revision and alteration. Here's what often happens when a fan watches a basketball game, a psychic gives a psychic reading, or a pundit discusses the election of a politician. During the game, reading, or election, there will be a lot of talk. Friends watching a game will discuss the plays, the players and their choices, who's injured, who's playing well, and so on. The psychic will start with broad and vague generalities on lots of topics, searching consciously or unconsciously for some reaction from the customer. And the pundit who has been invited to share her opinions with a news program will talk at great length about the various issues in the election, the politicians' choices, voter preferences, and so on. As events develop and in the time that follows, the mind engages in an active series of revisions, refinements, and model building about what is happening, what led up to it, and what is going to happen next.

Even though he may have said hundreds of things during the game, the basketball fan may begin to think about and emphasize the outstanding form of the point guard when that point guard starts scoring points. It's not hard then, after the fact, for the fan to think and genuinely believe it when he says after the game, "See, I told you Johnson was playing well and was going to be instrumental in their win. I called the game, and I predicted he was going to have a great season this year." In the days or weeks that follow the game, the fan tells and retells this story, and each time, the events of the game change slightly in the retelling as well as his account of his own performance in forecasting it and predicting Johnson's outstanding playing. Meanwhile, the hundreds of other comments he made during the game and his actual predictions from before the game get more and more remote in his memory. The psychic and the pundit do more or less the same thing. As it rolls forward through time, human consciousness constantly rebuilds a model of the world (including the mind's place in it) and folds in the rapidly changing information it gathers from moment to moment. As the world changes, your picture of what you thought was going on from five minutes ago, one year ago, or thirty years ago fades and is replaced. And we fabricate a coherent narrative at the cost of accuracy, consistency, and memory. In the world, current events replace recent history during which the focus of your current consciousness leaps about from one discrimination to another. And the narrative of events that you construct is heavily influenced by your expectations, your desires, your biases, and various psychological nuances.

At any given time, we are constructing a picture of the world based on the information we are acquiring through our senses about it. But those channels of information are highly selective and expectation driven. We don't see or notice everything, and we alter many of the things we do see. Eyewitness testimony is, as is often pointed out, highly unreliable, but we may fail to appreciate just how bad it is. Daniel J. Simons, a visual-cognition researcher at the University of Illinois, has created a number of experiments with shocking results. In one video showed to test subjects, a group of people, some in white shirts and others in black shirts, pass a basketball back and forth while rapidly changing position. Subjects are instructed to watch the video and keep track of the number of times the white team exchanges the ball. During the video, a man in a gorilla suit saunters across in front of the basketball players, looks at the camera, beats his chest, and then walks off screen. An amazing 56 percent of the test subjects, who were focusing their attention on the ball passing behind the gorilla, failed even to notice the gorilla standing in plain sight and waving his arms. Subjects who are shown Simons's video and instructed to count white-team passes are typically incredulous that the gorilla was there until they are shown the video again. The secret is ruined for you now, but show the video to someone else and tell them to count the number of times the black-shirt team passes the ball and see if he notices the gorilla.[30] In other research on change blindness, collaborators Simons and Levin had an interviewer stop a student on campus to ask questions, then the scientists replaced the interviewer *with a different person* when two workers carried a large board between the two people. A significant number of the students failed to notice that they were now talking to a different person.[31] If you don't notice a man in a gorilla suit jumping up and down in front of you as it is happening or the person you are talking to turning into someone else, how reliable is your memory going to be about something you think you saw thirty years ago?

Even when we see an event in the visual field, we often don't get the details right. How we notice things is a function of expectation, priming, prior experience, and the configuration of our sensory systems. Consciousness is a dark and distorting lens on reality. Matters are then made worse as those real-world events recede into the past. Now they cannot be observed and no information from them can be acquired directly. Now you've got to access your memory of your consciousness of the events from the time, which is doubly distorted. Your conscious awareness of some event on Tuesday at 12:01 may have been skewed. Later, you don't remember the event itself, rather, you recall your consciousness of the event. So, on Friday, when your access to the event goes through your memory of the skewed consciousness, your hopes of getting it right are even dimmer. And the story you tell three weeks later about what happened will be changed even more. Daniel Dennett's summary of the multiple drafts model of consciousness is worth quoting at length to appreciate what we have learned about the structure of consciousness in recent years.

> All varieties of thought or mental activity are accomplished in the brain by parallel, multitrack processes of interpretation and elaboration of sensory inputs. Information entering the nervous system is under continuous "editorial revision." . . . These editorial processes occur over large fractions of a second, during which time various additions, incorporations, emendations, and overwritings of content can occur, in various orders. We don't directly experience what happens on our retinas, in our ears, on the surface of our skin. What we actually experience is a product of many processes of interpretation— editorial processes, in effect. . . . These distributed content-discriminations yield, over the course of time, something rather like a narrative stream or sequence, which can be thought of as subject to continual editing by many processes distributed around the brain, and continuing indefinitely into the future. . . . Probing this stream at different places and times produces different effects, precipitates different narratives from the subject. If one delays the probe too long (overnight, say), the result is apt to be no narrative left at all—or else a narrative that has been digested or "rationally reconstructed" until it has no integrity. If one probes "too early," one may gather data on how early a particular discrimination is achieved by the brain, but at the cost of diverting what would otherwise have been the normal progression of the multiple stream Most important, the Multiple Drafts model avoids the tempting mistake of supposing that there must be a single narrative (the "final" or "published" draft, you might say) that is canonical—that is the actual stream of consciousness of the subject, whether or not the experimenter (or even the subject) can gain access to it.[32]

Dennett's account of our current understanding of the way a narrative of consciousness is constructed dovetails nicely with what we have learned about miracle testimony, supernatural beliefs, and memory. The multiple drafts model illustrates the organic, nonlinear, and constructive nature of consciousness. And it makes clearer how a subject's account of some event could be revised and altered. In turn, those revisions and any errors they introduce would be reflected in the testimony the subject might give.

SOCIAL CONFORMITY

Earlier, we considered the objection that whole groups of people do not have the same hallucination at the same time. Whole groups of people can readily come to believe that they have seen the same thing, even when it is a flagrant falsehood. The urge to conform to the expectations of your social group can have a powerful influence on such beliefs. In a now-famous study from 1951, Solomon Asch showed it is common for good sense to be eclipsed by the desire to confirm what the group thinks even if it is patently false. Researchers put a test subject in a room with a number of confederates who were all secretly instructed to give the same wrong answer out loud to a simple visual test. When the people around the subject confidently gave the wrong answer, he or she conformed his or her answer to the erroneous majority in about one-third of the cases. When there was no pressure to conform, the subject gave the wrong answer in only one out of thirty-five cases.[33]

We may be inclined to reject empirical conclusions that defy deeply intuitive convictions about how we think and form beliefs. When I imagine sitting in a room of people where many of them assert line A is longer than line B, and I can plainly see with my own eyes that it is not, I cannot imagine that I would simply conform with the group, and I certainly would not come to genuinely believe the group's manifest falsehood. But at this point, we should have had our confidence in the accuracy of our deeply felt intuitions shaken. The empirical research shows that our intuitions—our subjective sense of what we do, how we think, how we form beliefs, and how our memories work—cannot be taken at face value when so much empirical evidence undermines them. With evidence like we have seen about the fallibility of the human cognitive system under ordinary circumstances, the burden of proof for the advocate of the historical resurrection becomes considerable. What reasons do we have to think that the early Christians were so different from us to be immune to the normal mistakes, confabulations, and distortions that the rest of us commit? In light of the neurological phenomena of bereavement hallucinations, false and implanted memories, group conformity, and source amnesia, it is difficult to see how a resurrection or something extraordinary could *fail* to become parts of so many ancient religions. And the burden on someone who wants to defend the authenticity of the Jesus stories in particular is to argue that we have substantial evidence that none of these common psychological phenomena were at work with the early Christians, or that none of these possibilities are more likely than Jesus' actually returning from the dead, given the evidence.

IQ AND THE ADVENT OF RELIGIOUS STORIES

In addition to being subject to normal cognitive flukes and lacking information we have today, differences in intelligence amplify our doubts about the early Christians' ability to judge a real resurrection from a mistake. A person's intelligence quotient, or IQ, is "a very general mental capacity that, among other things, involves the ability to reason, plan, solve problems, think abstractly, comprehend complex ideas, learn quickly and learn from experience. It is not merely book learning, a narrow academic skill, or test-taking smarts. Rather it reflects a broader and deeper capability for comprehending our surroundings—'catching on,' 'making sense' of things, or 'figuring out' what to do."[34]

We once thought IQ was a relatively stable, inherited trait. But the evidence has accumulated that problem solving and critical-thinking abilities are much more responsive to environmental factors like culture and schooling than we thought. Richard Nisbett, a prominent psychologist at the University of Michigan, estimates that the effects of family, nutrition, schooling, home environment, and surrounding culture could account for as many as eighteen points of IQ.[35]

Furthermore, IQ has been on the rise. Intelligence quotient tests are regularly renormalized to keep the average IQ score at one hundred. James R. Flynn has demonstrated that over that period IQs have been increasing by about three points a decade, now dubbed the Flynn effect.[36] That is all to say that we are getting smarter, and it's not because humans are genetically or bio-logically changing that much. It's because our environment is changing. We have access to huge amounts of sophisticated information now, better nutri-tion, better healthcare, more affluence, improved education, higher literacy rates, and so on. We are getting smarter in two ways. First, we have more information and better access to it now than we once did—high-school kids are doing experiments with recombinant DNA in class and they know more than a high-school student of one hundred years ago did. But the environment is actually raising our intelligence independent of increased information. The IQ increases show that we can solve problems, reason critically, and employ cognitive strategies better now than we used to.

What are the implications of the rise in IQ if we project it backward in time? It means that the average person from three hundred or five hundred or one thousand years ago would be less mentally able than the average person of today. We will not assume a steady downward slope in the projection, but we can conclude that his average IQ would have been lower than ours. The reason is that culture, education, nutrition, healthcare, and other external factors play such a large role in making it possible for people to actualize the potential they have for being smart. And only in the last fifty to one hundred years have we brought the level of education and affluence up high enough for enough people to really start seeing large-scale effects.

The IQ problem raises serious issues for all of the historically based reli-gions. The people who founded the world's religions, on average, would have had distinctly worse reasoning abilities, would have been less able to compre-hend complex ideas, and would have had a worse comprehension of their sur-roundings. There would have been outliers, of course. Aristotle, Copernicus, Newton, and Kant would have stood out intellectually from their peers, and they would most likely still stand out among our modern, elevated stan-dards. But what about average people? The people who became believers in the major religious movements? If there were people two thousand years ago who thought they saw a ghost or miraculous, supernatural event, we might not blame them for their conclusions. They can't be faulted for not knowing what we know and not having the critical-reasoning capacities we have. Nor should we assume the claims they make about these events are false because they were less intellectually able. But it does bear on our assessment of these early Christians' reliability. We should not assume that if they were satisfied Jesus was resurrected or Muhammad was Allah's Prophet, then we should be satisfied, too.

It would be a mistake if our acceptance of their claims is predicated on an implicit or explicit assumption that the original believers would have been sufficiently thoughtful, reflective, objective, critical, and smart to figure out the truth. Considerations about the source's IQ are relevant to the extent that we take our justification for believing to be the fact that they believed. The reasons and the reasoning (or lack thereof) that might have led them to believe may not be sufficient for our believing. As soon as we uncover this assumption, it is obvious what a mistake it is. Would you readily accept the conclusions about the most important questions facing humanity—without question—from someone of today with an IQ of 60? Do you think she would be the most reliable, thoughtful, objective source of information you could find? The people transmitting the resurrection story to us were most likely equipped with less than ideal reasoning skills and cognitive abilities.

The suggestion here will be outrageous and offensive to some. But what other conclusion can we see? If we know that IQ is highly responsive to environmental factors and that those factors were worse in previous eras of history, then we know that IQs were lower—significantly lower—in those eras. And if we are getting our information about alleged supernatural events like miracles, invisible gods with magical powers, people coming back from the dead, and so on from these same people, then surely the facts about their mental capacities are relevant to our assessment of their reliability. We've got to consider the source; we should not make the mistake of assuming that they were just like us in all of the cognitively or epistemically relevant ways.

THE FRAME-OF-REFERENCE PROBLEM

From a broader view, this chapter has made it clearer how different the worldview of the first believers would have been. And it has made it clearer how many psychological factors would have helped create that worldview and contributed to its being mistaken. Those differences raise problems with our believing Jesus was resurrected on the grounds that they believed Jesus was resurrected. That is, we shouldn't believe what they believed because we can now see many of the factors that would have increased the early Christians' error rates. From their perspective (knowing and believing what they did) believing in the resurrection might have made sense; from yours, it does not.

The point of the discussion so far has not been to argue that the ancient believers were foolish, silly, or unreasonable (although some of them were, no doubt). The problem that emerges from this discussion is a peculiar problem of Christianity and other doctrines where the modern adherent bases her belief in some far-flung metaphysical entities and events primarily on the belief of others across some broad span of time. In this case, the ancient and modern believer are roughly believing the same thing, so to the extent that the modern believer founds his conviction on the ancient adherent's belief, he ends up believing it on similar *grounds*, for lack of a better term. But what constitutes sufficient or acceptable grounds for a belief: the available information, background beliefs, principles of evidence, and so on, all change dramatically over time. So believing what they believed will be out of synch with conclusions we accept that are couched in our world and the knowledge we have now.

The surprising implication is that what is reasonable changes as this background changes because a person's historical, scientific, cultural, and personal context changes. And in general, we have now seen why supernatural accounts of the world get less credible over time while natural ones get more credible. This is not to say that what is true, or what really occurred, itself changes or is relative. The bubonic plague was never caused by demon possession, even if that was the only justified explanation at the time. There is a fact of the matter about whether or not Jesus really came back from the dead. And the epistemic context for two different people may render believing the resurrection reasonable for one and absurd for another, just like a parent's and a child's perspective about Santa Claus differs.

The challenge we are accepting is trying to form a reasonable, consistent view about whether the things the early Christians said about Jesus are true.

And the result we are finding is that whatever the actual truth of the matter may be, it is not reasonable to accept the claim that Jesus came back from the dead on their reports and given the body of information available to us now.

THE FILTERS

With the goal of answering the question "Should I believe what they believed?" let us summarize the problems with the links in the chain between us and the alleged resurrection: the alleged witnesses, the repeaters, the authors, the copyists, and the canonizers. The problems raised in this chapter primarily concerned the alleged witnesses, the repeaters, and the authors, although many of them may have been at work on the copyists and canonizers, too. But we will consider specific problems with those last two links in the chain in the following chapters.

What are the problems we have seen? First, there is a general human-reliability problem. The abundance of miracle, magical, supernatural, and paranormal claims made by people who are mistaken, misguided, or deceitful shows that the general reliability of humans for testimony about these topics is vanishingly low. Lourdes, France, and the failure of prayer show that people are highly unreliable when it comes to reporting miracles. Even when we are being generous and grant that real miracles occur once and a while, people claiming to have seen a miracle get it right only once in millions of instances. The problem isn't really that miracles are rare but that mistaken miracle reports are orders of magnitude more abundant. The sources of miracle reports are staggeringly unreliable. Second, the early believers would have been highly disposed to generally believe in supernatural events. Their supernatural-belief threshold would have been very low. For Iron Age people, the world would have been full of mysterious forces, magical events, and spiritual entities; stories about supernatural happenings would have been common. Hundreds of the events you observe every day and know the causes of would have been complete mysteries to these early believers. For all they knew, headaches were caused by magic. The possibility that someone could come back from the dead would have seemed like common sense to them, with the right background information and expectations. And like other humans, they would have been strongly prone to attribute otherworldly powers to their religious leader.

We also now know that bereavement hallucinations are widespread and robust phenomena. When people are emotionally traumatized by the death of someone they care about, it is quite common to have strange episodes where we see the dead person, talk to them, or hear them.

Human consciousness and memory is an organic and unreliable method for recording events. We embellish, adjust, and edit. It is surprisingly easy for humans to acquire false memories that feel authentic and vivid. We are also prone to source amnesia. We have unreliable recall of where we heard something or how trustworthy the source is. We even co-opt the memory of events from other people, making them our own. Our expectations and goals can affect our observations to the point that even a dancing gorilla right in front of our faces goes unnoticed.

We have also seen that the constant revising of the narrative stream of events around us—and our participation in them—blurs the lines between reality and fiction. Our own misjudgment of our own abilities, such as the inverse relationship between confidence and expertise in the Dunning-Kruger effect, makes matters worse. The Asch effect leads people to believe or to say they believe claims that are manifestly false or that conflict with the evidence right in front of them. And contemporary research reveals that IQ would be much lower in previous centuries, further diminishing the reliability of reports from early Christians about fantastic miraculous events they thought they saw.

Furthermore, they were ignorant of the information we have concerning religious tendencies, religious group dynamics, human-cognitive flukes, psychology, and alternative explanations for paranormal beliefs. They were ignorant of the two thousand years of examples of allegedly supernatural events that turned out to be easily explainable in natural terms. In those two thousand years, we have learned a great deal about how human psychology works, errors in reasoning, problems in eye-witness reports, gullibility, mistakes, social-religious phenomena, and so on.

Early Christians would have been much less skeptical overall than many people who are good sources of information today are. (Regrettably, far too many people now remain unskeptical about similar matters.) They would not have been trained or practiced or even familiar with the notions of disconfirming evidence, alternative explanations, bias, and justification. They were deeply committed religious converts who were actively discouraged from being skeptical or critical about extraordinary claims made at that time. Many nonsupernatural explanations for ordinary and extraordinary natural events would not have been available to them.

APPLYING A CONSISTENT STANDARD

The Romans contemporary to Jesus believed in a wide range of omens, spiritual events, and supernatural phenomena. They also accepted the existence of a number of gods. But you don't accept their claims, probably because of the problems just outlined with believing the early Christians. Unless you are a historically minded Muslim or a Mormon who takes the stories about Joseph Smith's encounters with the angel Moroni to have actually happened, you would probably take a parallel argument to the one I have made against Christianity in this chapter against Roman superstitions, Islam, or Mormonism to be completely plausible. That is, you would accept that all these psychological factors and the general unreliability of human miracle testimony undermine the Romans and the foundations of Islam and Mormonism. Furthermore, there are many people today who are much better educated and who have a much better body of background information who make supernatural, miracle, and magical claims on a regular basis, yet you do not believe them. We are surrounded by smart, seemingly reasonable people making supernatural claims that we reject as suspicious, yet we accept comparable claims from utterly unreliable people in the first century.

In 1911, some Californians discovered a man named Ishi near Lassen, California, who was the last living member of an isolated tribe of Yana Indians. Anthropologists were fascinated with the case because he was one of the closest examples ever found of contact between a group of people that was virtually living in the Stone Age and people living in the modern era. Ishi achieved some level of assimilation and enjoyed some celebrity until his death from tuberculosis in 1916. Ishi was an expert archer, and he was accomplished at making stone arrowheads and shooting a simple bow. But Ishi also believed in a mystical land of the dead, where the souls of the Yana had a shadowy existence.[37] You might plausibly accept Ishi as a reliable source of information about making and shooting a simple bow and arrow, but no reasonable person would accept his views about the land of the dead merely on the grounds that he said it was real, even if he said he had been there and seen it with his own eyes. To accept the early Christians' claims about Jesus, God, and the afterlife would be a comparable mistake.

In sum, whatever sort of report they might make about religious or supernatural matters, the first-century Christians would have been resoundingly bad sources whose testimony should not be trusted. Here is a remarkable irony: even if Jesus had come back from the dead and had visited these people and they subsequently spread the story, from our position, we would not be able to accept the story because of the various considerations that erode the witnesses' reliability. Even if they were telling the truth, we should not believe them.

But suppose the resurrection did not happen. Consider the circumstances of a first-century peasant who has become a passionate follower of Jesus and who had already come to believe that Jesus possesses great power and is capable of various acts of magic. Then Jesus is executed in the midst of social unrest and instability among his followers, who are suffering acute emotions of loss, confusion, and fear. Shortly thereafter, like most people, some of the followers see or feel or hear something anomalous. After some excited comparisons in conversation of their experiences, which they would not have been able to explain naturalistically, the details of a vision of Jesus begin to be more and more vivid, and it seems to them more and more like something did happen. But the organic development of this now-vivid memory and its alterations are not apparent to the follower. Now suppose something similar is going on in the minds of some of the other followers, or the Asch effect is influencing their thoughts. As the weeks and years pass, the story is repeated and shared. The original followers and many new believers with powerful hopes continue to embellish and fortify the story unbeknownst to them. Some people even co-opt the story, coming to believe that it happened to someone they know, or even to themselves. The movement grows in popularity and influence, and after thirty or more years, an author writes down the amazing story he has been hearing about a man who claimed to be a god and who came back from the dead.

Within the context of the psychology and cognitive-science research we've been considering, our estimations of the reliability of the early believers should be greatly reduced. And several alternate, natural hypotheses suggest themselves over the view that the best explanation for the early Christians' stories is that they really did see a man return from the dead.

An objection remains to be considered here. When we raise worries about the reliability of historical sources regarding the resurrection, as we have done here, one of the concerns is that if we adopt such stringent standards for acceptable historical sources, we will be forced to reject many other historical claims that are widely considered to be reasonable. If we reject Jesus, then we will also have to be skeptics about Caesar's crossing the Rubicon, Lincoln's freeing the slaves, or the occurrence of the Holocaust.

First, it should be clear from the previous chapters that the evidence for the resurrection is simply much worse than the evidence we have for these other events. Second, and more importantly, we should recall a point from earlier in this chapter: the objection fails to acknowledge that people are demonstrably more reliable for some sorts of information than others. The point is so obvious, and so familiar that we scarcely notice how often we discriminate depending on the sort of claim. If some medieval source reports that Pope Gregory VII died in 1085, and that source is corroborated, we then accept the claim. But if that source reports the widespread view that holding a burning candle near an aching tooth will make the pain-inducing worms wither and fall out, we are justifiably incredulous, no matter how thoroughly we can corroborate that this was widely believed in 1085. Likewise, we would reject the people of this time period's widespread use of astrology and numerology for medical cures, planning crops, and political strategy. And notice that it does not matter how many sources we can find that show people in the period believed in astrology, numerology, trepanation for bubonic plague, and candle burning for toothaches. One thousand sources showing they believed these ideas do not make them even slightly more likely to be true than ten sources would. What we have seen is that for supernatural claims in particular, ancient sources are highly unreliable for a number of specific reasons. And those doubts should apply wherever they are relevant. They do not apply, for the most part, to our information about the major events in the life of Caesar. Many Romans did believe in magic, however. And many Romans believed that Caesar had magical powers. But the reasons outlined in this chapter are exactly why we should not believe them on those counts.

The task for the next chapter is to see how the layers and layers of doubts raised about the links in the chain between us and Jesus combine. When there are so many doubts at so many stages in the transmission, what is the net effect on the final reliability of the information? The short answer is that the prospects for the resurrection are going to get much worse.

Chapter 5

THE REPEATERS AND THE MONEY-BAG PROBLEM

W e have considered a number of problems that should substantially reduce our confidence in the reports about the resurrection from the alleged eyewitnesses. Errors at Lourdes, France; failed or unanswered prayers; and the frequency of other mistaken paranormal beliefs show us that people's error rates are very high. What we have learned about people's ignorance, receptiveness to supernatural claims, bereavement hallucinations, co-opted memories, false memories, embellished memories, source amnesia, social conformity, and IQ rates amplifies our doubts about the alleged eyewitness reports.

Many of our worries will also apply to anyone who repeated the story orally or who recorded it in writing on its way across time to the authors of the Gospels and then ultimately to us. But there are specific transmission problems to discuss regarding the repeaters—the people who would have been talking and spreading the Jesus stories for many decades before they were written down.

Bible scholars make a great deal of the accuracy of the Jewish oral tradition. In the rabbinic tradition, there was a practice of passing theological law by word of mouth and memory from master to student. A deliberate effort was made to communicate the information accurately and the practice was heavily emphasized as providing Jews with a vital segment of their religious traditions. Many students of the New Testament have defended the reliability of the stories conveyed about Jesus from their occurrence to when they were written several decades later by arguing that the stories were preserved carefully within the Jewish oral tradition.

There are several problems with this suggestion, however. First, the rabbinic oral tradition had a specific purpose that was antithetical in several ways
to the situation surrounding Jesus' resurrection story. The oral tradition was
preserved for exposition of a set of specific laws given to the Jews by God from
Moses. These laws were to be committed to memory and passed on in a very
deliberate fashion from rabbi to student under specific circumstances. And
the method was confined to these laws and some of their elaborations. It's
far-fetched, to say the least, to suggest the Jews would violate the centuries-
old customs of this tradition and quickly fold in a story about a renegade Jew
with some radical teachings that overthrow a number of vital Jewish religious doctrines. Suppose that last week, a Catholic priest in a small parish was
reported to have performed some new miracles and to have some important
new Christian teachings, some of which reject traditional Christian orthodoxy.
Consider the powerful resistance that would come from the Catholic Church
if a small group of the priest's followers suggested Catholics officially add a
new book to the Bible to record this priest's new miracles and new teachings.
What endows the rabbinic oral tradition with its authority and accuracy—its
conservatism, caution, exactitude, and parsimony—are the same reasons that
rumors about the subversive teachings and divisive miracles of Jesus would *not*
have been preserved in this fashion. Let us not forget that, as the Christian sees
it, the resurrection of Jesus is the undoing of traditional Judaism. Additionally,
modern Jews within the very same tradition that is alleged to have preserved
this essential information about the resurrection explicitly deny that Jesus
was resurrected. The Christian who would corroborate the resurrection in this
fashion cannot ignore the fact that Jews, rabbis, Talmud scholars, and modern
Jewish experts on the Jewish oral tradition emphatically reject the claim that
Jesus' resurrection was incorporated into Judaism in this way. The resurrection was not sanctioned or preserved in their oral tradition. If Jesus' resurrection and other essential Christian doctrines that overturn Judaism were
preserved by a time-honored and hallowed Jewish method, why does Judaism
persist and deny the resurrection and those doctrines?

Furthermore, only central parts of Jewish religious doctrines, such as laws
that were thought to have come from God, were designated for preservation
within the official oral tradition among rabbis. How does a story about a man

being resurrected fit into a procedure for preserving the elaborations of ancient Jewish law?

It is not known whether, how much, or which parts of the Jesus stories might have been sanctioned and included within Jewish law. Jesus' doctrines and his claims to divinity were hotly contested among the Jews and denied by many. Even if parts of the stories were preserved in this fashion, there were, no doubt, many other people talking, writing, and repeating ideas about Jesus. We do not know what sources (nor through how many) the information passed between the alleged events and their recording in the Gospels. And as we saw in chapter 2, the long period of liberal writing and communicating between early Christians that eventually created the thousands of documents from which the New Testament was compiled suggests a much messier, organic path taken by the Jesus stories. So the prospects seem dim for a strong defense of the accuracy of the Gospels in virtue of their transmission by the rabbinic oral tradition.

Yet, even the strongest defense of the oral tradition won't address many of the long list of problems we discussed in the previous chapter: the Lourdes problem, the low supernatural-belief-threshold problem, bereavement hallucinations, source amnesia, false memories, implanted memories, co-opted memories, the Dunning-Kruger effect, the invisible-gorilla problem, the Asch effect, the Flynn effect, and so on.

In either case, a significant problem with the transfer of information between people that is often overlooked is the cumulative effect of having information repeated again and again as it passes through different speakers. A simple example and some probabilities can illustrate this point. We can think of this example as a model of information transmission that will help us to understand the challenges of accepting the resurrection.

THE MONEY BAG

Suppose that a bag with a police escort arrives at a courthouse in Los Angeles. We can imagine that it is part of the evidence in a trial. A court clerk receives the bag, opens it, and finds a large sum of money. The clerk then asks some questions of the police officer who delivered it. As it turns out, the bag traveled from New York. Along the way, it was carried by three different police escorts, who each controlled it for a different leg of the journey. Let's also suppose that the manifest has been lost, so the clerk doesn't know how much money started the trip in the bag. The clerk does some checking and discovers there is some corruption in each of the three police departments that had custody, so the general likelihood that a given cop is completely honest in each of the three departments is 0.8. Let's stipulate that if a corrupt cop gets custody of the bag, he or she will take some money. And if an honest cop gets custody, he or she will deliver it to the next leg of the trip without taking any money. The clerk wants to answer this question: What is the probability the money that arrived in the clerk's office is the same amount of money originally found in the bag that left New York?

The answer is the probability that the first cop will take some money, multiplied by the probability that the second cop took some money, multiplied by the probability that the third cop took some, or $0.8 \times 0.8 \times 0.8$. The probability the amount that arrived in Los Angeles was the same as the amount that left New York is 0.51 (or 51 percent). If you add two more cops at the 0.8 honesty rate, this probability goes down to 0.32 (or 32 percent). And this is despite the fact that the *majority* of cops in each department are honest. If five cops with an honesty rating of 0.9 escort the money, there is only a 59 percent chance all of it will arrive at its destination. If seven cops with a 0.95 honesty rating escort it, there is only a 66 percent chance all of it will arrive, without any money being stolen. We can compare this system to a system that captures and relays information. It doesn't take many generations of copies from a copy machine, particularly a poor one, for the text of the original to become unreadable and for the information to be partially or completely lost.

Even when the individual links in the system are highly reliable, the cumulative effect of small error rates across multiple links quickly diminishes the overall fidelity of the system. And it doesn't take many links, even when they are 95 percent reliable, for the odds to drop off to the point that it is more likely the information or the money did *not* make it through than the probability that it did. If there were five cops relaying the money from departments that were 80 percent honest, you should conclude the money is *not* all there because there is a 68 percent probability that someone stole some along the way. Once we introduce multiple links and even just a very slight error rate, it is not long before the threshold is crossed and we should start assuming that what comes out of the system is not what went in.

Matters are made worse by still other variables. Suppose the clerk has no independent way to know what was put in the bag in the first place; she was just handed a bag. She would not know if it originally contained drugs, or diamonds, or cash, or bonds. She could ask the cop who handed it to her, or she could check the contents of the bag for some clue. Suppose there is a note inside the bag itself reading, "This bag originally contained $10,000." After she counts it and finds $10,000, can she now be assured all of the original contents of the bag made it to her safely? No, she can't. Notice that the note is part of the contents of the bag, too. For all she knows, there could have been $100,000 in the bag, or five kilos of heroin, or even a pardon from the president, and when one of the cops took $90,000 out or replaced the heroin with $10,000, the cop wrote the note and stuck it in there. Using the contents of the bag itself to determine the fidelity of the system that transmitted the bag is circular and completely unhelpful.[1] What the clerk needs is some independent (and trustworthy) source to corroborate the origination and transmission of the bag. If she put the money into the bag in New York herself and then flew to Los Angeles with it, keeping her eyes and hands on it all the way, then she could be more assured (assuming she can rely on herself and her memory).

Suppose it wasn't a cop who dropped the bag off in the clerk's office but just a stranger who left immediately after telling her the contents were important evidence for the trial. In this case, she has only the contents of the bag, but she doesn't know from where it originated, how many people through whom it passed, or how reliable any of them were. What would you think if you were on trial, falsely accused of a capital crime, and this mysterious bag that had passed through an unknown number of mysterious sources from a mysterious origination point was used as vital evidence to find you guilty, have you convicted, and send you to prison?

The point of the extended analogy is this: we are told by a book that has been transmitted to us across centuries and through countless unknown people that there were some important religious events that transpired circa 35 CE. Between those alleged events and their first recording in writing, thirty to one hundred years had passed. And we have only copies of those writings from about two centuries later still. During those years, we do not know how many times the story was repeated or through how many people it passed before it got to those who wrote it down.

We have some semi-independent means of rough secondary corroboration. We have other historical grounds to assess the oral-transmission tradition in Judaism at the time (leaving aside for the moment our previously discussed objections to the oral tradition). Part of our evidence involves using written sources to check the error rate of written stories versus orally relayed stories in different eras of history where we have both types of transmitted information. That is, we cannot conclude that the oral tradition is highly reliable merely because one of the assertions repeated within the oral tradition is that the oral tradition is reliable. We would need to have some fairly straightforward cases where a story originates and is communicated by both written and oral lines independently for some period. Ideally, the two versions would be kept completely separate, and then we could compare the two and check for divergence. Unfortunately we do not have any clear cases like this that are comparable to the Jesus story. We do know the stories about Jesus were spreading far and wide among the early Christians in the first two centuries. And while there may be some transmitters who have a higher fidelity than others, we are not sure who or how many sources the authors of the Gospel stories consulted. There may be a stream of information running through the Jewish oral tradition that is more reliable, but there can be no question that people will talk, and when people talk and repeat stories, we know they embellish, omit, alter, and improve the tale, either deliberately or unknowingly, especially if the story was about the demise and extraordinary return from the dead of a charismatic and loved religious leader.

When the story does get written down (which we would think would be an even more reliable method of recording), we can see that the story of Jesus' resurrection varies greatly among the Gospels. As Bart Ehrman says:

Not only did different Christian communities have different books—they had different versions of the same books. . . . Unfortunately, we do not have the originals of any of the books of the New Testament, or the first copies, or the copies of the copies. What we have are copies made much later—in most cases hundreds of years later.

How do we know that these copies were changed in the process of reproduction? Because we can compare the thousands of copies that we now have, which range in date from the second to the sixteenth centuries, to see if and how they differ from one another. What is striking is that they differ *a lot*. In fact, among the over 5,000 Greek copies of the New Testament that we have, no two of them are exactly alike in all their details. We don't know how many differences there are among these copies because no one has been able to add them all up. But the total is in the hundreds of thousands. Possibly it is easiest to put the matter in comparative terms: there are more differences in our manuscripts than there are words in the New Testament.[2]

And we also know a number of noncanonized sources that gave even more contrary accounts were deliberately excluded. So it is difficult to put much faith (pun intended) into some of the claims about the reliability of the verbal transmission of the stories. Again, think of a life-sentence decision in a court trial where you are the accused and your guilt is being decided on the basis of information coming through a transmission system made up of people. (And according to Christian doctrine, the decision involves your *eternal* reward or punishment.) Given what you know about the way people make mistakes, gossip, exaggerate for effect, embellish, and alter for a good story, are you so confident about the reliability of every single node of transmission that you would want your sentencing decision based upon it? Suppose you were a jury member and the sole piece of evidence for the defendant's guilt in a murder charge is the testimony of two to five men. The men claim they are scholars from a tradition that tells and retells important facts to each other and makes a careful effort to preserve them accurately. None of them saw the murder, but they all say it has been a part of their oral tradition, passed on to them for eighty years, saying that the defendant is guilty. Another man many years ago in their tradition told them that the defendant committed the murder. The charge is serious and carries execution as its punishment. Would you convict? Before you answer, think about the various errors in judgment we discussed in chapter 4.

We might be tempted to give generally high marks to an earnest person's reliability, particularly if he is taking pains to accurately communicate some important information. Part of our trust of others arises from what we know from our own experience and what we know about our own reliability. It seems to me that I am highly reliable about many things (and not others), and who would know better about it than me? But not only does careful research expose just how many cognitive tasks we are bad at but also how bad we are at noticing and acknowledging we are bad at them. Recall the Dunning-Kruger effect from chapter 4: in many cases, a person's performance is *inversely* related to his confidence.[3] Asking you if you are good at something produces answers that have very little to do with your real abilities. Students who are consulted about their performances on a test right after taking it give answers that wildly diverge from their real results. People persist in thinking they are good at a task even after it has been clearly demonstrated to them that they are not. Shoppers who are asked to evaluate the quality of a series of clothing items on a table will exhibit a strong bias in favor of the item on the right. And when asked why, they will say it is a better piece of clothing because of its construction, the material used, the stitching, the design, and so on.[4] What's particularly interesting here is that the shoppers have a strong bias, which they seem to be completely unaware of, and when they are asked to justify their choices, they fabricate an answer out of thin air without even knowing they are doing it. In fact, many will deny they have the bias, even after it is shown to them.

The research on this topic in recent decades, supporting a position sometimes called *anti-introspectionism*, is stunning. People's widespread presumption is generally something like this: "Surely I know what I do and do not believe. I also know why I believe it. I know when and why I change my mind. And when I have a feeling of certainty, then it can be trusted even more." The real picture is much dimmer. A large body of research, like the shopper study, shows that people are frequently poor judges of what they believe, what they feel, why they believe or feel it, whether they changed their minds, and why they changed their minds.[5]

WHAT ARE THE ODDS ON THE JESUS STORY?

In light of these points about supernatural reports, we can clarify some points about the resurrection's reliability. The police in our money-bag story transmitted the bag, but the bag did not originate with them. By analogy, the Jesus resurrection story allegedly originated with some eyewitnesses. Their reliability should be considered separate from the reliability of the repeaters. Our assessment of the reliability of the alleged eyewitnesses should be informed by our general knowledge about people who claim to have seen miracles, and the other things we now know about human psychology.

The picture is still oversimplified, but we can sketch it out this way. If the claim that some event of supernatural origin came through one eyewitness and was then transmitted three times before being written down, the probability that the output of the sequence is true will look something like this:

$$0.0000167 \times 0.8 \times 0.8 \times 0.8 = 0.000008 \text{ or about eight in one million.}$$

If one person tells a miracle story and the general reliability for miracle stories is 0.0016 percent (from our Lourdes discussion in the previous chapter), and then that story passes through three other people who all happen to be 80 percent reliable in their transmission of the information, then the odds are exceedingly small that the end result can be trusted. Even though these people assert it is true, the variables affecting their reliability show it is much more likely to be false.

Suppose we are much more generous about people's reliability with miracle reports, and we grant that in one-tenth of the cases where someone says she witnessed a miracle she actually did; and when other people then repeat that story, they are 90 percent reliable; our equation would be $0.1 \times 0.9 \times 0.9 \times 0.9 = 0.07$ or seven in one hundred. So a miracle report in these circumstances is still orders of magnitude too unlikely to be accepted. This ignores the impact of many of the problems with their reliability, which we discussed in the previous chapters. Furthermore, it is simply not reasonable to think that 10 percent of all miracle claims are true. Even the review board at Lourdes would agree. No one who has listened closely to themselves or others retelling a miraculous story will think that they achieve 90 percent fidelity. But note that even if we allow these exceedingly generous estimates on our simple model, the Jesus story is far too unlikely to be believed.

Also note that we are being generous by accepting that the real miracle rate at Lourdes is .0016 percent. We have been accepting that the miracles declared to be real by the Lourdes Medical Bureau are in fact real. This panel is made up of appointed clergy and doctors who selected themselves to be on the panel. Many of the alleged real miracles in Lourdes, France, don't stand up to any serious outside scrutiny. Typically, enthusiasm, lack of objectivity, con-flicts of interest, wishful thinking, the placebo effect, and other natural causes have played a role in such cases.[6] If we reduce the number of real miracles at Lourdes (as we should) to a still-generous five, and lower the reliability of the transmitters or add a few more links, then the result is 0.000000021 or twenty-one in one billion for the probability that a miracle report conveyed to you in this fashion is true.

We have a very rough picture of a range of values we might attach to infor-mation about the resurrection of Jesus coming through a simplified system. And it should be clear that our confidence in the Jesus story in a system like this is many orders of magnitude smaller than it needs to be for us to take it seriously, even when we are overly and unjustifiably charitable. On our simple model, given what we know about the original reporting and the transmission of these stories, it is exceedingly unlikely that they are true.

More sophisticated models of probability employ Bayes's theorem, which tells us that the net effect of others giving the same or similar testimony is to bolster our confidence in the story if the reliability of each of the additional testifiers is greater than 0.5.[7] That is, suppose you attach an initial probability to the occurrence of some event or kind of event, and then one person comes and tells you it has occurred. Suppose you figure the odds of winning the lottery are one in one million and then someone you know but who you've come to distrust as a reliable source (e.g., reliability = 0.3) tells you that a friend of his just won the lottery. The odds of winning the lottery are very low and since you find this distrustful person's testimony actually to be a greater indicator that a claim is false, you should come away thinking the supposed friend of his did not win the lottery. However, if you assign a relatively high probability to an event, say the probability that some American soldiers will be killed in Afghanistan today is 0.9, and then a newscaster who is generally very reliable (reliability = 0.9) reports this event to you, then applying Bayes's theorem will indicate that it is probable some American soldiers were killed in Afghanistan today. Bayes gives us an extremely useful way to quantify what's often intuitive in assessing probabilities. But it also helps us to clarify the variables when the picture gets too complicated to trust our intuitions.

In our example so far, we have modeled one person testifying at the beginning of the chain, and that information gets transmitted through several repeaters, one at a time, before it gets to you. Defenders of the historical case for the resurrection will insist that there were multiple witnesses and multiple lines of transmission. The result of the more simple model I have sketched out, because of the general unreliability of miracle testimony and noise in the system, is that the odds are very good the event did not occur. What happens when more lines of testimony inform us that the same thing happened? According to Bayes, it depends on the reliability of those lines of information. If these additional sources have a low reliability (under 0.5), then the net effect of their adding to this improbable story will be to reduce its probability. If those sources have a high probability (over 0.5), then their contribution will be to upgrade the story's probability. The exact numbers and degrees to which a given source changes the probability depend on the case and the exact numbers we assign to the various values.

Despite the technical approach, this makes some sense. If one (reliable) person tells you something highly unusual happened, you might not be as inclined to accept it until several more say the same thing. Multiple independent lines of corroboration satisfy us about most things, especially events that are not too uncommon. But the acceptability of the result will depend on how unlikely the event is to start with and how reliable each of the testifiers is.

So what is the net effect on our simple model of the added consideration that other people reported the resurrection story? Many people appeared to believe it; there were different witnesses and different lines of information. Doesn't that give us the independent corroboration we need in the money-bag case? No, it doesn't, but the explanation as to why not is complicated. Without doing the math using Bayes's theorem, we can say the following. In the first equation (A), what really drags down the overall reliability rating is the extraordinarily low reliability rating for the first link in the chain, the originator of the miracle story. If that number is low, and we have seen why it is, then that dramatically reduces the reliability of what comes out the other end of the system. This makes sense; even if you have a very good transmission system, if you put garbage into it, then you get garbage out. In simple terms, it won't matter if the fidelity of the connecting links is perfect, if the claim that gets put into it is probably false, then the claim that comes out of it is probably false. What we are wondering about now is what happens to the output if there are more originators who seem to corroborate the story. The answer is that if their reliability for reporting miracles stories is as low as our example, then they don't help much.

How many lines of information do we have about Jesus? Mark, possibly Q (the additional source from which Matthew and Luke borrowed that is now lost), and John are the only early written sources. According to Bible scholars, Matthew and Luke use the text of Mark for their information, so that disqualifies them as independent lines of information. Paul, in First Corinthians, Acts, and elsewhere, repeats that Jesus had been resurrected and visited his followers. But those are not alleged to be accounts of eyewitness reports the way Mark is typically thought to be. But even by being generous, we have possibly four lines of information: Mark, Q, John, and Paul.[8] It seems unlikely that they were all independent. It is quite possible that some of the same people repeated the stories that the author of Mark and Paul both heard. Too much is unknown about who talked to whom. Some pro-resurrection accounts argue that the authors of the Gospels were the followers for whom the Gospels were named, that Paul saw Jesus himself, and that Paul spoke directly to some of the alleged eyewitnesses.[9] But these claims do not appear to be widely accepted outside evangelical circles. And with the compounding effects of doubts and the long list of challenges we discussed in the previous chapter, even this overly optimistic picture of the written reports is not enough to salvage the resurrection. Every week there are cases on the news where thousands of the faithful claim to witness some miraculous event at a shrine, a church, or a mosque that turn out to be mistakes.

What we have seen in the preceding chapters is that we have a number of very strong indicators that the reliability of miracle testimony for first-century

Christians would have been astronomically low. Psychological and social factors erode the extent to which we can trust them, and the Lourdes, France, example indicates that overall human reliability in these cases is very low. First-century Christians would not have had knowledge of the relevant facts to help them assess what was happening. It would even appear, given recent research, that their IQs would have been significantly lower on the whole than ours, making it even harder for them to sort out the events in question. And we have seen how easily many people can come to believe the same mistake. Whatever else we may think about them, the same worries apply to each one of these four other sources of information about the return of Jesus; they are highly unreliable resources of information too, so their contributions to the information that arrives in our hands does not significantly shift its reliability for the better.

And the whole affair is made much more complicated and difficult to believe by the addition of centuries of unknowns in the transmission of information from the early believers to us. Even if the first witnesses were highly reliable, we have seen that the doubts introduced by transmission problems tip the balance and force us to reject the results.

It should be clear that even with our partially completed account, the case against Jesus' resurrection is vastly overdetermined; we have seen several doubts, objections, or problems that are enough to justify our rejecting the resurrection individually. In conjunction, their effect is disastrous. The values we have found to assign to these various factors show that the likelihood we should assign to the resurrection is not favorable. It is not reasonable to believe a claim is true when all of the indicators give it a probability of many millions to one that it is true. You should not believe that you will be infected with the Ebola virus today, or that Paris Hilton will be elected president, or that there are one billion dollars' worth of gold ingots in the trunk of your car hidden by smugglers. And you should not believe that a man named Jesus came back from the dead in 35 CE.

It is true that the histories of the people and the transmission of the information are much more convoluted than the simplified model we have constructed from Lourdes and money-bag examples. But in the rough sketch of the facts as we have them, it appears that no amount of details will be enough to elevate this probability to even warrant suspending judgment. The convolutions and the multitude of unknown variables make the outcome worse.

Chapter 6

ABDUCTED BY ALIENS AND A FALSE MURDER CONVICTION

We have now seen that by our own standards, the criteria leading us to deny witchcraft at Salem, Massachusetts, should lead us to deny Jesus' return from the dead. And we've also seen a number of specific reasons why the people in Jerusalem or in Salem cannot be relied on when it comes to miracles and magic.

But for many, sympathy for the Jesus story will persist. We might be willing to reject witchcraft, ghosts, astrology, and a host of other supernatural allegations, particularly after considering the evidence we discussed in the previous chapters. But somehow, for many of us, the Jesus story still seems different. The same doubts and problems don't apply. The Jesus story doesn't feel as alien or foreign, so it's hard to feel the pertinence of the points that have been made so far.

Part of the reason for this persisting double standard is because the Jesus story is embedded so deeply within Western culture. When we consider religious doctrines, superstitions, or cultural practices that seem exotic to us, the strangeness (and unreasonableness) of them is easy to appreciate. For a non-Haitian, it is hard to fathom how killing a chicken in a Haitian voodoo ritual could possibly give us reliable information about the future, and it is so strange (to most people) that rejecting it on the basis of its dissonance with the rest of what we know is easy. But when we are surrounded by a set of ideas, when they are in our collective cultural history, in our holidays, in the stories we read as children, and in a thousand other places in our lives, even the strange becomes commonplace, normal, and natural. If you sneeze in a room full of people, there will be an instant chorus of "Bless yous," but there may be no one in the room who is aware that the practice may have arisen from a medieval fear that when you sneeze, your soul can be thrown out of your body, making you vulnerable to being taken over by devils and demons. The truly bizarre aspects of our cultural practices and beliefs vanish with our daily exposure to them. The surreal becomes normal and unremarkable.

Furthermore, when we are ideologically and emotionally committed to a set of ideas, it can be very difficult to view them objectively and acknowledge their weaknesses. Bias, as we have seen, can be difficult to detect, particularly when it is our own.

So, part of the challenge to become clearer, more consistent, and more rational thinkers is uprooting the Jesus story from its privileged and familiar place so that we can see it with fresh eyes. One way to do this is to preserve the important aspects of the story as closely as possible, but to reframe it in a way that divorces it from its familiar cultural context in order to improve our prospects for evaluating it objectively.

Suppose a stranger comes up to you. He introduces himself as Matthew and says he has a very important story he wants to tell you. There is a particular claim in the story that he thinks is very important for you to believe. But before he tells you the story, he informs you of some details about how he came to know about the story. As it turns out, the events he wants to relay to you didn't happen to him. He didn't see them. In fact, it isn't clear whether he has actually met or spoken to the people immediately involved in the story. The events in question actually took place a long time ago, and the story then passed through an unknown number of people before it got to the people who told him the story. But he's quite sure that these people are trustworthy. They were all honest and well intentioned, Matthew assures you. He talked to some of them and listened closely to the story they told. And he has heard that they were all passionate believers who were utterly sincere when they relayed the story.

As he thinks about it, Matthew realizes that there are some other important details. "Now that I think about it," he says to you, "the real events in this story actually happened hundreds of years ago. And there were some people who then retold the story for many decades before it was written down. But we don't actually have the original documents where it was written down, either. What we have are some copies of copies of copies of those original documents, where the original documents were based on retellings of retellings of retellings of the original story. I'm not sure, really, how many people there were in all of these intermediate steps between the actual events and us. I'm sure they were all trustworthy, however, and they were all completely convinced about the authenticity of the story. And there are no reasons to doubt it from contemporary sources." It occurs to you that from what he is saying, most or all of the people involved in the transmission of the story were zealous believers. You realize that if there had been some other relevant details or contrary evidence, it doesn't seem likely that it would have survived unaltered.

You ponder all these layers of questions and unknowns as Matthew prepares to actually divulge his important story. It concerns another man, call him Jones. Matthew tells you a lot of things about Jones, but the most important and central claim of the story is that Jones was abducted by aliens and disappeared off the face of the earth.

You have been told a story by someone who appears to be honest and sincere, and who seems to believe the story's truth without question. But he admits there have been many people, many hands, and many years between the events in question and you. And the central claim he wishes you to accept as true is that someone was abducted by aliens and never came back.

What's the reasonable position to take with regard to Jones's alien abduction? I think there's no question that any reasonable person would reject it. Reasonable people would not even bother to suspend judgment about it. Typically, suspending judgment is the rational response when there seem to be equally compelling bodies of evidence for and against a claim. Surely your evidence in support of Matthew's assertion that Jones was abducted by aliens is not equal in force to your evidence that no such thing happened and that there is some other, more probable explanation. Matthew seems like a trustworthy guy, but there are just too many unknowns, too many questions about the transmission of the story. And the story itself involves a claim that is simply outrageous and utterly unlike anything you have ever seen or heard. Even if a close friend who you know and trust came to you and tried to convince you that she had been abducted by aliens herself, you would be skeptical. Even without the information-transmission problems in the Jones story, the claim is one you would reject unless it met a high burden of proof. Furthermore, you don't need to know what really did happen, or where or how the story might have been altered, in order to be justified in disbelieving the story. By themselves, the questions you have and the problems in the story are enough to justify rejecting it without an alternative explanation. Given the obscurity of the event, it seems unlikely that anyone could ever really know what, if anything, happened.

Many believers will acknowledge that the alien-abduction story is preposterous, but they will argue that Jesus' resurrection is different. It is consistent to believe the latter while rejecting the former. I have deliberately stated this analogue to the Jesus story in uncharitable terms for a reason, because the way to argue for a division is to show that there is some important difference between the two cases that makes one silly but the other reasonable. If you are inclined to reject the analogy here because the Jesus story and how you came to know it are importantly different from the alien-abduction story, then here is the challenge.

Suppose there are some crucial differences (let's call them X, Y, and Z) between the cases, and these differences make it reasonable to reject the alien-abduction story while accepting Jesus' resurrection. Once we know what the alleged differences are, we can test them by altering the alien-abduction story to match. Apply the X, Y, and Z differences and see if it becomes reasonable to believe that Jones was abducted by aliens on the basis of the new story. Improve the alien-abduction story in any fashion you like that would make it more analogous, as you see it, to the resurrection. If there are features of the Jesus story that are missing in the alien-abduction story, then add them. Make Matthew a person of unquestionable integrity and honesty. Add in that Matthew personally interviewed and recorded the story from some people who claimed to have seen the alien abduction. Add in that you meditated about it and a powerful and convincing voice in your head or a feeling in your gut assured you the abduction story is authentic. Suppose Matthew introduces you to four of his friends, Mark, Luke, John, and Paul, and they all concur about the alien abduction of Jones. But to make the cases match the Gospels,

Mark, Luke, John, and Paul will all have to give different versions of the alien-abduction story. And Paul says he learned about the alien abduction from a voice in his head he heard when he had a powerful seizure and vision while he was walking to work. Before that event, Paul was a famous skeptic with a television show who routinely debunked alien-abduction stories the way James Randi or Michael Shermer have done.

A believer may wish to add this detail: suppose that some of the other believers were later persecuted and killed for believing that Jones left this planet with aliens. There's a widespread view among believers that some of Jesus' followers were persecuted or killed for their beliefs after Jesus died.[1] Surely a mistake, a delusion, a hallucination, or an ordinary social phenomenon could not have produced such commitment in people.

The historical believer may wish to add the martyrdom point to the alien abduction story to bring it more in line with the resurrection, but this is a weak point that will not help the case. Being willing to make sacrifices, endure persecution, or even die for a mistaken belief or an unworthy cause is a lamentably common human trait. After he died in 2009, there were reports that at least twelve of Michael Jackson's passionate fans committed suicide. In 1997 in a compound in San Diego, police found thirty-nine members of the Heaven's Gate UFO cult dead from suicide. They were convinced that suicide by phenobarbital and asphyxiation would lead to the rendezvous of their incorporeal souls with a spacecraft in the tail of the Hale-Bopp comet. Over nine hundred followers of the charismatic cult leader Jim Jones committed suicide or were killed in the Jonestown, Guyana, disaster in 1978. These cases, and regrettably many more, show that we should take a willingness to kill oneself for the sake of some radical religious principles as an indicator of cult manipulation, delusion, derangement, and overzealous obsession, not, as so many Christian apologists have done, as a measure of accuracy. A person consistently applying the Christian argument would conclude that the dedication at Heaven's Gate shows there really is a space craft in the tail of the Hale-Bopp comet. Having people sacrifice themselves for a cause is more strongly correlated with its being misguided than with its being true.

The alien-abduction story relayed by Matthew is fictional. And the point is we can change it any way we want in order to get it to cross the threshold from unbelievable to believable. But we are restricted in that we can only change it in ways that make it parallel the Jesus case more closely. If Matthew had video of the event or alien artifacts, and if an exhaustive investigation by impartial observers had been conducted, that would bolster Matthew's case. But none of those are true of the Jesus case. The guiding question for the revisions is: Are the things that would need to be added to Matthew's arguments in order to make the alien-abduction conclusion reasonable also true of the Jesus story we have?

Now the question before us, once the suitable revisions to the alien-abduction story have made it parallel in every important respect to the Jesus story, is: *Does it become reasonable to believe?* The answer for every historical-resurrection argument I can find is a resounding no. Even when the historical evidence for the resurrection is presented in the most flattering light, there is far less there than what we would need to show that someone had been abducted by aliens.

It's not that we should categorically reject the claim that someone was abducted by aliens. There is a body of evidence that could, in principle, be sufficient to prove it. But the gap between that information and the information we have about the resurrection is staggering. For example, you probably think the claim that there is a space craft in the tail of the Hale-Bopp comet is false. Now consider the evidence you would want to see before you would change your mind. It is no less extraordinary to claim that two thousand years ago a man in Jerusalem, who was also a divine being, came back from the dead and then transcended this plane of existence to return to an all-powerful supernatural being that created all of reality. Now consider the gap between the hypothetical evidence that would convince you of the Hale-Bopp space-craft and the actual evidence we have for the resurrection. See? You already don't believe in Jesus.

Trying to construct the analogy to an alien abduction brings out another interesting problem for the Jesus case. On the surface, how would you evaluate the general likelihood of the existence of aliens (which perform abductions) against the likelihood that there is a supernatural being in another plane of existence that violates the natural order in our world and removes humans from here to there? Which is more initially plausible, as you see it: aliens or magic?

The existence of aliens, even abducting ones, seems to me to be far more initially plausible. That is not to say they are probable or reasonable to believe. But aliens would fit into the world we know. I think the hypothesis that there are other material beings with physical powers somewhat like our own and that inhabit a different part of the galaxy or universe fits more readily into the rest of what we know than magical, transcendent, supernatural beings. On a similar note, if you had some exotic, hard-to-diagnose medical symptoms, you would more readily accept a doctor's claim that you had a very unusual disease rather than her claim that you were inhabited by demons.

A number of factors could lead someone to disagree or have different intuitions about aliens and magic. Depending on his background information, someone might think that they are equally likely, or that the magical/supernatural possibility is greater. Background information, prior beliefs, and personal experience give people different initial assumptions of plausibility (I won't pursue that tangent). But if I am correct that we should prima facie rank aliens as more plausible than magic, then there's another problem for the Jesus case. Suppose we alter Matthew's hypothetical abduction story to the point that it would become reasonable to accept the conclusion. If aliens, all other things being equal, are more plausible than supernatural beings, then the case for the resurrection of Jesus would have to be *even better* than the embellished alien example. Presumably, Matthew's alien story would need to be substantially improved before you would accept it. And it would have to be embellished in ways that are simply not parallel to the meager information we have about Jesus in the Bible. And even if the two cases were parallel, the evidence for the Jesus story would need to be much more substantial in order to be minimally acceptable, given the initial implausibility of the supernatural-being hypothesis.

In the end, the alien-abduction thought experiment shows one of two things. Either it will become painfully obvious that the believer is guilty of engineering ad hoc, Bible-stretching justifications in favor of the Jesus story, or it will become clear that the sorts of additions needed in order to make Matthew's alien story reasonable are not true of the Jesus case. I think the example will make it clear that the believer's ideological and emotional commitment to the Jesus story and the high level of cultural familiarity has led said believer to adopt a double standard of justification.

MURDERER!

Let's consider one more alternative model of the Jesus story that brings out the problems with believing. Suppose you have been falsely accused of committing a murder many decades ago. There is very little evidence connecting you to the murder except the testimony of four people, named Mike, Monty, Larry, and Jacob. Your defense attorney puts each of them on the witness stand and interviews them one at a time. During the questioning, several important facts are revealed about their belief that you committed the murder. None of the four actually saw you commit the murder. They've never met you before. But each one of them heard some stories from some other people saying that you committed the murder. But it cannot be established that these other people were witnesses either, and they are not available to be questioned. None of the four knows how many times the story was repeated or passed around before they heard it. They heard that a lot of people were witnesses to the murder, but again, none of those people is available and it is not known who they are. The murder happened thirty years ago, and Mike, Monty, Larry, and Jacob heard about it because the accusation that you did it has been talked about and remembered over all these years by these other unavailable people.

It also turns out that Mike and Larry got a lot of the story from Monty. They believe you did it on the basis of Monty's telling them that you did and possibly some other sources. Furthermore, when the attorney tries to get the details straight about what happened at the crime scene, none of them tell the same story. The important details (which they all got from other people) are different in every case.

At one point, the prosecution puts a man named Perry on the stand, and he affirms that you did it, too. But he admits he wasn't there and he did not see it. Rather, he had a powerful vision during a trance or a seizure while he was walking down the street one day, and a voice he heard told him that you committed the murder. Or, for those so inclined, we can improve the story so that Perry claims he saw you do it himself.

The prosecuting attorney makes an attempt to assure the jury that you are guilty because there are lots and lots of people out there who believe it because they heard it from Mike, Monty, Larry, Jacob, and Perry. But the judge prohibits it because "Everyone knows that it is true" is not an admissible form of evidence in court. It is not clear why the judge allowed the hearsay evidence of the five men to be heard in the court in the first place.

The prosecuting and defense attorneys close their cases. The jury promptly convicts you of murder and sentences you to death.

Does this sound like fair grounds upon which to convict a person?

A murder charge and conviction are no less important in their impacts on a person's life than the changes that Christians believe we should enact in our lives for Jesus. The fact that in this case you have been falsely accused helps to illustrate how serious it is to draw the wrong conclusion on such flimsy evidence. If the accused in the example actually had committed the murder, then a conviction on the basis of Mike's, Monty's, Larry's, Jacob's, and Perry's testimonies might not seem as wrongheaded. Justice would have been accidentally served. But we don't want the defendant's actual guilt to cloud the issue: if it is not reasonable to conclude that person committed murder on these grounds, it is no more reasonable to believe that two thousand years ago, a person came back from the dead on similar grounds, especially since such a resurrection matters so much.

Suppose we debriefed the jury members after the trial and asked them about their decision, and when we raise doubts about what the jury had done, some of the members said things like, "Well, I know that the evidence was really sketchy, but in the end you just gotta have faith. And I have faith in my heart that he did it and deserves to go to prison for the murder." Would that make the decision better or worse? Some of the others said things like, "I was raised Lutheran and we were always taught that he committed the murder. That's just the way I was raised. So when it came time to decide, I just went with that." One of the other jurors said, "Yeah, the evidence for his guilt was really weak. But I just figure that it's a good bet to find him guilty anyway. I mean, it could be wrong, but you never know—he might really have done it. There's a one in a billion chance that he did it. So if I convict him, then I will have done the right thing and justice will be served." And another juror says that he just went along with the others to keep his grandmother happy.

There will be complaints about this comparison, no doubt. "The cases aren't the same because in this case the person is accused of something bad, a murder, and it is a false accusation. But Jesus' resurrection is true." Or, the false murder conviction unfairly prejudices our intuitions against the conviction. There are two problems with these responses. First, the false murder charge is analogous because it and the Jesus belief are both decisions of great import. What matters is that what is decided on the basis of the information at hand will have an enormous impact on a person's life. There's no question that believing in Jesus does have a radical effect on people, and there is no question that millions of believers think that it should have that effect on you. If believing in Jesus seems like a minor, trivial matter to you, then perhaps you should rethink the implications of it. But even so, believing something irrationally is irrational, no matter how big or little the belief is. With the resurrection case, what we are concerned about is getting it wrong. So, the false murder charge is not so disanalogous if it turns out the resurrection did not happen but someone decides on the (poor) evidence that it did.

Second, if the source of a person's conviction that Jesus' resurrection happened is based on the testimony of Matthew, Mark, Luke, John, and Paul, then complaining that the murder case is different because it is a false charge is begging the question. The point is that we don't know whether or not Jesus came back from the dead except on the basis of their words, so we can't then assert that we are sure their words are accurate *because* Jesus came back from the dead. If the resurrection claim is false, then the cases *are* analogous, and that is the possibility we are worried about. If the resurrection did not happen, then the believer has drawn a momentous—but mistaken—conclusion on the basis of analogous evidence.

Someone may think an important disanalogy here is that committing murder is an awful thing, and the injustice of falsely convicting the defendant is not parallel with the consequences of believing a false resurrection story. Even if Jesus wasn't resurrected, many people think it is laudable to believe. How can it be a bad thing to believe something so wonderful or so spiritually and morally beneficial, even if it doesn't have sufficient evidence? As Daniel Dennett has pointed out, we believe in belief.[2] It is widely held that we ought to believe or that disbelieving is a bad thing we should discourage in ourselves and in others.

However, it is crucial that we isolate this sort of enthusiasm for believing from the question of whether the evidence gives us epistemic justification for the conclusion. Whether believing is beneficial is an entirely distinct matter from whether the conclusion is implied by the evidence. I would derive benefit from believing that if I eat more than two thousand calories in a day, I will instantly drop dead. That benefit is irrelevant to whether there is good evidence for believing it. Benefits derived from believing create incentives, but they are irrelevant to the truth of the claim. If it turns out the argument for the resurrection must be completed by "Besides, it is good for you to believe it anyway," then we have to conclude that the historical argument fails. And that has been my thesis from the start.

There is a disanalogy here that actually makes the case for Jesus worse. To make the murder trial more in line with the Jesus case, Perry would have to tell his vision story about twenty years after the alleged murder. Ten to twenty years later, Mike, Monty, and Larry would come to the courthouse and give their stories. Then a full ninety years after the alleged murder, Jacob would show up and give his account of the murder. And since the ending of Mark detailing Jesus' return from the dead was added decades later from yet another unknown hearsay source, we would have to change Monty's testimony accordingly.

Add that Mike, Monty, Larry, Jacob, and Perry would not be able to give their stories in person nor could they be cross examined. The best the prosecuting attorney could do is to find some copies of copies of copies of the story that the five of them wrote down. The original papers where they told the story of your involvement in the murder have been lost, but the attorney assures the jury that all during the decades of copying and recopying what they wrote down, the utmost care was taken to be diligent and careful. The judge happens to be napping when this happens, so he doesn't rule these copies of copies of copies of hearsay evidence inadmissible in the case.

CONCLUSION

In this chapter, my goal has been to lever the Jesus story up out of its comfortable and familiar place in our cultural backgrounds so that we can examine it more objectively. Now we have several analogous cases—the Salem witch trials (from chapter 2), an alien abduction, and a flimsy murder conviction—that illuminate the problems (and strangeness) of the Jesus case.

The alien-abduction story is a graphic demonstration that if a claim is being made that we initially take to be highly implausible or outrageous, then the quality of the evidence in its favor matters. The quality of evidence should always matter to us, but with an outlandish scenario like alien abduction, it becomes especially clear. It is also clear that whatever sorts of improvements in the evidence we would demand in order to buy in to the alien-abduction story, those same points cannot be found in favor of Jesus' returning from the dead. The scanty evidence we have for Jesus' resurrection falls far short of what would be needed to make it believable. It should take a lot more to prove an alien-abduction story than what we have concerning the resurrection—and that is the undoing of the Christian view.

The flimsy murder conviction is jarring in a different way. When we recast the Jesus story in a way that activates our sensitivity for injustice—especially about the prospects of being wrongly convicted and executed for a murder—the problems for the evidence for Jesus are overwhelming. It would be unjust and irrational to convict someone of murder on the basis of such deplorable evidence; how is it any more reasonable or just to accept a story about Jesus that would have radical, *eternal* life-altering implications? We should be applying the same standards in church that we apply to spaceships in comets, alien abductions, and criminal charges.

Someone may be tempted to bite the bullet about some revised account of the abduction or courtroom stories. That is, someone may insist that once we do get the alien-abduction story and the evidence for the murder charge into exact parallel with the relevant aspects of the Jesus story, then we should accept their conclusions. The critic may insist that we must be reasonable and consistent, and we cannot simply accept my undefended assumptions that alien abductions are outrageous. There must be a point at which these claims become reasonable, and the Jesus story crosses that threshold.

The problems here, as I see it, will be comparable to the bite-the-bullet problems we saw concerning the Salem witch trials in chapter 3. If X, Y, and Z amendments to the alien-abduction story make it reasonable (and X,

Y, and Z are true of the Jesus accounts), then the advocate will have lowered his standards of proof to a level that produces a number of negative results. Lowering the standards of proof here will open the floodgates to a wide range of other extraordinary claims that are demonstrably or obviously false. Some of those other miracles or religious claims one will be forced to accept in order to be consistent will be contrary to or incompatible with the Jesus story on various levels. On the other hand, expressing a general principle of evidence that simply lets Jesus in but keeps the others out will require ad hoc engineering or special pleading.

Chapter 7

THE COUNTEREVIDENCE PROBLEM

I t is often harder to reason clearly about what is not in front of us than to think straight about the visible or the tangible. When we are trying to form a justified conclusion on some matter, vital information that might have otherwise disproven an idea can elude us in a number of ways. Sometimes our own psychology is at work against us, such as when we settle for evidence that is merely consistent with a favored hypothesis because it is easy and satisfying. Sometimes the sources from which we get our information adjust, tilt, or filter it so that we only get a partial picture of the real state of things. This chapter addresses what is likely missing from our information about Jesus.

The short statement of the point is that there are good reasons to think that we do not have the full story regarding Jesus, particularly, potential counterevidence to his miracles. Arguments for the resurrection often focus on the details that are present in the Gospels, but it is the information that is likely missing that is vital to our drawing a reasonable conclusion about the resurrection that is most important. If there had been any information supporting a view of Jesus that is contrary to what we now see as essential Christian doctrines, it is unlikely it would have survived the transmission process across the centuries. To understand how these vital pieces of information may have eluded us, let us consider a few hypothetical cases.

Suppose a police detective named Ortega is investigating a murder where a man named Reynolds has become a suspect. Reynolds did not commit the crime, but, for some reasons we do not need to pursue, Ortega has some hidden motives or impulses, of which she is not aware, to implicate Reynolds. As Ortega compiles evidence surrounding the murder, unbeknownst to her, she subtly sifts, filters, and adjusts the evidence. Ortega asks a lot of questions about some issues, particularly about Reynolds, and not about others. Ortega investigates Reynolds vigorously, while neglecting to check up as carefully on suggestive leads concerning other suspects. Ortega even leaves out some important facts from the file concerning Reynolds. When Ortega gets information suggesting Reynolds's guilt, she more readily accepts it, and she applies excessive critical scrutiny to any counterindications to Reynolds's innocence, and so on. There is a substantial body of research showing the subtle and pervasive effects of desire on belief formation; "judgments about information people do not want to believe will be more sensitive to information quality than will judgments about information they do want to believe."[1] Like Ortega, we frequently engage in a biased reconstruction of the evidence in favor of some preferred conclusion.

We could even imagine that in creating a case file, Ortega doesn't actually include any false claims, but the kinds and amount of information she includes implicate Reynolds more than anyone else. Ortega then presents this body of subtly tilted (but more or less accurate) information to District Attorney Michaels. Under the assumption that she has received all of evidence that is relevant in one way or another concerning Reynolds's guilt, District Attorney Michaels concludes that Reynolds is guilty and proceeds to make a compelling case to the jury. The jury eventually arrives at the (probably) justified, but mistaken, conclusion that Ortega is guilty. They are all operating on the good-faith assumptions that the detective did a thorough and balanced job of investigating the case and that the district attorney presented them with all of the relevant facts.

Consider another case. Suppose a nurse named Chevalier is helping to treat a patient named McMaster. Chevalier has some of her own ideas about medicine, illness, and diet. As people will do, she's become enthusiastic about the idea that too many dairy products in peoples' diets leads to high blood pressure and atherosclerosis. She has talked to McMaster on many occasions, she's seen McMaster's file, and she's now passionately convinced that McMaster eats too many dairy products and, as a result, now has atherosclerosis. She's sure that it would help him greatly if he could get treated for that and eliminate dairy products. So, either intentionally or not, as she compiles information about McMaster and adds it to McMaster's medical file, she guides the information toward what she knows will make a convincing case for McMaster's high cholesterol and atherosclerosis. In this case, we can imagine that Chevalier does add some information to the file that she knows to be false, and she deliberately excludes some information that is accurate, but her intentions are positive; she only wants what is best for McMaster and she thinks that these falsifications are necessary to get him the right treatment. She's so sure about her conclusion that she doesn't really think of what she has done as falsifying. As she sees it, she has merely clarified and expedited vital treatment of a real problem. A doctor named Lee picks up the file, consults her medical manuals, carefully studies all the information and comes to the (probably justified) conclusion that McMaster has high cholesterol and atherosclerosis.[2] The other information, the real data that was present without Chevalier's interventions, never comes to light, and Lee is never the wiser. The placebo effect kicks in, and the treatment McMaster gets for his fabricated syndrome happens to have some accidental effect on his real problem, and eventually he feels better and is declared cured. Nurse Chevalier grows even more confident about the excess of dairy products in people's diets and its negative effects.

There are several important details about the nature of good evidence that are illustrated in these two cases. First, tiny differences in the way the search for evidence is conducted can have profound effects on the conclusions that emerge from this evidence. Second, the person gathering information may or may not have a deliberate, conscious intent to misrepresent. He or she could genuinely believe that they are gathering all of the important information and then transmitting it accurately and completely. Nevertheless, vital counterevidence is left out that would prove the opposite conclusion. Third, the effects of bias and the influence that a favored conclusion exert on our minds in the search for evidence can be very subtle and hard to detect in others and even harder to see at work in our own minds. Fourth, the search phase is pivotal not just for the person doing the investigating but also for everyone else who then comes to accept the conclusion on its basis. And the ill effects of a mistake, an omission, or a misrepresentation get amplified as more and more people come to believe. If the first person gets it wrong, then *everyone else down the line* gets it wrong, too, unless they can detect or uncover the problems. Fifth, the examples above demonstrate that a discrepancy between the original purpose for gathering and recording the information and the purpose that it ultimately gets used for could also lead to significant misrepresentations of the facts. Ortega is trying to implicate Reynolds; Michaels is trying to achieve justice. Chevalier is on a campaign against dairy products; Lee is trying to cure McMaster. The people who are downstream in the process, like the jury, have the presumption that the purposes guiding Ortega and Chevalier in gathering and recording the information roughly match their purposes when they set out to draw the correct conclusions. Michaels, the jury, and Lee want all of the relevant facts, not just those that support the conclusions that Ortega and Chevalier are after. So the people making use of the information at the end of the transmission put it to use for a different purpose than the one for which it was originally compiled, and with a disastrous effect on the truth and justice. Michaels, the jury, and Lee assume that the picture they are getting about Reynolds and McMaster is the whole picture, with all the relevant details included that would be necessary to make a well-informed and accurate decision. But the deck has been stacked in favor of a particular (wrong) outcome.

Furthermore, the people at the receiving end of this constructive process are never the wiser about how the process went off the tracks. District Attorney Michaels and Dr. Lee have reasonable expectations not only that the information relayed through the detective and the nurse was true, but also that it was, in some relevant respects, complete with regard to the issues at hand. Consciously or unconsciously, they presume that if there had been some vital facts present that would have *refuted* the conclusions they drew, then that information would have been in the cases as they were presented to them. That is to say, the district attorney would assume that if Reynolds had a compelling alibi, then Ortega would have passed that information along.

These considerations lead us to the counterevidence principle:

It is reasonable to draw a conclusion C on the basis of a body of information E only if it is reasonable to believe that the evidence that would show the opposite conclusion, if there were any, would have been included in E.[3]

That is, it is not reasonable to accept a conclusion merely because I have some evidence that is consistent with its truth. If that evidence is filtered, slanted, selected, or otherwise misrepresentative of all the relevant facts, then it may appear to support the conclusion, but a better search and a larger, more complete evidential picture would have made that clear. If disproof or counterevidence for the conclusion I am reaching would not manifest itself in the information I'm considering, then I have got no business thinking that the conclusion is justified or true on that basis.[4] That information would not have indicated anything else. Dad isn't justified in concluding that Junior is an outstanding student by only considering the B on the report card where the rest of the grades are Fs. Your brother shouldn't conclude that his clever new system for beating the house at blackjack works by only considering his wins.

A more subtle problem arises when the conclusion happens to be true, and the evidence that I have seems to justify it, but details about the way the information was collected, if I had known them, would undermine my confidence in the inference.

A conclusion that accidentally lines up with the facts and that was based on a flawed body of evidence is no more justified than a false conclusion. It's the procedure that got you there that justifies a conclusion, not the separate question of its truth.

If we draw a conclusion C on the basis of evidence E, we want the counter-indications or contrary evidence to C, if there are any, to be present and taken into account in E. The search phase in the belief-formation process should be as inclusive as possible and not biased in favor of any particular conclusion.

Nowhere is the failure to recognize this principle more obvious than in the excitement over the so-called Bible Code and various other alleged paranormal phenomena. Enthusiastic believers in the Bible Code feed the entire text of the Bible, page by page, into a computer program that actively searches for any strings of letters in a vertical, reverse, or diagonal line that are meaningful. *Never mind that if you change the font, the translation, the language of translation, or the page size, the vertical and diagonal arrangements of letters are all completely altered.* By discarding millions of nonsense strings of letters, they can find numerous words with this process. Then they proclaim they have found a hidden message magically buried within the text. *Never mind that we could get similar results with a cookbook.* They present only the hits and none of the misses to support their claim.

The same mistake regularly produces attention in paranormal pop culture about the Mayan predictions of the end of the world in 2012, Nostradamus's "remarkable" visions of the future, and burned-toast images of the Virgin Mary. Burn enough toast or waste enough time scouring thousands of pages of Nostradamus and you can find what you're looking for. It also helps to be able to go searching for these "predictions" after the fact from vague, metaphorical, and poetic passages that are ripe for hedging, "interpretation," or spin. And it turns out that a significant minority of the population in every generation believes that the end of the world is coming shortly.

The mistake is also apparent if your brother tells you about his clever system for winning at blackjack, and he also tells you about several instances where he won large pots of money using it. But you would have a different view if you found out that overall, he lost as much money as other players not using the system, and that his winning rate is same as theirs.

Consider another hypothetical case that fails to satisfy the counterevidence principle. Suppose Dr. Lee is evaluating McMaster (this time without Nurse Chevalier's interference). Numerous tests have been done on McMaster and the results are all compiled in his file. Without anyone's knowledge, a crucial machine in the lab that evaluates blood has broken down during the night so that it reports that every blood sample submitted to it tests positive for hepatitis. Lee reads McMaster's file carefully, including a lab report from the broken machine, and concludes (wrongly) that McMaster has hepatitis. Naturally, Lee assumes that if McMaster did not have hepatitis, then the blood-test results would be negative.

But if Lee knew that the machine was broken, then she would withhold judgment until better evidence was available or draw her conclusion without the lab report. And she would make a better decision if the search phase had been better. In this case, there is no deliberate manipulation of the information, no conscious misrepresentation, no lying, and no deceit by any person. And the problem in the body of evidence could be quite hard to detect. (Suppose that the blood-testing machine *broke down again* and began functioning well the next day.) We probably wouldn't fault the doctor for drawing the hepatitis conclusion if she didn't know about the broken machine. For her, we can imagine that it is reasonable to assume that the machinery in the lab is working. But the point is that there are facts that run counter to the evidence as she sees it, but she is misled by their omission. And now, just the fact that the information on which she based her decision is unreliable would be enough for her to retract her conclusion; Lee doesn't need to see a negative test result from an unbroken machine in order to withhold the now-dubious conclusion that McMaster has hepatitis. And if Lee went ahead and treated McMaster for hepatitis knowing that the diagnosis was faulty, we would think she was guilty of making a gross mistake.

THE COUNTEREVIDENCE PRINCIPLE AND THE MIRACLES OF JESUS

Now we have a valuable principle for information gathering and belief formation, and we have seen some of the important ways that it applies. What are the implications for the case of Jesus?

The problem for the Jesus stories is that we should doubt that our information is even nominally complete enough to draw any conclusions about his miracles or his divinity. We have good reason to think that many, most, or even all of the people involved in the compiling and transmitting of the information about Jesus would have played roles like Detective Ortega, Nurse Chevalier, the broken blood analyzer, or your gambling brother. At any number of points in the transmission from Jesus' alleged return from the dead until we read about it two thousand years later, a variety of conscious or unconscious human interventions, as well as institutional forces, would have filtered out the sorts of counterevidence that, had they been present, might have undermined the resurrection. So our counterevidence principle is not satisfied with respect to the evidence for Jesus' resurrection.

To see the problems, we need a brief recap of some of the highlights from chapter 1 about what happened to the story over the years. Jesus allegedly returns from the dead after his execution around 30 to 35 CE. By word of mouth, an unknown number of stories spread among believers for several decades until the authors of the Gospels wrote their versions of it (derived from word-of-mouth stories they had heard) thirty to ninety years later. Those manuscripts, along with thousands of others that proliferated among the growing groups of Christians, are copied and recopied for two hundred or so years until the canon of the books of the Bible as we now know it (more or less) begins to be sifted out in the late 200s. The actual copies of the Gospels that exist today are from this period. In the surviving copies of the manuscripts we have from this period and later, there are thousands of differences that we know about from deliberate alterations, editing, copying mistakes, ecumenical and spiritual adjustments, and harmonizations. No two copies of any of the documents we have are the same. During canonization, the other noncanonical stories and writings are rejected, abandoned, destroyed, declared heretical, or otherwise discouraged.

Recall from chapter 2 Kurt and Barbara Aland's statement about the way the texts were treated:

> Until the beginning of the fourth century the text of the NT developed freely. It was a "living text," unlike the text of the Hebrew Old Testament, which was subject to strict controls because (in the oriental tradition) the consonantal text was holy. And the NT text continued to be a "living text" as long as it remained a manuscript tradition, even when the Byzantine church molded it to the procrustean bed of an ecclesiastically standardized and officially prescribed text. Even for later scribes, for example, the parallel passages of the Gospels were so familiar that they would adapt the text of one Gospel to that of another. They also felt themselves free to make corrections in the text, improving it by their own standards of correctness, whether grammatically, stylistically, or more substantively. This was all the more true of the early period, when the text had not yet attained canonical status, especially in the earliest period when Christians considered themselves filled with the Spirit.[5]

We can find evidence for a great deal of winnowing, adjusting, and excising in the various texts of early Christianity that occurred with the explicit purpose of creating a single coherent canonical set of writings. The Bible that we now have coalesced over the centuries through a process that deliberately tried to minimize contradictions, eliminate alternative accounts, lessen dissonant details, and exclude information that did not fit with core Christian doctrines.

Furthermore, the ecumenical, evangelical, and spiritual purposes for the texts grew and morphed over this period and led to further changes.

So when we start to think about what might be missing from the accounts of Jesus' life in the context of our lessons about the counterevidence principle, a number of problems manifest themselves.

First, people who "are motivated to arrive at a particular judgment or conclusion engage in a biased memory search to access hypotheses, inference rules, and instances from past behavior that are most likely to support their desired conclusion."[6] The followers of Jesus would have been just as guilty of these distortions as we are, perhaps more so given the Iron Age problem, the IQ problem, and some of the other issues considered in chapter 4.

Second, the people who first transmitted the information may or may not have had a conscious intention to misrepresent the events; nevertheless numerous influences could have led them to leave out vital counterevidence. We know very little else about the authors of the Gospels, but it seems unlikely that their inquiry into the Jesus question was even nominally skeptical or investigative. They were believers. They had drawn their conclusions about what had happened to Jesus and they wrote to communicate the conclusion, not to gather a broad body of evidence that would then serve to inform an educated decision about the events. Detective Ortega in the earlier example was engaged in a formal investigation for evidence, and we saw how the effects of bias impacted the results. Ortega was part of a process with the district attorney, the jury, and the judicial system with a rigorous set of rules for every step of the process to insure the truth emerges. How much worse would the results be in a case where dedicated and passionate believers in a particular conclusion were responsible for gathering the information, communicating it, writing it down, and then preserving it for everyone else? If Ortega couldn't get it right, how could we expect the Bible account to be more reliable?

Third, we know that for centuries the deliberate purpose of many of the people involved in the preservation and propagation of Christianity was to foster a particular set of beliefs. The Apostle Paul is frequently quite explicit about his intention to fortify belief and to discourage doubt in response to the considerations that might be leading believers to change their minds. For Paul and many of the people responsible for the Jesus story, the goal is to get people to believe;

doubting is treated as an obstacle to belief that must be overcome or stamped out. When your purpose in approaching the evidence is to secure a prior-held belief, your treatment of it is different than if your purpose is to gather all of the relevant information and then draw the conclusion, whatever it might be, that is best supported by the evidence. The difference between the two projects can be difficult to detect. Consider, for example, the number of university faculty who put Marx's *Communist Manifesto* on their syllabi with the latter goal but who have been accused of pursuing the former. I can say the same for making articles about atheism required readings in a Philosophy of Religion course.

Fourth, the effects of bias and the influence that the favored conclusion of Jesus' resurrection would have had on the process can be very hard to detect. We have seen how people working hard and acting in good faith can be grossly misled. We do not need to impugn anyone with sinister motives to see that even if a person were doing what he took to be his very best, the results can be grossly misleading. Many believers resist alternatives by asking, "Why would the disciples hide the body or lie or engage in such a grand deception? They had so much to lose." People's motivations for lying are often backward and perplexing, and the comment belies a naïve presumption about applying rational analysis to them. Furthermore, there is just too much we do not know. But what we have also seen is that a person does not need to lie deliberately for the truth to be lost. We often don't understand the influences that are at work in our own thoughts. We know even less about what is going on in the minds of others. With information such as what we have about Jesus, there is too much we do not know about what has happened to it as it moved through so many people. It is common for external or internal causes of belief to be present, but people are not aware that the factor had the effect on them. They fail to notice the change, they deny that their beliefs changed, or they even explicitly deny that the causal factor that changed their beliefs had any influence on their views.

Fifth, if there were mistakes, omissions, or misrepresentations in the early stages of the process, the effects on belief in the minds of others would be amplified down through the centuries and across billions of believers.

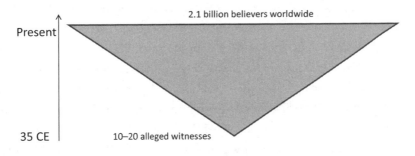

Figure 7.1. A movement with billions of believers today rests on the fragmented, hearsay reports from a tiny handful of dedicated followers who are alleged to have seen Jesus returned from the dead.

Consider that with 2.1 billion believers worldwide basing their belief on what a handful of people said two thousand years ago, the slightest change in what even one of them said would have reverberated up through history with massive effect.

What purposes did early retellers have? There is no simple answer to that question, especially since we do not know how many people retold it or where the Gospel authors got their information. But it is clear in the Gospels and in the other early writings that the intent of the authors is to spread the good news, to foster belief, to encourage faithfulness, to keep people strong in believing *against the possibility of doubt*, and to create new converts. One central purpose was to get people to believe that Jesus was the Messiah, not to facilitate the formation of a well-justified conclusion that might have run contrary to Christian doctrine. The explicit goal in much of the early literature was directly opposed to the intent of the counterevidence principle. The early believers' intentions were to fortify conviction among followers and to create new ones. The goal of evangelism is to spread an ideology, the goal of sound reasoning is to foster a critical-thinking methodology that endorses the claims that are justified and true, regardless of their ideological conformity.

In their own way, the early believers may have presented what they took to be evidence. They asserted that Jesus had come back from the dead, they retold the events, they noted that other people saw the events and believed, and so on. But all of that has only a nominal resemblance to what we now mean by *evidence*. Doubting and disbelief themselves were actively discouraged *in principle*. In Romans, Paul praises Abraham for believing that he will have a son with God's help, despite Abraham's advanced age and Sarah's inability to have children (Romans 4:18–21). When Thomas, who has his doubts about the stories of Jesus' return, finally sees Jesus for himself, Jesus scolds him: "Have you come to believe because you have seen me? Blessed are those who have not seen and have believed" (John 20:29). The dissent, skepticism, and critical analysis that potentially could have rectified the situation have been actively discouraged in much of Christian history. It hasn't been uncommon within Christian movements (and other religious traditions) to treat disbelief as heretical and then punish it with death or torture. The legacy of condemning doubt persists in our culture, as we saw in chapter 1, in the form of strong social disapproval.[7]

We must keep in mind that it will take another sixteen centuries or so before humans begin to fully appreciate the need for an active search for *disproof* for a hypothesis, when Francis Bacon publishes *Cogitata et Visa* in 1607 and *Novum Organum* in 1620. The Enlightenment (which Bacon ushers in) and the development of the scientific method teach us that justification for a hypothesis depends more upon the results of our efforts to disprove it than on evidence that merely appears to be consistent with it, and that the search for evidence must take into account the various biases, filters, fallacies, and distortions that might affect the search for evidence itself. Recall the scholars mentioned in chapter 3 who condemn the spirit of the Enlightenment as running contrary to the Christian faith.[8]

Given what we do know about the history of the information itself, we can safely infer that the principles of a sound evidence search were not satisfied during the early acquisition and transmission of information about Jesus. Excited, enthusiastic, and passionate converts in an Iron Age culture (with all the limitations that it would impose on their minds) were actively trying to suppress doubts and get people to believe. And many of these same people were responsible for the composition, editing, and propagation of the written manuscripts that were essential to their movement. Their purposes would have been fundamentally at odds with the counterevidence principle whether or not they were aware of it and even if they harbored no ill intent.

QUESTIONS TO SHARPEN THE PROBLEM

We have good reasons to doubt that the record is impartial and objective. And the people who recorded and transmitted the Jesus miracles did not have the conceptual tools, investigative methods, principles of good evidence, or background knowledge that would be necessary to adequately evaluate and represent the phenomena. I began this chapter by claiming that thinking clearly about what is not present can be harder than thinking clearly about the stuff we can see. Some questions about the process that brought the information to us can help draw the boundaries around what might be missing.

Were the people surrounding Jesus and the ones giving the accounts of the miracles that he is alleged to have performed impartial, objective observers? Would they have been free of the impulses to consciously or unconsciously distort, sift, or assimilate with bias that the rest of us are so prone to? Would the dedicated Christians who transmitted the stories about Jesus down through the centuries have the goal of preserving all the information about him, including evidence that would have undermined the authenticity of Christianity if it had been present?

Consider the alleged witnesses; the people who repeated the story and the authors who ultimately wrote it down, as well as the other people who have played a role in the transmission of the stories. Were all of those people well equipped with the tools and cognitive abilities to detect fraud or identify self-deception? Did they understand the value of having careful investigations into paranormal claims? Did they know, eighteen hundred to two thousand years ago, how often claims about the paranormal, about miracles, and about supernatural events are mistaken? Did they understand how frequently people giving eyewitness testimony, particularly about matters in which they are passionately and personally involved, unconsciously distort evidence, sift for confirmation, and ignore counterevidence? Did they know what sort of questions to ask and what aspects of the case to investigate in an alleged paranormal event? Did they know about bereavement hallucinations? If they had had one, would they know what was going on? Did they understand how strong the influences of social conformity are on belief formation?

Suppose that the Jesus stories were known to be false by someone who had figured out that something else had happened. Would the evidence of the Jesus stories' falsity have survived centuries of faithful adherents' active culling, adjusting, and protecting of them?

Do we have reasons to think that the people who relayed the stories across the centuries had the goal of preserving all of the relevant evidence, including information that might suggest that the miracles were not authentic? Was our counterevidence principle satisfied for any of the people between us and Jesus? Was it satisfied for *every* person in that chain leading to us? Is the principle of disconfirmation satisfied for us when we consider the information we have about Jesus in the Gospels?

I believe the answer to all of these questions is no. Even if the answer to some of these questions is no, then a reasonable person would be forced to withhold judgment about the truth of the Jesus miracles on the basis of the Gospels. At the very least, a conservative approach would suggest that we just don't know the answers to many of these questions. And if that is correct, then the evidence that we have concerning the Jesus miracles is not adequate to support the conclusion that they were real. So it is unreasonable to believe that Jesus was a supernatural, divine being on the basis of the New Testament Gospels.

SOME COUNTEREVIDENTIAL POSSIBILITIES

We can clarify the problem by thinking of some counterevidence that might have been available but that may not have been originally discovered or recorded or, even if it had, would not have survived the long history of transmission. Let's consider several possibilities.

Suppose there had been a hoax concerning the miracles of Jesus. Perhaps after his execution, some of the disciples conspired to spread some impressive stories and stage an empty tomb. Suppose that there were people who knew about the hoax and even made some protests about the misrepresentations. Would we expect reports or information from those whistleblowers to have survived and made it into the body of evidence concerning Jesus' miracles or resurrection we have today? Believers sometimes give a circular rejection of this possibility: a hoax doesn't fit with the information of the Gospels, which, by hypothesis, would have been part of the hoax. But it is important to note that I am not defending the hoax alternative here. Our question here is: If there had been a hoax, would any indications of it have survived two thousand years of transmission through the hearts and minds of zealous believers in the Christian tradition? There appear to have been a number of influential people in the church from an early time who did not believe that it was a hoax. So if they had heard that it was, or if they encountered some substantial evidence that it was, would they have made that information part of the essential set of doctrines in the church tradition? Would that information have made it through all the people who were ever in a position to influence what was passed on and what was not? Suppose there was never an empty tomb at all. Suppose Jesus was buried there and the body remained there. But the enthusiasm and the ardent desires of the disciples got the better of them in the months, years, and decades that followed before the Gospels were written. The movement gained momentum; thousands, then millions of people became converts, and a religious institution built upon the veracity of those stories came to be the primary mechanism of preserving and propagating the stories. Would we expect that information about the tomb would survive through the centuries of that process and end up accurately represented in the information we have today?

The objection will be, "How could people claim or believe that the tomb was empty when the disproof was right there in front of them?" But it's not hard to imagine how people living hundreds of miles away might believe it without ever bothering to check for themselves or ever being able to check for themselves. It is not hard even to imagine people living in the same city believing it, especially dedicated followers. Elvis Presley's and Tupac Shakur's graves do not deter those who believe the two men live on. Despite reports of his death, rumors about Michael Jackson's survival began to surface within days, and mere months later, there were already thousands of passionate believers. Pictures of Jackson's body, coroner's reports, and eyewitnesses do not seem to deter in the slightest those who think he is alive.[9] If stories about Michael Jackson's survival can spread so quickly and be accepted by twenty-first-century Americans with a relatively high level of education and broad access to information, how much more likely would it be for something similar to happen two thousand years ago among superstitious, uneducated, and deeply religious peasants? Have any of the parties in this dispute checked in the graves of Presley, Shakur, or Jackson?

Suppose the few people who claimed to have seen the miracles of Jesus hallucinated, exaggerated, embellished, and filled in missing details, and then their memories shifted (as we saw in chapter 3 is so common). Given the body of evidence that we have today and the history of how it came to us, should we expect to find some indications about what really happened in the Bible? If one of the early believers was overcome with guilt years later, long after the movement had been well established, and confessed that he hadn't really seen anything that day when Jesus was alleged to have visited them, would that confession have become part of the record of Jesus that we have now, centuries later?

Some of these examples clearly show that we should make a distinction among alternatives to a resurrection that the early believers would have had the conceptual tools to recognize or discover and alternatives that would have escaped their grasp. Imagine a medieval healer trying to ascertain the causes and mechanism of the bubonic plague during its outbreaks in early fourteenth-century Europe. Without modern bacterial theory and an understanding that the bacterium was carried in the blood from rats to humans, and even with the best available evidence at the time, he would be able to form only a dim, inaccurate picture of the problem. It would take until the nineteenth century for scientists to develop the conceptual tools, instruments, method of investigation, and knowledge base that would make it possible to understand what the disease was and how it was transmitted. A thirteenth-century healer, who thinks that there are four vital humors that govern health in the human body—black bile, yellow bile, phlegm, and blood—concludes that the patient is suffering from an imbalance of his black and yellow bile and prescribes foods that are cold and leeches for bloodletting. The point is that even the best available body of evidence at the time would not have revealed the truth because of inadequacies in the available investigative tools, concepts, or background knowledge. If epileptic seizures, disassociated states, bereavement hallucinations, schizophrenia, or bipolar disorder (all of which are common psychiatric problems) played a role in what the early Christians believed, they would not have had the slightest clue about what was really going on when strange things began to happen to them. Without the necessary conceptual tools, the background knowledge, and the ability to investigate the appropriate aspects of a phenomenon, one cannot hope to form the sort of evidential picture about it that would lead to accurate conclusions.

Dr. Julie Holland worked for years as a psychiatrist on the night shift at New York's infamous Bellevue Hospital. In an interview for National Public Radio, she describes some of the symptoms of bipolar disorder:

> You don't need much sleep. You've got a lot of energy, and sometimes you can get hyper-religious. You might think that you're Jesus or God or that God has spoken to you, or you've had a vision, you've had an epiphany. Epiphanies are very common in mania, in the same way that epiphanies can be common in somebody taking a psychedelic drug.
>
> You know things—you can sort of, you can see the big picture. You pull back and see the macro. Everything's connected. It all makes sense to me now. And a lot of times when I would see manic patients at Bellevue, they would remind me of people who were tripping, who had been sort of enlightened, and you can also see this, I think, in people who have had sort of religious epiphanies.
>
> So [for example,] the idea that everything is interconnected and everything makes sense. . . . A lot of people may have thoughts like this, but they don't share them, and when you're manic, sometimes your filter is gone and you tell everybody what you're thinking and feeling, and that's really, you know, where you can end up at Bellevue. . . .
>
> When someone's manic, it's more about how they can influence the world. . . . They've written a manifesto they want to share with everybody, or they've figured out an answer that needs to be—you know, they need to enlighten other people. It's much more about how they can have an impact on the people around them as opposed to how the environment is having an impact on them.[10]

Now imagine a first-century follower of Jesus—Paul's overwhelming visions on the road to Damascus come to mind—having one of these episodes and trying to understand it.

Overall, about 5 percent of adults in the US population have serious mental illness. And 46 percent of US adults will have some mental disorder during their lifetimes, including schizophrenia, personality disorders, mania, bipolar disorders, and others that are frequently associated with powerful religious components.[11] The rates would have been higher among the people in the first century because they would have had no real medical treatments or knowledge base, and the symptoms would have been utterly mysterious. For them, the best explanation of psychogenic blindness, lightning strokes, migraines, seizures, hysteria, hyperreligiousness, hypermoralism, and auditory and visual hallucinations would have been very different than the best explanation from our perspective.[12]

Suppose that when the authors of the first Gospel accounts of the life of Jesus began to record the events, the Christian movement had gotten established in a number of towns and the hopes of a great many people hung in the balance. So either knowingly or unknowingly those authors subtly adjusted, improved, aligned, or embellished the stories they had heard. Would we be in a position now, with the body of evidence we have in front of us, to find the indicators of those subtle—or maybe not so subtle—adjustments or to compare them to some other more accurate account of what had happened? In the cases where we have been able to compare manuscripts originating from a common early source, we have been able to find some of these sorts of alterations. How many more are there that we do not know about?

Suppose that Jesus had given a sermon in which he said something like, "The stories you have heard about my being the Son of God, and the reports about my performing miraculous feats have been created by some of my overly enthusiastic and imaginative followers. I am nothing but a normal person and I am not a divine being." And suppose that these enthusiastic and imaginative followers ended up being the primary sources we now have for information about Jesus. Would we expect to have a careful and accurate record of this sermon from Jesus now?

It won't be adequate here to respond by arguing that Jesus would have never said something like this in one of his sermons or that such comments from Jesus are inconsistent with what we know about his sermons, his life, and his mission. It will be circular to argue that a hoax, a stolen body, or a mistake does not fit with the details of what we know about Jesus in the Gospels. The question is then, if something natural like this had happened, would we expect for any substantial indicators of it to have survived the transmission process to reach us? Arguing that they didn't reach us misses the point. It is reasonable to expect that given the history of transmission, the information we now have about Jesus' sermons and his life and mission will have a certain character that will present him in a certain fashion. It would be blatantly circular to use the possibly misrepresentative information to argue that other accounts about him aren't accurate.

Suppose that someone happened to be in the area of the tomb and saw some Roman teenagers sneaking in and stealing the corpse during the night— we can imagine that they were the same sorts of teenagers we have today who hang around in cemeteries, vandalize headstones on Halloween, listen to The Cure and Bauhaus, and wear black eyeliner. And later the person who saw them take the body told many people about what he had seen. Given the history of the body of information that we have about Jesus now, would we expect to find a careful account of that grave-robbing incident within the evidence we have now about the life of Jesus? What if no one had seen the body being stolen?

Suppose that a group of Roman teenagers had stolen the body and no one saw it or ever reported the incident, not realizing what a profoundly important event it would become. In several of the Gospel accounts, and in the non-canonical Gospel of Peter, one or two "angels" are found inside the tomb. In John, Jesus himself is found in the tomb. Suppose that these "angels" were the grave robbers caught in the act, or that Jesus was alive there all along and that the people checking the tomb made a mistake.

Again, we should not get distracted from the central point with a debate over whether there was a deliberate hoax or mistake. Efforts by some skeptics to prove on the basis of the Gospels that something like this happened are also off the mark. The point of considering these counterevidential possibilities is *not* to argue that the evidence from the Bible supports one of them better than a real resurrection. The more fundamental questions here are the following: If something other than a real resurrection had happened, would we expect that the early believers would have been aware of it? If they had been aware of it, would they have communicated successfully that alternative to other people in the movement who *did* believe that a real resurrection occurred? Would those others have believed the natural explanation? If that information had been known, would it have been completely and accurately recorded in the stories and writings that were circulating among the early believers? And would that information about the non-supernatural explanation of what happened have made it through centuries of active editing and copying of the manuscripts so that we could consider the total body of evidence and decide for ourselves what the most likely events were? I think that we have good reasons to think that the answer to *all* of these questions is no. The counterevidence principle has not been satisfied for the resurrection.

We know how commonly belief persists, even in the face of refutation. In our own day, reports of Bigfoot, the Loch Ness Monster, and crop circles created by aliens in the English countryside abound and have become a part of the collective Western consciousness. But information that decisively debunks them remains virtually unknown. A member of the Patterson expedition that produced the first famous film footage of Bigfoot has confessed that they faked it with a basketball player in an ape suit.[13] The photographer who took the first picture of Nessie has confessed that he faked it with some foam and a toy submarine in order to embarrass a London newspaper.[14] And the two Englishmen who for decades created crop circles under cover of darkness have confessed their prank.[15] True believers in all three phenomena have persisted and given elaborate justifications for why we should disregard all of these confessions. You have heard of Bigfoot, the Loch Ness Monster, and crop circles, but you probably didn't know about the confessions and debunkings. Even after James Randi went on *The Tonight Show* and demonstrated that Peter Popoff's faith healing "miracles" were performed with a hidden radio receiver, Popoff's followers continued to proclaim his innocence, and attendance at his services scarcely diminished.[16]

If the possibility that a mere hoax could be responsible for a movement as vast as Christianity seems unlikely, consider that exposure of the Loch Ness

Monster, Bigfoot, and crop-circle hoaxes have not deterred millions of true believers in the slightest.

From this, we see it would not be an adequate response to any of the alternatives to argue that the evidence we have shows that no such thing happened or that the persistence of so many believers proves that it must be real. The question before us now is about the body of evidence itself and what we should reasonably expect to find in it, if one of those alternatives was true. Appealing to the body of evidence itself to corroborate the completeness of the body of evidence is, as we have seen, circular. If you begin to suspect that the score-keeper in the football game between the Devils and the Falcons is padding the score in favor of the Falcons, someone cannot simply point to the scoreboard to prove that the Falcons are winning. If it turns out that the Falcons' coach, who has been caught doctoring the score in the past, is keeping the score in the scoring booth, then the current score is even more suspect.

Clearly, the answer is that we would not expect to find the counterevidence in question within the information we have, given its origins, its transmission, and the nature of its transmitters. Furthermore, the alternatives we are describing are common and plausible scenarios that we see happen frequently as people tell and retell stories, gossip, and try to recall events from the past. If the miracles had not been authentic, would we would not expect to find indicators of inauthenticity within the records of those miracles sustained by the Christian church. It is also true that if Jesus really had been resurrected and there was no significant counterevidence available to his original followers because the resurrection was real, then we might also expect to find a lack of that counterevidence in our information. But the absence of that information cannot by itself be taken to show that there was no natural explanation. We must consider the best overall explanation for the account we have, along with the rest of what we know about people. As far as we know, there was no substantial investigation of the Jesus miracles conducted by a disinterested third party. The people relaying the story did not know how to conduct such a thing. They would not have known about the wide range of alternative explanations for these sorts of testimonies. And they would not have known about many of the sorts of signs to look for if something natural could explain it. And finally, if there had been any sort of serious investigation or corroboration of these miracle claims, and if that investigation had revealed something suspicious about them, we would not expect to find that counterevidence or any of those indicators in the body of evidence we have today.

Consider that, for the most part, the institution of Christianity has been the sole record keeper and source of information for many centuries regarding these texts. The people copying, preserving, and sustaining the Gospel accounts have been dedicated believers within the Christian church. A pessimistic reading would suggest that we have had a case of the fox watching the hen house for many centuries, and our primary means of confirming or disconfirming whether any chickens have been eaten is by checking with the fox itself. We would not go to a pharmaceutical company that has the sole patent on a drug and that controls all of the information about its effectiveness to cure cancer and simply take its word for it about how good the cure is. As a teacher, you would never walk out of a testing room full of students who all have their notes and books sitting in their backpacks and then just check with them about whether they cheated while you were gone. You would be foolish to get all of your information about the progress of the war effort from the government waging the war and simply believe it without question. Imagine if we simply accepted his claim of innocence every time someone accused of a crime denies his guilt with passion and sincerity. We shouldn't be inclined to take his word on faith alone, especially when the answer is so important.

CONCLUSION

In this chapter, we have discussed some hypothetical evidence that, if it had existed, would have refuted or at least raised serious questions about the authenticity of the stories about Jesus' resurrection. The larger lesson here is that when we have a hypothesis that we suspect is true, our first question should not be, "Is there any evidence that is consistent with it?" Rather, we should ask, "If the hypothesis is false, how would that manifest itself in ways I can detect?" We should not treat the hypothesis as justified until we figure out what might show that it is mistaken; and then we should aggressively pursue the possibility of disconfirmation. But we have good reasons to think that the evidence concerning Jesus and his returning from the dead is fundamentally lacking in this regard. What is not present in the Bible turns out to be more important than what is present.

We can make a useful distinction here between a search phase with a belief orientation and a search phase with a truth orientation. Psychologist and critical-thinking researcher Jonathan Baron describes *actively open-minded thinking* with a truth orientation. It consists of "(1) a search that is thorough in proportion to the importance of the question, (2) confidence that is appropriate to the amount and quality of thinking done, and (3) fairness to other possibilities than the one we initially favor."[17] When a search for information has a belief orientation, the thinker looks for that information that would corroborate the belief he already favors. He has the process backward: the belief determines and guides the search instead of starting with an unbiased assessment of a broad, inclusive body of evidence and having the best justified conclusion emerge out of that process as a result. When the early Christian writers were sharing their stories and ideas, they were often engaged in shoring up the flagging beliefs among their movement's followers. The point of their exchanges was to create a particular belief, namely that Jesus had returned from the dead and was the Messiah. They were not intent on preserving the full body of information that might have undermined their whole movement.

The lesson of this chapter can be readily understood in terms of Baron's third condition. Would the believers who ground the modern Christian's belief have treated the other possibilities to Jesus' divinity with the appropriate fairness? The answer from prior chapters and this one has been no. As we saw in chapter 3, there were many alternatives of which they simply would not have been aware. They could not have known about the placebo effect, or about double-blind controls, or how to conduct a full-scale modern scientific investigation. Nor would they have understood how wishful thinking, suggestion, peer pressure, mistakes, delusions, inattention, prior expectations, misunderstanding of the events, revisions, hedging, vagueness, and confirmation bias can all influence someone to believe that something extraordinary happened when it did not. They would not have appreciated that, in general, small samples of information are less trustworthy. The more evidence that can be gathered the better. If a miracle was to occur, all other things being equal, we would have better evidence if there are more people who attest to it. Early Christians would not have fully appreciated that a few passionate believers with a great deal of investment in the cause of the miracle claim are not as reliable (or not reliable at all) as a large group of impartial, autonomous people. And the history of the Christian movement leads us to think that other possibilities that they might have been able to grasp would have been systematically suppressed, neglected, or overlooked.

First-century believers would not have understood that impartiality is one of the most important rules of the evaluation of empirical data in a scientific investigation. Those with a vested interest in one outcome or another should not be responsible for the gathering, recording, evaluating, or preserving of the evidence. James Randi has investigated thousands of cases of alleged paranormal, pseudoscience, and alternative-medicine claims. The single biggest problem he finds, and the cause of the inevitable downfall of all of them, is that enthusiastic believers, adherents, and people with powerful interests in a positive outcome are responsible for the "investigating" of the phenomena in question. So, not surprisingly, given that people have such an uncanny knack for finding what they are looking for, they conclude that a phenomenon is real and that it is resoundingly supported by the evidence. Randi has despaired more than once from having to explain the most rudimental elements of the principles of double-blind testing. And time after time, when more rigorous controls are applied, the evidence that seemed to be there during the earlier, sloppier investigations evaporates. But the early Christians would not have been fully aware of the depth of these problems or their frequency among humans. It would be centuries before humans would begin to appreciate the point, and—as James Randi's busy schedule shows—we are still struggling with it.

Many of the early Christians may have done their best with the tools and information available to them. But the question is not about whether they were justified given what they saw or heard from others. Recall that District Attorney Michaels and the jury were justified in convicting the defendant, given what they knew. Nor is it about whether the early Christians believed what they reported. The real question is about whether you and I now, two thousand years later, are justified in concluding that the Jesus miracles occurred on the basis of the information that those people left for us. Deeply flawed epistemic agents and processes stand between us and the truth about Jesus. We should refuse to believe on the basis of the early Christians' belief because of the many problems with how they thought and how they would have formed their belief in Jesus.

What should be clear now is that by a reasonable standard, the body of evidence we have is actually quite poor. So that brings up another issue for the next chapters: if it is God, after all, who is producing and preserving the evidence in question, surely it would not be challenging for him to have made the case for the authenticity of the Jesus miracles much better than it is. It seems obvious that if an omnipotent and omniscient being had intended that people in later centuries should come to believe in the authenticity of the Jesus stories, it would have been a trivial matter to bring about evidence that was vastly better than what we have now. And since the evidence is so poor it seems far more likely that God had nothing to do with it. But what the evidence does manifest is the unmistakable marks of the foibles, limitations, biases, and fallacies of human psychology.

Chapter 8

WHY ARE ALL OF THE GODS HIDING?

The layers of doubt brought out by the previous chapters raise an important question. At the very least, even if someone is not convinced to doubt the resurrection by anything that has been said, it should occur to her that the case for the resurrection and the reasons for accepting Christianity could be *better* than they are.[1]

Suppose the almighty creator of the universe with the power to control every aspect of reality had sought to achieve a state where all or most normal, thoughtful adult human beings could reflect on the evidence available to them and come to believe that he exists. Could such a being create a state of affairs where a person with our powers of reasoning (or better ones!) could consult the evidence and arrive at a justified, reasonable, and compelling conclusion that God is real or that Jesus was resurrected from the dead? Could God have brought it about so that the historical evidence for the resurrection turned out better than what we've got? Achieving these goals would be a trivial matter for such a being. I am not all-powerful, all-knowing, or all-good, yet I can make my existence perfectly obvious to humans. I might even be able to arrange it so that people two thousand years from now got sufficient information about some event to draw a reasonable conclusion about it. Could God have given Christianity a better foundation? We have compelling historical evidence for believing that George Washington was the first US president, for the occurrence of the Civil War, for the eruption of Mount Vesuvius that destroyed Pompeii, for the existence of the Babylonians, and for thinking that Newton discovered the universal law of gravitation. So far, this book has focused largely on the inadequacies of the case for the resurrection. In this chapter, we can consider the improvements that would have made the story about Jesus' resurrection much more plausible.

MIRACLES! NEW AND IMPROVED! BIGGER! BETTER!

A problem for the believer is it appears that if God had been in charge, the miracles could have been better, and if God had sought for us to believe on the basis of those miracles, they should have been better. Consider a few obvious improvements for performing better miracles that would have helped alleviate the various concerns undermining the miracles of Jesus for us. If God was interested in proving something with miracles, here is a good place to start:

1. *Objective, impartial observers.* The claim that a violation of the laws of nature has occurred should not be evaluated or investigated by committed, zealous believers. Humans have a powerful tendency to affirm the conclusions they desire to be true. The virtue of double-blind testing procedures in science is that they help us prevent undue influence by wishful thinking, conflicts of interest, hedging, confirmation bias, and sloppy thinking. The person who deeply wants the conclusion to be true should not be the same person who investigates the evidence that might prove it to be false. Many people claim that there are miracles happening on a regular basis now. It would be a relatively easy matter to have an independent panel of objective evaluators such as doctors in the case of a healing miracle who examine the evidence before and after an alleged healing without any leading or suggestive information about what they are looking for. Show them the x-rays, the blood tests, or the CAT scans before and after someone is alleged to have been healed of a brain tumor, for example.

2. *More evidence.* In general, small samples of information are less trustworthy. The more evidence that can be gathered, the better. If a miracle was to occur, all other things being equal, we would have better evi-

dence if there are more people who attest to it or more evidence to support it. A few emotional believers with a great deal of investment in the cause of the miracle claim are not as reliable (or not reliable at all) as a large group of diverse, autonomous people. If God has the goal of proving his existence through miracles, he would need to make them evident to a great many, well-educated, skeptical people who do not already believe. And it would certainly be within the abilities of an all-powerful being to do it.

2. *Go big.* The larger the scale of a miracle, the greater the possibility that it can be corroborated, confirmed, cross-checked, and witnessed. A small miracle—a spiritual leader making a golden ring appear in his palm (which is an old magician's trick)—is going to be more difficult to confirm, more likely to be faked, and less indicative of some real violation of the laws of nature than a large one. With small miracles, the rest of us are merely likely to get hearsay, anecdotal evidence, conflicting stories, and poor transmission of the information. A miracle that appears to everyone could be vastly more effective. And surely an omnipotent God or even just a very powerful God would be up to the bigger task. If the goal is to bring Jesus back to demonstrate his divinity to all of humanity for the rest of history, then why just show him to a handful of his devoted followers for a few fleeting moments? Why not parade him around to everyone on the planet for decades, or centuries, or forever?

3. *Take human fallibility into account.* The power of suggestion, social pressure, and peer expectation can be very influential in getting people to believe that something special or extraordinary has happened. As we saw in chapter 3, dozens of psychological studies have shown that it takes very little prompting and only slight suggestions to get people to fabricate stories, to deny what they have seen with their own eyes, and to come to genuinely believe something that is a mistake. Any miracle claim is going to be up against this psychological background that will create challenges to its authenticity. Surely God would know the limits and pitfalls of human psychology better than anyone.

4. *Make it better than tricks that are easily faked.* Stage magicians have

devised ways, through entirely natural means of trickery, to perform feats that are stunning for what they appear to be. They make large objects, such as cars, disappear and reappear. They make people disappear and reappear. They appear to be able to levitate, walk on water, and transport from one location to another instantly. The ability of con artists and performers to do these tricks casts substantial doubts on any alleged miracle that resembles them. Wouldn't it be perverse of God to bring about a real miracle but have it be the sort of thing that is easily duplicated by a teenager with a magic kit or a magic how-to book, and thereby completely obscuring its significance and occurrence?

5. *Make it something an almighty being would do.* Too many of the miracles that people allege are idiosyncratic, local, and selfish. High-school football teams pray fervently for God to help them win the upcoming game while the other team does the same. A rap star gives thanks to God for the modest success of his latest CD. A woman at the convenience store wins $500 with a lottery ticket and claims that her prayers have been answered. Joe Nelms has been opening recent NASCAR races with prayers that thank God profusely for Fords®, engines, Sunoco™ racing fuel, and his smoking-hot wife.[2] Even if God did play some role in these events, it's difficult for the rest of us to believe that the omnipotent and omniscient creator of the universe takes such an active interest in the outcome of a football game between the rival high schools in Ottumwa, Iowa. Consider how baffling it would be if God had played some role in the success of a rap album while ignoring the genocide of millions of innocent people in Rwanda. Even resurrecting a dead man so that he can talk to a few dozen or even a few hundred of his followers and then vanish is a tiny, insignificant act against the context of what an all-powerful God could do.

6. *Miracles aren't merely fortuitous events.* Events that are merely fortuitous for the person considering them, like having a baby or surviving a car wreck (especially since many pregnancies go awry, and many people die in car wrecks), even if they really are the result of God's violating the laws of nature, just aren't going to be convincing to anyone

who thinks about it very much. These sorts of events don't look special at all when viewed from a distance. In fact, they appear to be completely predictable and ordinary—every day there will be some people who will survive car wrecks, especially with seatbelts and airbags, and every day there will be babies born, especially when people have unprotected sex. Couldn't I throw a ball up in the air and just as well claim that its coming down is a result of my divine powers? If it were going to happen anyway, can't everyone equally claim credit for it, and doesn't that show that no one gets credit for it as a miracle?

7. *Feelings aren't enough.* Powerful feelings of awe, religious significance, excitement, and enthusiasm themselves are not indicators that something special has happened in the world. We have too many examples of cases where people got very worked up over things that turned out to be mistakes, deceptions, or just insignificant events. Recall that in history eclipses have been treated as indicators of profound supernatural significance. Presumably, God would have the ability to do something more than induce such feelings in people, and he would know how much those feelings cloud the truth.

8. *Pick a better audience.* As the first-century Christians living in the Iron Age saw it, the world was infused with magical and supernatural events. Their minds and lives must have been overrun with spooky events, spirits, supernatural forces, mysteries, and frightening possibilities. Virtually none of the facts about nature that you take for granted was a part of their knowledge base. They didn't know that such a thing as oxygen exists, they didn't know that infections are caused by viruses, they didn't know that it gets dark at night because the earth is turning, they didn't know what made water boil, and they didn't know that there are no evil demons. The vast majority of them did not know how to read or write. The average life expectancy was twenty to thirty years because of their ignorance of medical science, basic hygiene, and public sanitation. If you were God and you were going to pick an audience with the intention of proving your existence and communicating your desires, you almost could not find a more gullible, easily impressed, and more ignorant group. It would take

surprisingly little to completely stun them—a *toaster* would appear to be a wondrous, miraculous artifact from heaven.

9. *Beware of the placebo effect.* The placebo effect is well documented in human beings. When they have the expectation that they are getting treated for a medical problem, the expectation itself has a substantial effect on their state and their reporting of their state. A minimum requirement for even the most modest over-the-counter cold medicine is that it must demonstrate effectiveness significantly beyond the placebo-effect level. If it does not, the Food and Drug Administration will not allow manufacturers to claim any real capacity to treat illness. The effects felt in many putative spiritual cures, alternative medical therapies, faith healings, and alleged miracles are undoubtedly the placebo effect. If you were God and you were performing miracles, you would need to do better than that. And presumably, you would have the power, the knowledge, and the will to do so.

The problem is that as far as we can determine, *not a single alleged religious miracle in all of human history* satisfies these modest, reasonable, and obvious suggestions. Yet they are the sorts of requirements that even a fourteen-year-old high-school science student understands and learns how to investigate empirically. These are some of the minimal criteria for publishing in a science journal. How can it be that the most powerful, most knowing, and morally perfect supernatural being in the universe does not do any better? Here's another case where our double standard in favor of Jesus is exposed. We insist that these requirements be met in order to test the efficacy of an over-the-counter cold medicine, but we utterly forget them in church on Sunday morning.

If the all-powerful, all-knowing creator of the universe had sought to make his existence known and reasonable through the Bible, he could have done a better job. We can readily imagine a hundred ways in which the case for God on the basis of the Bible could have been better. It seems quite clear that if there were a God who desired belief in him on the basis of the evidence, then we would find abundant, compelling evidence to that effect.

Since he didn't, Christians are left in a difficult situation. They might argue that there are mitigating circumstances that made it impossible for God to have given us a better body of evidence. Or perhaps God does not want to reveal himself. Daniel Howard-Snyder and Paul Moser offer a list of reasons that God might have, including the following possibilities. Maybe revealing himself is not a high priority; it is not something he wants. Remaining hidden enables people to freely love, trust, and obey Him. Coercion is incompatible with love. Being hidden prevents a human response based on improper motives like the fear of punishment. Being hidden prevents humans from relating to God and their knowledge of God in a presumptuous way. God's being hidden allows us to recognize the wretchedness of life on our own, without God, and to stimulate us to search for him with the appropriate attitude of contrition. If he revealed himself, then it would not be possible to have the real risk associated with passionate faith. If he revealed himself, then the temptation to doubt would be reduced or eliminated. Doubt makes religious diversity possible and gives us opportunities to assist others and ourselves in building personal relationships with God.[3] We can call this position *hidden theism*.

While these are fascinating suggestions, I think they fail for a variety of reasons. But arguing against these justifications for divine hiddenness is not my goal here. Hidden theists are to be commended, however, for acknowledging what atheists have been arguing for all along: there are not sufficient evidential grounds for concluding that God is real. The problem is that these explanations of God's hiddenness cannot be reconciled with the view that the resurrection or God's existence are historically evident. The advocate of the historical resurrection and the natural theologian cannot have it both ways. She cannot, on the one hand, argue that God's existence or the resurrection is the reasonable outcome of a non-question-begging, objective analysis of the arguments and evidence while also endorsing justifications of divine hiddenness like those on the list. She cannot insist that God's existence or the resurrection is manifest and reasonable while also claiming that God has his reasons for withholding his existence from serious inquiry. Either God's existence or the resurrection is justified by our epistemic situation or it is not. And the very fact that the arguments for God and the resurrection are so embattled, weak, complicated, and unconvincing, even to other believers, works against them. If the believer appeals to some carefully constructed and subtly nuanced version of the cosmological argument, or to exhaustive historical research, she faces the much harder challenge: God would have given us much more to work with if he had wanted us to arrive at belief by this route. There is no way to reconcile a view of God as seeking our belief with reasons for belief that could have been so much better. What mitigating circumstances could possibly interfere with his getting what he wants?

The hidden theist might argue that humans—not God—have meddled with and corrupted the body of evidence, making it not as compelling as it could have been. Perhaps the most popular answer on Howard-Snyder and Moser's list is that God refrains from revealing himself because it would compromise our freedom; more evidence, proof of miracles, or revealing himself to us directly would prevent us from freely choosing to have a relationship with him.

But the "freedom to choose" position and the historical resurrection position are deeply incompatible. By withholding more compelling evidence or better historical grounds for the resurrection in order to preserve freedom, God is leaving ambiguity and doubt. To preserve freedom is to insure that the historical evidence for the resurrection is *not* sufficient to show the resurrection. You can't both maintain that the only or best explanation of the historical evidence is that the resurrection happened, *and* that there is room for us to choose to believe or not to believe. The historical evidence for the existence of Abraham Lincoln does not leave room for a reasonable person to legitimately doubt his existence. To do so would be irrational and wrong. If God left room for us to choose about the resurrection, then the historical evidence for it is inadequate. If history shows that the resurrection happened, then we are not at liberty to (rationally) not believe it.

Furthermore, I can't see how my acknowledging the existence of Abraham Lincoln, for example, compromises my freedom in any way. Doing so doesn't constrain my real choices any more than your walking into a room where I can see you constrains mine. While it may prevent me from reasonably believing that it did not rise, the sun's rising doesn't limit my freedom in any important sense that I can detect. The freedom to not believe is a peculiar notion. Evidently, having direct confrontations with God didn't compromise Abraham's ability to choose to sacrifice his son Isaac when God ordered it. It didn't compromise Satan's freedom to choose, or Adam and Eve's, or Noah's, or Mary's.[4] If God can directly reveal himself to them, and so many others in history, why not more? If Abraham can have as much direct access to God as he had and then still be capable of freely rejecting God's commandment to sacrifice Isaac, then how would better evidence for the resurrection compromise our freedom?

GOD DOESN'T WANT YOU TO BELIEVE THE BIBLE

We might even pursue further the notion that God could have made the evidence better. In light of its evidential shortcomings, if someone believes on the basis of the Bible, then it would appear that she is believing in a fashion that is contrary to God's will. If God had intended for people to believe on its basis, he would have made the evidence much better. He did not, so that must not be what he intended. Furthermore, by attempting to construct a reasonable case for God's existence or for the miracles of Jesus on the basis of the Bible, the believer is doing something that God himself does not appear to be seeking. It would appear that she is distorting, obfuscating, or violating God's intentions. She is actively undermining God's plans, whatever those plans might be, and adding to the general confusion, controversy, and grounds for nonbelief. By seeking to achieve something that God himself does not want (and could have easily achieved if he had wanted to), it appears that she is thwarting God's intentions.

HIDDENNESS

The possibility of better evidence for God has motivated some positions known as the argument from nonbelief or the argument from divine hiddenness from authors such as Theodore Drange and J. L. Schellenberg.[5] What's novel about Drange and Schellenberg's approach is that they are taking the long, difficult struggle for proof of God or Jesus itself as evidence that there is no God or that Jesus was not who he said he was.

There are layers of problems with the Christians' claim that God wants us to believe. Purportedly, God seeks the spread of Christianity (and, by extension, these arguments will apply to other religions with expansionist, evangelical doctrines). But the spread of Christianity has not occurred on a scale or in a fashion that would befit the all-powerful creator of the universe. One would expect for him to get what he wants. We are not in circumstances where the existence of God is obvious or reasonable to all or most people who consider it. And the primacy of Christianity and the divinity of Jesus are not evident to as many people as one might expect if that is what God sought.[6]

Certainly there are a great many people who believe. But there are a great many who do not. There are billions of Buddhists, for example, who do not believe in the existence of an all-powerful creator God. And certainly in human history we can find billions more people for whom the existence of such a being was not obvious or reasonable. There are even many believers who are doubtful about God's existence being obvious, proven, or clearly indicated by reason. When polled, a great many of them respond that belief in God can come only through faith.

Belief in God could be more widespread, and an omnipotent God who had the intention that people should believe in him could have done much more to achieve that end. So the absence of belief and evidence themselves are taken as evidence that there is not an omnipotent God who seeks widespread belief.

ATHEISM

In chapter 1, I said that many aspects of the argument against Christianity and the resurrection could be expanded into a broader argument for atheism. Now we can see one of those expansions. Notice that the problem of divine hiddenness or the argument from nonbelief works against other religions, too. In fact, if you are a Christian, it may work even better. That is, suppose that a Muslim insists that Allah is real and that, furthermore, Allah has goals and plans for us, there are things he wants from us, he wants us to believe in him, he wants us to become Muslims and acknowledge that Muhammad is his one and only Prophet, and so on. The internal inconsistency of the position ought to be troubling. If Allah is a real, all-powerful being, then it would be a trivial matter for him to achieve those goals better than he has. If you are a Christian, or if you are a non-Muslim, you probably deem the plausibility of Islam to be low. You don't accept those claims, you don't have those beliefs, and you don't have the recommended sort of relationship to Allah. If Allah is what they say he is, then he could have done more to help us reach the desired state of believing. Assuming he is real, it would be perverse, capricious, and unjust for Allah to then judge you and condemn you for failing to believe. So these facts suggest that what the Muslim is saying about Allah's power and goals must be mistaken. There's something deeply amiss in the internal coherence of the story. And that contradiction counts against the plausibility of the story.

So the argument against Islam may help the Christian to see the problem with the internal logic of the scenario she is arguing for. And if it works with Islam, then it works against Christianity and any religious doctrine that claims some powerful divine being is real. The problem casts suspicion on every religious movement that asserts the existence of a being whose existence could have been more obvious and that has the power to bring it about. Why are all of the gods hiding? Without satisfying answers to that question, being doubtful about the existence of such gods is justified. The believing Christian now must argue on non-ad-hoc grounds, and without special pleading, that there are absolving reasons that explain away this internal problem for Christianity and that those same absolving reasons cannot apply to Islam and other religions.

The advocate for the historical resurrection of Jesus is in a serious bind. He's got to maintain first that the historical evidence shows us that the resurrection is real and second that the God responsible for the resurrection is one who is capable of making that historical evidence much better than it is but didn't. He's got to argue that we should believe the contentious and weak case for the resurrection, but, furthermore, we should not be puzzled by the weakness of that argument in the light of God's omnipotence. The position undercuts itself. The believer embraces the following: (1) the historical evidence forces us to conclude that the resurrection was real, (2) but, admittedly, God could have made the historical evidence much better than it is, and (3) this internal gap or incoherence does not count against the plausibility of the historical argument.

What reasons can the believer offer to defend the third point? If the evidence for the resurrection could be better, and if making it better was within God's power, then God's leaving the resurrection in the state it's in does not make sense. An additional problem is that whatever reasons or justifications the believer might give for God's not making the evidence better, they cannot be derived from the historical case without circular reasoning.

> *Critic:* Why isn't the historical evidence better?
> *Believer:* Because God wants X.
> *Critic:* How do we know that God wants X?
> *Believer:* From the historical evidence.

This sort of reasoning is as bad as this example:

> *Believer:* I believe that God is real.
> *Critic:* But why would you believe this?
> *Believer:* Because the Bible says he is.
> *Critic:* Why believe what the Bible says?
> *Believer:* Because God wrote it.

Ironically, the conclusion we are being asked to accept on the basis of the historical evidence actually undermines the case from the historical evidence since the sort of God that the evidence is alleged to prove would have provided better historical evidence.

A larger case for atheism can be extrapolated from the problem here for Christianity. Suppose that members of a religious movement maintain that the existence of some powerful god and its goals or laws can be known through their scriptures, their prophets, or some special revelation. If the capacity of that god is alleged to be greater than the effectiveness or quality of those scriptures, prophets, or special revelations, then the story they are telling contradicts itself. "We know our god is real on the basis of evidence that is inadequate for our god." Or, "The grounds that lead us to believe in our god are inconsistent with the god we accept; nevertheless, we believe in this god that would have given us greater evidence if it had wished for us to believe in it."

Given the disparity between the gods that these religious movements portend and the grounds offered to justify them, the atheist is warranted in dismissing such claims. If the sort of divine being that they promote were real, the situation would not resemble the one we are in. A far better explanation is that their enthusiasm for believing in a god has led them to overstate what the evidence shows.

There are a number of justifications for a wider atheism, but here is one. Unless some evidence is forthcoming that befits the inference to an all-powerful supernatural being, the atheist is justified in preferring the naturalistic account of the origins of these religions. Notice that atheism is also justified if Howard-Snyder and Moser are right about the possible justifications for God's hiddenness. The irony is that even if God is real, believing that he is not would be the only conclusion justified by the evidence if God refrains from revealing himself for some of the reasons they have given. The other side of their list is that no one can be faulted for drawing the conclusion supported by the evidence in a situation where God has taken such deliberate measures to make it appear as if there is no God. If Howard-Snyder and Moser's God is real, then apparently he wants the evidence to support atheism.

Chapter 9

WOULD GOD DO MIRACLES?

I t is time to reframe the issue of God and miracles. Let us consider them from the other side and ask two questions that rarely get asked: First, if a miracle occurs, could we infer that God was responsible for it? And second, if God were going to act, would he act by means of miracles? That is, is a miracle the sort of thing he would do?

MIRACLES AS EVIDENCE FOR GOD

So far, we've looked at whether we should believe that Jesus' miracles happened. Let us now suppose that they did. What could we then infer? Too often it is taken for granted that if miracles really do occur, then proof for the existence of God is in hand. We seem to assume that if there really was a Jesus who did and said all the things he is purported to have said, then we would have compelling reasons to think that the God of Christianity is real. If Jesus was resurrected from the dead, then Christianity would be vindicated from the arguments of the previous chapters. Similarly, we may assume that if our prayers are answered, then God must be listening.

Many atheists and nonbelievers have been just as guilty of buying into these assumptions when they have expended energy arguing that there really was no Jesus, or that the virgin-birth motif was common among various first-century religious sects, that the Bible contains internal inconsistencies, or that there was no intelligent designer of life on Earth. The background presumption often seems to be that if there was a Jesus, or if his mother was a virgin, or if the Bible is consistent, or if there were a nonnatural cause of life on Earth, then theism must be true, or even that Christianity itself has been proven. Skeptic Evan Fales has said that were an undeniable miracle to occur such as the stars in the sky suddenly realigning to spell "Mene, Mene, Tekel, Upharsin" thus making headlines all over the world and sending astronomers into a frenzy, then "that would convince me of theism (or polytheism); no other explanation is remotely plausible."[1]

What has been missed in many of these discussions of miracles is that even at their best, they do not show the existence of an all-powerful, all-knowing, all-good being, nor do they rescue Christianity. The view that there is an almighty creator God who performs miracles is riddled with conflicts.

Since Hume, the debate about miracles has largely focused on whether such events ever occur or whether it is ever reasonable to believe that they have.[2] We should remain open to the possibility that a person equipped with good tools, adequate concepts, and sufficient means of investigation could be in an epistemic position (albeit rarely) where believing miracle testimony is reasonable. What we have seen in previous chapters is just how far short the actual evidence for the resurrection falls. I am conceiving of miracles as violations of the laws of nature;[3] so suppose that a real miracle occurs and we had overwhelmingly positive evidence that it did. Now what?

First, I will consider to what extent the occurrence of a miracle could be construed as evidence for the existence of an omni-God. Would it be reasonable to take a miracle as an indicator that a single, supernatural and personal being of infinite power, knowledge, and goodness is responsible? Even in the best-case scenario, however, the argument from miracles to God is vastly underdetermined. But there is an underlying problem that is much worse; if a miracle occurred, we could be sure that an omnibeing did not do it.[4]

WHAT WOULD A MIRACLE SHOW?

What seems to have infused our thinking about miracles is some slipping between necessary and sufficient conditions. If in order to perform a miracle, a being must be omnipotent, omniscient, and infinitely good, and if we had compelling grounds to believe that a miracle had occurred, then we would have compelling evidence that God exists. The problem, however, is that while these properties appear to be sufficient to perform miracles, they are not necessary.[5] A lesser being could perform one; therefore, we can't make the leap to an omni-God.

According to the Christian faith, the relationship between Jesus and God is complicated. The Christian God is, by all accounts, an omni-God. He is all-powerful, all-knowing, singular, personal, and infinitely good. He also possesses a number of other properties that distinguish him from the omni-Gods in other traditions, such as Islam. Jesus is alleged to have been his son. Jesus was divine, but he was also a man, by the Christian doctrine. The extent to which he was a man and lacked the status of a full omnibeing is a point of some controversy. God, if he had chosen, could have resurrected or not resurrected Jesus, and the miracles of Jesus were, either directly or indirectly, God's doing. In this chapter, we are interested more in God and his connection to miracles than in Jesus. So I will speak of God's performing these miracles, although locally, acts like healing the sick were said to have been performed by Jesus. There were other miraculous events, more often in the Old Testament, such as the burning bush or the destruction of Sodom and Gomorrah, which have been more directly attributed to God. It is God's acts that we are interested in here.

What could we infer about the cause from the occurrence of a real miracle? Is omnipotence required to violate the laws of nature? No. Consider these two events, both violations of the laws of nature: First, someone walks on water. Second, all of the nuclear-fusion reactions driving the burning of every star in the universe are stopped and all of those stars are instantly rendered cold and inert. It is reasonable to think that walking on water could take less power than what would be required to stop all fusion reactions for all stars. In part, it seems that the former would take less power if we were to try to accomplish it by acting within the framework of natural law. Using physical means to try to bring about the former event would, I think, be less difficult than trying to bring about the second.

Admittedly, it could be a poor analogy to draw conclusions about how much supernatural power is required for different acts from how much natural power would be required. Another argument is convincing: a being could have the power to perform one violation of the laws of nature and not another. Imagine two supernatural entities, one who could do only those miraculous feats that Jesus is said to have performed, and another who could do all of the Jesus miracles and infinitely many others as well. Surely the latter would be more powerful, on a reasonable account of power, than the former. We could imagine that some force is able to make a human walk on water or to stop the sun's burning only once and only for a moment, but never again. The laws of nature would be violated in these cases with less power than omnipotence because, presumably, omnipotence would include the power to perform all of these acts, as well as many others, at any time. A source that could only make someone walk on water, stop the nuclear reaction of the sun once, or perform any other miracles except reverse the flow of time, would not be omnipotent. So omnipotence is merely consistent with miracles. But were we to come across compelling evidence that a miracle occurred, at most, that might suggest to us that there *could* be an omnipotent force that was responsible—but a being with less power could have done it as well.[6]

Is omniscience necessary in order to violate the laws of nature? No. You could have an unintelligent but very powerful being that violates the laws of nature to burn a face on a fish stick because it thought that would make people believe in it.[7] There have been a few times when something on my car wasn't working and I tinkered around with the components that I figured were responsible without knowing what they do or how they work. And then, after messing around with the settings on the carburetor, or taking some fuses out of the fuse box and putting them back in, or checking the oil, the car started working properly again, much to my surprise. So there are times when I have managed to fix my car, but I was largely in the dark about how I did it, what I did, or what was wrong in the first place. There's no reason in principle to deny that this same sort of thing could be going on with a being that intervenes in nature to bring about miracles. Perhaps the being sort of faked it, tinkered blindly a bit, and the results seem to have come out the way it wanted (or not!). In fact, this sort of God hypothesis might make much more sense of the examples of miracles that are so frequently given: statues bleeding from the eyes, statues drinking milk, high-school football teams winning their championships, and fish sticks bearing the image of Jesus. Omniscience appears to be consistent with miracles, but it is not necessary.

Is omnibenevolence necessary to bring about a miracle? Again, the answer is no.[8] Typically, we think that miracles are fortuitous events. But Satan's torments of Job at God's behest were clearly violations of the ordinary course of nature. Presumably, if Satan hadn't engaged in his challenge with God, then Job would not have miraculously lost all of his livestock, had his wife and children die, developed boils all over his body, and so on. Left to the normal course of nature, Job's life would have been much less unpleasant. So miraculous events need not arise from good sources or have good effects.

Miracles that appear to accomplish good ends seem to be consistent with infinite goodness, but omnibenevolence is not necessary.[9] Many of the miracles we have been told about seem to reflect good will, such as Jesus' healing the sick, curing blindness, or feeding the hungry. But are they indicative of infinite goodness, infinite justice, or moral perfection? Again, not by themselves. Would any single, finite miracle indicate infinite goodness in the author? No. I have some degree of good will, and sometimes I act on that basis and do kind or loving things for others. But for the rest of the time, apathy, distraction, selfishness, or indifference set in and my actions don't reflect much goodness at all. So singular or even multiple miracles that seem to have good results may be consistent with infinite goodness, but they are not sufficient to indicate it. Like the omnipotence examples above, a good miracle could be the result of a momentary lapse into goodness by a being that is otherwise indifferent or even malevolent.

Far from suggesting infinite goodness, miracles—even ones that do great good—seem to suggest that the responsible party is *not* omnibenevolent. Many miracles are presented as good: Jesus is alleged to have healed a crippled man so that he could walk again, Jesus cured a group of lepers, and he miraculously fed thousands of hungry people. Similarly, many people are alleged to have been miraculously healed at Lourdes, France. Muhammad is said to have supernaturally multiplied food and drink on several occasions in order to feed hungry masses. God is reported to have parted the Red Sea to save the Israelites.

The problem is that at any given moment on the planet, now and when these miracles are alleged to have happened, there are millions or even billions of other people who are not being cured, healed, or benefitted by miracles. So any miracle that we attribute to an infinitely good God is problematic because it would indicate that God is out there and, under *some* circumstances, will intervene in the course of nature to achieve some good end. But there are all of these other cases where he does not help. The occurrence of a miracle, particularly one in the midst of so many instances of unabated suffering, cannot easily be reconciled with an omnibenevolent source.

What can we infer about the source from a miraculous event? Were some supernatural force to alleviate some cases of suffering and not others, it would not be obvious that the source is infinitely good. On the contrary, if a doctor travels to a village with enough polio vaccine to inoculate one thousand children but gives only ten of them the shots, throws the rest of the vaccine away, and then watches the remaining 990 die or be crippled, we would conclude that doctor is a monster, not a saint.

Christine Overall makes a step toward the same conclusion, "If Jesus was the Son of God, I want to know why he was hanging out at a party, making it go better [turning water into wine], when he could have been healing lepers."[10] But we can press the point further. Suppose a miraculous event suddenly heals all the lepers in the world today. Presumably, an omnibenevolent being would have done it sooner. Why not yesterday? And what about the Nazis in Auschwitz murdering over one million people in 1945, or the bubonic plague ravaging and killing millions in Europe during the 1300s?[11] We are left with this question: There are vast amounts of comparable suffering in the history of sentience that were not and are not being alleviated by miracles. How could we possibly infer infinite goodness, love, or kindness in some supernatural source that has shown the ability and the willingness to fix a select few and knowingly ignore the rest? Overall has the correct answer, "a being that engages in events that are trivial, capricious, and biased cannot be a morally perfect God."[12]

Many believers, especially those with a familiarity with the debate over the problem of evil, will insist that there could be reasons from the divine perspective that justify God's miraculously alleviating some suffering while allowing other instances to persist. That is correct. There could be some absolving reasons, but there may also be no absolving reasons. And the question here is that if one apparently good miracle occurs and some comparable ones do not, then can we reasonably infer that the cause *is* infinitely good or morally perfect? The believer's point here is that the cause *could* be omnibenevolent. But we can't reliably infer that it is or must be. At the crime scene, we cannot infer from the fact that the murderer *could* be a man or a woman that it was, indeed, a woman.

A positive argument for omnibenevolence will not arise from any finite good act. Quite the contrary, we would expect that infinite goodness, knowledge, and power in a being would preclude its doing only part of the job. If some being saw fit to fix one evil in the world, then there are evils worth fixing from its perspective. In the inductive problem of evil discussion, William Rowe has called these, "instances of intense suffering which an omnipotent, omniscient being could have prevented without thereby losing some greater good or permitting some evil equally bad or worse."[13] If a miracle achieves some good end, the responsible party has apparently found the situation to be a case where it could prevent suffering without losing a greater good or allowing an equal or worse evil. But it also could be that what appears to be a miracle arising from benevolence is actually motivated by hatred and will produce far more suffering later even though it creates some temporary happiness now.

It is reasonable to think that if there is one instance that warrants a miraculous intervention, then there are more. There are many others that look just like it, and there are many cases that appear to be worse. But they have been ignored.

James Keller develops this point into a moral argument against God's performing miracles on the following grounds. "The claim that God has worked a miracle implies that God has singled out certain persons for some benefit which many others do not receive," Keller argues, "implies that God is unfair. . . . More specifically," he continues, "there may be two cases which are similar in all ways that seem relevant, yet in one case there will be a recovery (which some deem a miracle) and in the other case no recovery."[14] The unfairness charge is that for one person to receive miraculous assistance while someone else whose situation resembles the first in every important respect doesn't, would be unjust. And an infinitely good being would not be responsible for such injustices.

A person confronted with a miracle finds himself in the following situation. Here's a case of the laws of nature being violated, possibly in order to rectify a case of what appears to be pointless evil.[15] There are many other cases now and in the past of what appear to be pointless evils that were not rectified. Lots of them resemble this one in all the relevant respects that I can think of. And many of them are far worse and even more worthy of being repaired. What is reasonable to conclude about the possible goodness of the source behind this miracle? If it is omnibenevolent, then it would have fixed those other evils, too. So if this event arose from some supernatural source or sources, it is reasonable to conclude that it or they are not omnibenevolent.

Ironically, the challenge to God's existence presented by inexplicable suffering is made worse for the theist who alleges that God performs miracles. Every case where someone claims that her prayers led to her rapid recovery from terminal cancer, or that his piety helped bring back a loved one safe from the fighting in a war zone shines a light on all the other cases of suffering that went unabated despite heartfelt prayers, decent lives, and fervent piety.

There's another way in which miracles create trouble for the believer. God is alleged to be all-powerful and all-knowing, so there is nothing that he does not know. There is no situation or event that he would not have foreseen as well as it could be foreseen. There will be no surprises, no accidents, or no unanticipated eventualities. The world will unfold the way he intended, in perfect accordance with his omnipotence and omniscience. And he won't be subject to changing his mind, having doubts, adopting a new plan, or changing to suit the circumstances.[16] So what is God accomplishing when he performs a miracle? He can't be changing something he didn't anticipate, it can't be that he has changed his mind about some aspect of his plan, and it can't be that the way he arranged the world in the first place needs to be adjusted because he didn't get it right the first time. God would have gotten it exactly right from the start. So how can we reconcile a miracle, which significantly alters the course of the laws of nature and the events that he had already set in motion with God?

For the theist, it would strain credulity less to argue that God is all-good and loving without the complications that miracles introduce. That is, the believer in these cases would have less explaining to do and could possibly make more sense of the compatibility of a world that does not have these local, arbitrary miracles than a world where one person wins the lottery, or has a cancer tumor vanish, or is the sole survivor of horrible accident, while wars, famine, plagues, and drought kill millions elsewhere. If an omni-God performed no miracles, one might offer up some generalized account of gratuitous suffering like John Hick's soul-making theodicy wherein the inflexibility of the laws of nature builds moral and intellectual virtue in us. A good God wouldn't alter the course of nature, according to this popular view, because it gives us the opportunity to help others, to show generosity and love, and to acquire knowledge of the world.[17]

So, if we try to derive God's omnibenevolence from miracles, we have several challenges. First, there's the wider problem of reconciling God's goodness with all the staggering amounts of suffering in history that went on without intervention. An omnibenevolent being wouldn't do a partial job. So a miracle actually suggests that the source is not omnibenevolent. Second, attributing miracles to God undermines the soul-building theodicy to reconcile suffering with God's existence. Third, a miracle suggests an alteration in the unfolding of events in a world that should have been the best of all possible worlds to start with.

CAN WE GET A SINGULAR, PERSONAL GOD FROM A MIRACLE?

Should we assume that a force that can violate the laws of nature is a single, personal being that possesses a consciousness with goals? Many religious traditions are dominated by the view that their god is a singular being with no peers and has dominion over all, as well as the view that their god forms direct, personal relationships with us. In order to cause a miracle, must the cause have the capacity to love, hate, forgive, become angry? Again, the answers are no. Couldn't there be a blind, unthinking, unconscious force that is powerful enough to interrupt the course of nature? Violating natural laws does not require being sentient, being aware, or having any of the personal traits that we typically attribute to God any more than felling a tree does: lumberjacks and lightening are both capable.

Reading particular intentions, consciousness, purpose, or personhood from an anomalous event that violates the laws of nature is hard because none of those appear to be necessary for that interruption to occur. Even if the source has conscious intent, it may be more than one being. The occurrence of a violation of the laws of nature could have come from ten, one hundred, or ten thousand sources working together or even in conflict. At the very least, one would need to give an argument based on some considerations beyond the miracle itself that the best explanation is that some single, personal force was responsible rather than many sources and rather than one that is blind and unconscious. The occurrence of a miracle might be consistent with a single supernatural force and that force being a person, but it will not be positive evidence by itself.

The critic may object at this point that if it is a person, in the form of a human, as Jesus was alleged to have been, and if that person performs a miracle and then claims to be a supernatural agent, then we would have evidence that the source of the miracle is a person. What else could be needed beyond a person performing a miracle to show that the miracle's cause is a person? And who else but an omnibeing could be responsible?

But we must be careful here and not simply grant what needs to be proven. That someone who appears to be a conscious agent with purposes claims that an anomalous event in nature arises from the exercise of his will doesn't imply that it did. It will take a great deal more to show that he is the cause, that he has control over the cause, or that the event should be understood in only the manner that he instructs. In Mark Twain's *A Connecticut Yankee in King Arthur's Court*, Hank, a modern American, time travels back to 528. He recalls that there is a solar eclipse and fakes being able to control it to demonstrate his magical powers to King Arthur's court to keep them from killing him. If we see a miracle occur and there is a person who claims to have been responsible, then his claims about what the event means are more pieces of evidence that a reasonable observer would have to take under consideration and evaluate. Humans are fallible. There are cases where alleged psychics or paranormalists seem to genuinely believe that they have extraordinary powers, but even they don't realize that what is occurring has a natural explanation and source. Sometimes palm readers and fortune tellers are able to pick up on subtle body-language cues, facial expressions, and other discrete indicators without being aware that it is these cold-reading techniques that are giving them information instead of their alleged paranormal abilities. If something natural is happening, then the agent may or may not understand what it is. Similarly, if something supernatural is happening, the agent may or may not know what is happening, why, or how. Even if there is a voice from the heavens that claims to be the source of the miraculous event, it may not be. Jesus might have known no more than we do about the real origins of the events that he thought he was able to command with his will.

So if I have compelling evidence of a miracle before me, and my goal is to draw some reasonable inferences about what sort of cause may have brought it about, I cannot leap to the conclusion that it is omnipotent. Nor should I infer that the cause is all-knowing or all-good. I shouldn't hastily draw the conclusion that the cause is a single, personal, conscious being either.

While the occurrence of a miracle might appear to be consistent with the existence of an omni-God, or, perhaps, a Christian God, they don't support those stronger conclusions any more than my lifting a bag full of groceries, balancing my checkbook, and giving a homeless person five dollars prove that I'm God. It would seem that God could pick up the groceries, do the math, and spare five dollars. But since so many other lesser natural or supernatural beings could have been responsible, the stronger conclusion for the existence of an omni-God is grossly underdetermined by miracle evidence.

The occurrence of a real miracle is consistent with any number of possible supernatural explanations, with many of them different from or even incompatible with the existence of the omni-God of classical Western monotheism. The evidence is consistent with the responsible force or forces being supernatural but having less than divine properties. It could have been (natural) aliens with more power, knowledge, and goodness than us, but less than God. It could have been a lesser (supernatural) god's mistake, a blind tinkering, or a deception. It could have been the Tooth Fairy; Santa Claus; Sobek, the Egyptian crocodile god; or Gefjun, the Norwegian goddess of agriculture. What's the status of the God hypothesis in the midst of all these possibilities when we consider our miracle? It has nothing special to recommend it from the miracle alone.

These limitations of miracle evidence raise another more fundamental question: Is it even consistent to attribute miracles to an omnibeing? That is, our presumption has been that the divine attributes are sufficient for performing miracles—God could do miracles if he so chose. But there are compelling reasons to think that an omnibeing would not perform miracles. So if we believe one has occurred, we should conclude that God *did not* do it.

GOD WOULDN'T DO MIRACLES; GOD ISN'T AN UNDERACHIEVER

Consider the question now from the other side. Assume that there is an all-powerful, all-knowing, all-good, singular, and personal divine being. What sort of acts would it engage in? That being's actions will perfectly and completely achieve that agent's purposes. Its acts will achieve their ends as fully as they can be fulfilled. The resulting state of affairs will be the perfect manifestation of that agent's will. There won't be any restraint from some external force. There won't be any knowable solution or knowable fact or knowable outcome that such a being wouldn't be aware of. The results will not dissatisfy that being because it still desires something that cannot be had, or because it cannot obtain its goals.

So generally, we should assume that if some anomalous event occurs, and that event is the result of the exercise of an omnibeing's will, then the state of affairs produced through that event will be completely and exactly what that being sought to achieve. The results will be as perfect a fulfillment of that being's will as can possibly be achieved. There are cases where finite beings like ourselves seek to accomplish some goal that is beyond our power, or, out of ignorance, we employ the wrong means to accomplish our ends. So the results may or may not reflect good intentions, competence, knowledge, and ability. And the results may or may not succeed at getting what we wanted. But an omnibeing will not fail to achieve its desired ends for lack of ability, incompetence, or ignorance.

Consider two computer-programming students, Smith and Jones, working on a homework project to produce some output Y from an input X using a programming language. Smith creates a circuitous, inefficient, clumsy, and unnecessarily complicated program that fulfills the required task with hundreds of lines of code—the programming equivalent of a Rube Goldberg machine. Smith's program produces the Y output from input X, but it takes lots of time, and the program contains lots of unused and unhelpful features. Jones is smarter than Smith and has a more powerful command of the means at her disposal. She finds a simple, elegant, efficient solution that achieves the same output with a few dozen lines of code with no wasted time and no unnecessary features. The instructor would rightly give Jones the better grade; she has enacted a better solution to the problem. By extension, an omniscient, omnipotent being would achieve the most elegant and effective means to achieve its ends. Omniscience would grasp that solution perfectly, and omnipotence would enact it without any restraint. We would also expect, if that being is infinitely good, morally perfect, or omnibenevolent, then it would have only the highest, most noble, most appropriate goals as targets for the exercise of its will, whatever those might be. As a result, we shouldn't expect lesser, insufficient, or ineffective acts from such a being. A priori, we wouldn't expect to see minor gestures, insignificant events, or trivial results. Unhappy outcomes arise from the actions of a being that lacks foresight, ability, judgment, or virtue.

Since, as we have seen, the typical miracles that have been alleged in history could have been brought about by a force or forces that are not all-powerful, all-knowing, and all-good, God would be acting far below capacity if he had done them. Miracles would amount to trivial acts for God. A mere violation of the laws of nature is vastly less than what such a being could accomplish if it chose.

Miracles are more superficial, ineffective, and indirect means for achieving ends than an omni-God would enact. Consider some of the purposes that have been connected to miracles. If God has the goal of instilling belief, inspiring faith, fortifying resolve, discouraging misbehavior, or enforcing commandments, it takes very little imagination to conceive of more direct, effective, and sustained means of achieving those ends. As Ted Drange has argued, if these were God's goals, then it would have been a simple matter to directly implant belief into all people's minds or to perform more spectacular miracles that would convince more people. Jesus could have reappeared to everyone, not just a handful of easily discredited zealots. Millions of angels disguised as humans could have spread out and preached the word behind the scenes. Or God could have protected the Bible from defects in writing, copying, and translation.[18]

Walking on water, turning water into wine, and raising the dead are underpowered, inelegant, clumsy solutions to the various goals that are typically attributed to God when we reflect on what an omnibeing is capable of. Jesus could have given a more conclusive demonstration of his divinity to more people than raising a single dead man, or destroying a fig tree that had no fruit in front of a handful of already converted witnesses. Jesus' resurrection as it has come to us was an isolated event. No one seems to have seen the stone being moved or the body being reanimated. Only a few people saw the tomb afterward. And only a tiny group of people had a close encounter with Jesus when he returned (and the first written report of that visit doesn't surface until 150 years have passed).

Without exception, the miracles that have been presented in Christianity as well as in the rest of the world's religions have been ambiguous, underdocumented, obscure, contentious, underwhelming, and divisive. It takes very little imagination to envision events that would have been vastly more appropriate and effective for a divine being. An infinitely powerful being could have just *saved* the Israelites instead of exacting the prolonged conflicts with the pharaoh of Egypt involving plagues, murdering children, parting the Red Sea, and so on. An omnibeing could have achieved whatever ends for humanity it had in mind with the entire Jesus saga, whether it is universal belief or redemption. If God's intention was to foster confusion and strife, however, that end was accomplished quite effectively. Believers themselves bicker endlessly and split into tens of thousands of hostile factions over the specific meanings, the events, and the implications of the Bible stories. When we consider the alleged miracles of history with a sufficiently broad conception of what divine power and knowledge would be, no other goals besides divisiveness and confusion can be reasonably inferred.

Consider the problem this way. For all of the alleged supernatural miracles in history, natural facsimiles that are undetectable as fakes to anyone but an expert can be performed readily by even mediocre magicians and illusionists. David Copperfield makes the Statue of Liberty disappear on television. Penn and Teller catch bullets in their teeth. Chris Angel walks on water in a swimming pool and floats in the air over the Luxor hotel in Las Vegas. Imagine the social and religious impact these ingenious, natural illusionists could have had among the superstitious, poor, and uneducated masses of New Testament Palestine. Religious leaders such as Billy Graham, Rick Warren, Peter Popoff, Robert Tilton, Joel Osteen, Pat Robertson, and Jerry Falwell use cruder, more transparent trickery and deception to win the hearts of millions of people and in doing so acquired vast wealth from educated, modern people. My point is not to suggest that Jesus was merely performing sleight-of-hand tricks, although that is certainly a possibility. My point is that surely an omni-God, were he seeking to manifest himself through miracles, could do better than feats that look just like sleight-of-hand tricks that are so easily faked. It is more reasonable to conclude that an infinitely powerful, knowledgeable, and good being would not perform miracles than to attribute acts to him that an ordinary illusionist could effectively fake.

The culture of religions, miracles, and paranormal phenomena is so mired in fabrications, frauds, and confusions that if God were to perform a real one it would stand the same chance of exoneration as the one innocent man who is mistakenly jailed. Just like every other prisoner, he claims he is innocent. Couldn't an omnibeing do better than that? Would he allow himself to be so grossly mistaken, maligned, and misunderstood?[19] Why would he make the message ambiguous and impotent and then bury it in history in the midst of so many false miracle claims that look just like it?

If some miraculous event occurs, features of it might at first appear to be consistent with omnipotence and omniscience, but then if we consider the larger picture, that event appears to be less impressive. Whatever God was trying to accomplish, aren't there more effective ways to do it? Couldn't this act have been bigger and smarter? And if so, then the fact that it isn't bigger, smarter, or better gives me convincing evidence that was not God who was responsible. If a reasonable person is confronted with a miracle, she should think: "If God were attempting to demonstrate his existence to me, there would be no obstacles." But this miracle is insufficient to that task. So this miracle was not performed by God and does not show his existence. He would do much better than this if he were trying to demonstrate his existence.[20]

Similarly, if God were attempting to accomplish good in the world, then there would be no obstacle to his achieving much more of it than this miracle does. Suppose that thousands of the sick get healed, or the hungry get fed, or the Red Sea parts to save the Israelites. None of these miracles accomplishes nearly as much as God could. So it would also be implausible to conclude that a miracle is a manifestation of his infinite power or love.

In many examples, God punishes with miracles. Lot's wife gets turned to a pillar of salt for watching the destruction of Sodom and Gomorrah when God commanded her not to. The view that Hurricane Katrina was sent by God to punish sinners in New Orleans has been popular among American evangelical preachers. If God were attempting to exact some punishment or retribution through a miracle, then it would be grossly inconsistent to arbitrarily single out some individual for lesser misdeeds while ignoring so many others, particularly when the misdeeds of others are so grievous. An omnibeing could achieve vast, effective, balanced punishment, so it would be unreasonable to conclude that this miracle is God's punishment.

In general, if God were attempting to accomplish anything unambiguous in the world, then he could. But miracles are ambiguous. So miracles cannot be God's attempt to achieve any clear goal. He would do a much better job of accomplishing a clear objective, if that's what's going on here.

If a reasonable person has thought through the implications of what it would be for an omnibeing to act, the reaction should be something like, "That's it? That's the best you've got? How am I supposed to believe in an omnibeing on the basis of *that*? Any old demigod could do *that*." These considerations will plague all of the interpretations that we devise for the results of a miracle so long as we credit God for the action. We will not be able to conceive of any way in which this outcome could be an omnibeing's project. And if there does not appear to be any way that this could be God's act, then it is reasonable to conclude that God did not do it.

We should infer then that at the very most, if a real violation of the laws of nature occurs and we have good reasons to believe it, the strongest conclusion we could get from that evidence is some force greater than us but less than God was responsible. We should not infer from a miracle alone that the cause is a single, personal being with infinite power, knowledge, and goodness.

One objection the Christian may offer to the argument that God would not perform miracles is that God's motives and plans are mysterious to us, so we shouldn't conclude that some real miracle was not brought about by him. If a miracle occurs, we should be agnostic about the responsible party or parties instead of accepting the stronger conclusion that God didn't do it. God's knowledge and power will be too far beyond our comprehension for us to be confident that we could tell the difference between his actions and some events that appear to have limited scope. In effect, if God acts, then we won't understand it, so we should refrain from drawing strong conclusions about how God will act.

Before we analyze this rebuttal, it should be noted how far we have come here from the common position that miracles provide us with evidence for the existence of God. This critic seems to have acknowledged many of the limitations of the case in favor of a divine author—a difficult position for most Christians and many other religious believers.

If real miracles were to occur and we knew it, should we be agnostic about the possibility that an omnibeing did it? The mere possibility being argued for by the Christian doesn't amount to much. What the critic is suggesting is that there is an infinitely powerful, knowing, and good being out there, and from its perspective there are limiting factors or reasons that motivate it to perform actions that are indistinguishable from our perspective from the actions of a lesser being. The "beyond our comprehension" stretches credibility here. The argument I have given takes the notion of God very seriously and explores the implications of what it would be to have God's power, knowledge, and goodness. We have some concrete reasoning to think that when those properties manifest themselves in the world, the results should not look just like the results that a being who doesn't have those properties would achieve. The critic is pressing for a suspension of judgment about how God would act on the possibility that some unknown factors would confine him to acting in a decidedly un-God-like fashion. Without some more substantial explanation or some positive reasons to think that such limiting factors are real, the possibility is not enough to overcome the incompatibilities that have been outlined. We have several substantial reasons to doubt that an omnibeing would act by means of miracles. The nebulous possibility that it has some reasons that we don't understand might justify our holding off concluding that an omnibeing would not perform miracles if (1) we were sure on other, independent grounds that such a being exists, and (2) we had good reason to think that it performs miracles. The biblical grounds, as we have seen, are not sufficient to the task. (We will consider the frequently offered "faith" answer in chapter 11.)

Furthermore, notice that the believer cannot claim that miracles are evidence that God is real while simultaneously asserting that the motives, goals, power, knowledge, and goodness behind those miracles are mysterious and inaccessible to us. If we cannot read off some properties of the responsible force from the event, then we cannot claim to have proven the existence or character of that force.

CONCLUSION

Many of the discussions between believers and nonbelievers about miracles have missed some fundamental points. Even if miracles are real, neither omnipotence nor omniscience nor omnibenevolence are necessary in order to perform them. Nor should we assume that the cause of a miracle is a single, conscious, personal being. So even if one happens, we won't be able to infer God's existence from them. I have also argued that an omnibeing would not employ miracles to achieve its ends. Therefore, the occurrence of a miracle should not be construed as evidence for the existence of God.

The problems for Christianity created by this analysis of miracles are momentous. Jesus is thought to be the son of God, and through Jesus, God is alleged to have given expression to his will. The resurrection of Jesus and Jesus' other miracles are widely accepted by Christians to be manifestations of and proof of his divinity. But by considering the sorts of acts in which an omnibeing would engage, we have seen that we just cannot make sense of connecting miracles to the will or actions of a being that has the properties that

God is alleged to have. In earlier chapters, we saw that our evidence for the resurrection of Jesus is too flimsy to be trusted. But now it's clear that even if the resurrection and the other miracles of Jesus are real, there are good reasons to think that they cannot be attributed to God. Moreover, if Jesus' miraculous acts are disconnected from God, then Christianity is undermined on one of its essential doctrines.

By extension, all religious movements that assert the existence of a god whose capacities outstrip miracles are undermined. Miracles don't cohere with omnibeings. So there are more reasons to be skeptical about a whole class of theistic beliefs. With these theistic beliefs undermined and with natural explanations as better accounts of the origins of these religions, the justification for atheism grows broader and deeper.

Chapter 10

FIVE HUNDRED DEAD GODS AND THE PROBLEM OF OTHER RELIGIONS

In 1922, H. L. Mencken wrote an essay called "Memorial Service" in which he sought to make a point about the preponderance of gods and religions in history that have fallen out of favor. Mencken gives a long list of these gods. I have supplemented Mencken's compilation for a list of five hundred (there are many more).[1]

Aa, Aah, Abil Addu, Addu, Adeona, Adjassou Linguctor, Adjinakou, Adya Houn'tò, Agassou, Agé, Agwé, Ahijah, Ahti, Aizen Myō-ō, Ajisukitakahikone, Ak Ana, Aken, Aker, Äkräs, Aku, Allatu, Altjira, Amano-Iwato, Ame-no-Koyane, Am-heh, Amihan, Amon-Re, Amun, Amurru, Anapel, Anath, Andjety, Anhur, Anit, Anu, Anubis, Anzambe, Apsu, Arianrod, Ash, Ashtoreth, Assur, Astarte, Aten, Atum, Ayida-Weddo, Ayizan, Azaka Medeh, Azaka-Tonnerre, Azumi-no-isora, Baal, Bacalou, Badessy, Bagadjimbiri, Bahloo, Baiame, Bakunawa, Bamapana, Banaitja, Ba-Pef, Baron Cimetière, Baron La Croix, Baron Samedi, Barraiya, Bata, Bathala, Bau, Beltis, Beltu, Belus, Bernardo Carpio, Bes, Biame, Biamie, Bilé, Bimbeal, Binbeal, Boli Shah, Bossou Ashadeh, Budai, Bugady Musun, Bugid Y Aiba, Bunjil, Cai Shen, Ceros, Chenti-cheti, Chimata-No-Kami, Chi You, Chun Kwan, Cihang Zhenren, City god, Clermeil, Congo (loa), Consus, Cronos, Cunina, Dagan, Dagda, Dagon, Daikokuten, Damballa, Dan Petro, Dan Wédo, Daramulum, Dauke, Dea Dia, Dhakhan, Diable Tonnere, Diana of Ephesus, Diejuste, Dimmer, Dinclinsin, Dragon King, Dragon King of the East Sea, Duamutef, Dumu-zi-abzu, Dzingbe, Ea, Ebisu,

Edulia, Efile Mokulu, El, Elali, Elder Zhang Guo, Elum, Engurra, Enki, Enma, En-Mersi, Enurestu, Erlang Shen, Erzulie, Ezili Dantor, Fan Kuai, Fei Lian, Feng Bo, Four sons of Horus, Fūjin, Fukurokuju, Fu Lu Shou, Fu Xi, Furrina, Futsunushi, Gargomitch, Gasan-abzu, Gasan lil, Goibniu, Gong Gong, Govannon, Grand Bois, Gran Maître, Guangchengzi, Guan Yu, Gunfled, Gwydion, Hachiman, Hadad, Hakudo Maru, Han Xiang, Hapi, Hapy, Heka, Hemen, Hermanubis, Hermes, Heryshaf, Hoderi, Hongjun Laozu, Hoori, Horus, Houyi, Huang Feihu, Hung Shing, Iah, Ibong Adarna, Iho, Iku-Turso, Ilat, Ilmatar, Imhotep, Imset, Iron-Crutch Li, Isis, Istar, Isum, Iuno Lucina, Izanagi, Jade Emperor, Jar'Edo Wens, Ji Gong, Julana, Jumala, Jupiter, Juroujin, Kaawan, Kagu-tsuchi, Kalfu, Kalma, Karakarook, Kara Khan, Karei, Kari, Karora, Kerridwen, Khaltesh-Anki, Khepri, Khnum, Khonsu, Kidili, Kini'je, Kitchen God, Kmvum, Kneph, Kōjin, Ksitigarbha, Kui Xing, Kuk, Kumakatok, Kuski-banda, Kuu, Ku'urkil, Lagas, Lan Caihe, Lei Gong, Leizhenzi, Lempo, Ler, Leza, Li Jing, L'inglesou, Llaw Gyffes, Lleu, Loco (loa), Lü Dongbin, Lugal-Amarada, Maahes, Ma-banba-anna, Mademoiselle Charlotte, Maîtresse Délai, Maîtresse Hounon'gon, Maman Brigitte, Mamaragan, Mami, Mamlambo, Manawyddan, Mandulis, Mangar-kunjer-kunja, Marassa Jumeaux, Marduk, Maria Cacao, Maria Makiling, Maria Sinukuan, Marinette, Mars, Marzin, Matet boat, Mawu, Mayari, Mbaba Mwana Waresa, Meditrina, Mehen, Melek, Memetona, Menthu, Merodach, Mider, Mielikki, Min, Molech, Mombu, Morrigu, Mounanchou, Mulu-hursang, Mu-ul-lil, Muzha, Naam, Nana Buluku, Na Tuk Kong, Naunet, Ndyambi, Nebo, Nehebkau, Nergal, Nezha, Nga, Ngai, Nin, Ninib, Ninigi-no-Mikoto, Nin-lil-la, Nin-man, Nio, Nirig, Ni-zu, Njirana, Nogomain, Nuada Argetlam, Numakulla, Num-Torum, Nusku, Nu'tenut, Nyan Kupon, Nyyrikki, Nzambi, Nzame, Odin, Ogma, Ogoun, Ogyrvan, Ohoyamatsumi, Ōkuninushi, Olorun, Omoikane (Shinto), Ops, Osiris, Pa-cha, Pangu, Papa Legba, Peko, Perkele, Persephone, Petbe, Pie (loa), Ple, Pluto, Potina, Ptah, Pu'gu, Puluga, Pundjel, Pwyll, Qarradu, Qebehsenuef, Qingxu Daode Zhenjun, Qin Shubao, Ra, Raijin, Randeng Daoren, Rauni, Resheph, Rigantona, Robigus, Royal Uncle Cao, Ruwa, Ryōjin, Saa, Sahi, Samas, Sarutahiko, Saturn, Seker, Serapis, Sesmu, Shakpana, Shalem, Shangdi, Shango, Sharrab, Shen, Shennong, Shezmu, Shina-Tsu-Hiko, Simbi, Sin, Sirtumu, Sobek, Sobkou, Sōjōbō, Sokk-mimi, Sopdu, Sousson-Pannan, Statilinus, Suijin, Suiren,

Suqamunu, Susanoo, Tagd, Taiyi Zhenren, Tala, Tam Kung, Tammuz, Ta
Pedn, Tapio, Temaukel, Tenenet, Tengu, Tenjin, Theban Triad, Thoth, Tian,
Ti-Jean Petro, Ti Jean Quinto, Tilmun, Ti Malice, Tirawa Atius, Todote,
Toko'yoto, Tomam, Tororut, Tu Di Gong, Tu Er Shen, Tuonetar, Tuoni,
Ubargisi, Ubilulu, U-dimmer-an-kia, Ueras, Ugayafukiaezu, U-ki, Ukko,
UKqili, Umai, U-Mersi, Umvelinqangi, Ungud, Unkulunkulu, Ura-gala,
U-sab-sib, Usiququmadevu, U-Tin-dir-ki, U-urugal, Vaisravana, Vaticanus,
Vediovis, Vellamo, Venus, Vesta, Wadj-wer, Weneg, Wenshu Guangfa
Tianzun, Wen Zhong, Wepwawet, Werethekau, Wollunqua, Wong Tai Sin,
Wuluwaid, Xargi, Xaya Iccita, Xevioso, Xuan Wu, Yama, Yau, Yemaja,
Youchao, Yuanshi Tianzun, Yuchi Jingde, Yunzhongzi, Zagaga, Zaraqu,
Zer-panitu, Zhang Guifang, Zheng Lun, Zhongli Quan, Zhu Rong, Zonget.

In closing, Mencken says, "They were gods of the highest dignity—
gods of civilized peoples—worshipped and believed in by millions. All were
omnipotent, omniscient and immortal. And all are dead."[2]

Mencken, as he was prone, is making more of a rhetorical point here than a
careful philosophical one. What does Mencken's "dead" mean here? He means
that people believed in all of these, but they were never real. More recently,
Richard Dawkins, Daniel Dennett, Sam Harris, and Christopher Hitchens,
among others, have made a similar appeal: "An atheist is just somebody who
feels about Yahweh the way any decent Christian feels about Thor or Baal or
the golden calf. As has been said before, we are all atheists about most of the
gods that humanity has ever believed in. Some of us just go one god further."[3]

How do these dead gods cast a doubtful light on Christianity? How is it
that all of these so-called dead gods have any bearing on one particular religion's claim to worship the one true, living god? Many nonbelievers seem to
appreciate the point immediately when it is suggested, but many Christian
believers are unphased. The believer's retort is often along the lines of, "Those
other gods aren't real, and they never were. My God is the one true God, not
a primitive superstition."

In this chapter, we will discuss the argument lurking behind the list of
dead gods and the "I'm just an atheist about one more God than you are"
comment. There are some compelling reasons to doubt Christianity here, and
theism in general, but they need to be drawn out with some care.

CAN TEXTUAL EXEGESIS SETTLE THE QUESTION?

One of the common responses to the Mencken's and Dawkins's challenges is to appeal to some holy scripture for an answer. The Christian thinks that what's wrong with the other religious traditions and what's right with Christianity can be found by carefully reading the Bible. The Muslim appeals to the Koran, the Mormon refers to the Book of Mormon, and so on. A Christian might not find it challenging that so many people worship what amounts to, as she sees it, false gods. Her God commands us to have no other gods before him and not to engage in any form of idolatry. Furthermore, the five-hundred-plus other religions don't use the Bible, so their gods aren't real. What the Bible says about a divine being can be trusted; the other religions don't have that. For one reason or another, Christianity is superior to them.

More narrowly, when disagreements between different sects of Christians—Lutherans, Jehovah's Witnesses, Baptists, Episcopalians, Catholics, nondenominational Christians—break out, the method is often the same: check the Bible. They argue, cite passages, and pore over the text in an attempt to settle their disagreements over who is really the true Christian and who has got the correct doctrinal tenets. The presumption seems to be that if we can just get clear on what the Bible *really* says, then all questions will be answered about which gods are real and what God's nature is. Someone who is an adherent to one sect thinks that the problem with all of these other sects or religions is that they are failing to understand all of the relevant Bible passages or that they are misunderstanding what the passages mean in context.

Is there one true Christianity? A single doctrinal interpretation of the Bible that perfectly reflects God's will better than all of the other Christian sects? And does the Bible give an answer to the five-hundred-dead-gods problem? The arguments over the text belie a naïve presumption that there is such a thing as a single, clear doctrine that can be distilled from the text. We really have no reason to accept the presumptions behind this approach to addressing religious questions. Consider the problem from the outside. Atheists have left these inter- and intra-religious debates behind. They see whole religious movements disagreeing over who is reading and understanding their books the correct way. Between the sects within religions, there is widespread disagreement about which is the correct way to understand a passage and its relevance to the movement's doctrines. For example, endless disputes unfold about the real lesson we should learn from Abraham's test of faith when God commanded him to kill Isaac, or the meaning of Jesus' miraculously withering the fig tree that had no fruit. To think that more analysis of the book will ultimately put the correct answer into focus is misguided and credulous. Thousands of years and staggering amounts of analysis have not produced any widespread agreement about these issues, even among the believers themselves. Quite the contrary; the endless splintering of religious movements into antagonistic sects over doctrinal disputes suggests that more scrutiny of the texts has created great disagreement and strife. Given that so many believers from different sects and movements have disagreed for so long about so much, continuing to scour the texts in hopes of finding the one right answer, whatever that may be, seems pointless.

Texts never give us some unadulterated, interpretationless access to deep truths about reality. A text is always mediated by the background, the predispositions, the biases, the confusions, the goals, and the expectations of the reader. It just isn't possible to read a book—especially one that is as stylistically diverse, metaphorical, and ambiguous as the Bible—and not find some of what you put in there yourself.

If we have great numbers of people all bickering over the correct interpretation of a text or, by extension, whole religious movements disagreeing about who has got the right God and the right text, then we have to ask this question: Will prolonged analyses of any text actually produce a definitive answer to that question, or is the attempt to find the one right interpretation of the only acceptable religious text itself wrongheaded? We have to conclude that it is the latter. More study of the book that one favors within one's preferred doctrinal tradition will not excavate an accurate picture of reality on any topic.

Let's consider the idea that textual study will reveal answers. So what would it mean to have a better interpretation of the sacred texts? Maybe it would mean the interpretation adheres more closely to the author's intentions. Perhaps we could make some headway on this front, assuming that the author had a set of clear, consistent intentions and that the author was able to communicate those well. If not, then we'll have no hope of finding these intentions in the text. A problem, however, is that many literary theorists, constitutional scholars, historical philosophers, and art critics will tell us that the author's intent may or may not be what's important, meaningful, or useful about a text, even if we could figure out what it is. Listen to artists or authors talk about their works and compare that to your impressions of their works before you heard them and you'll appreciate the difference. Often artists' ideas about what they are doing completely diverge from the impact they have on us. And the way an artist's explanations of what a work means evolve over time suggests that not even the artist knows what the deeper significance is. The personal meaningfulness is largely a subjective and personal creation.

But there's a more serious issue here. Suppose we manage to excavate the author's real intentions behind the words; then what? What does that tell us about the world? What does that tell us except that the author intended to communicate X and Y? With the Bible, the question of what Paul or Moses or the author of Matthew intended to accomplish when he penned his words is vastly different from the question of whether what he says is true. When a mentally ill man at the stoplight mutters to you about alien invasions and mind control, he sincerely intends to warn you about the impending doom from outer space, but the truth is independent of his heartfelt avowals and has to be ascertained by some metric other than "What does he mean?" We should replace the "What does he mean?" with "Whatever he means, do we have any independent reasons to think that it is true?"

Prolonged debates about whose form of Christianity is the right one are like English professors arguing over who is the one true Frostian. Imagine one of them reading a couple of Robert Frost poems, citing several passages in support of an interpretation, and then announcing that he is the one true, real Frostian, the one who has the only accurate interpretation of the text, and all the other fake, misguided students of Frost are going to hell for their refusal to see the light.

For the believers, the presumption through all of this, and the reason why they often invest so much energy into understanding the text, is that it contains the real words of God and some truths about reality, so if we can figure out what it says, we will have the deep answers straight from the divine source.

Some recent empirical investigations are revealing about what might be at work here. Researchers found that people are much more prone to bestow their own views about social, ethical, and religious matters on God than they were to attribute those views to other people. That is, I'm more prone to say that God's beliefs are like mine, but I'll acknowledge that George Bush's or Bill Gate's views are different from my own. Neuroimaging also showed that "reasoning about God's beliefs activated areas associated with self-referential thinking more so than did reasoning about another person's beliefs. Believers commonly use inferences about God's beliefs as a moral compass, but that compass appears to be especially dependent on one's own existing beliefs."[4]

In one of the most revealing studies, researchers manipulated a subject's moral views about some topic by having the subject write and deliver speeches for or against some position. The subjects' attitudes about the position varied in parallel with the position he or she was assigned to defend, not surprisingly. When you have to think hard about the other side of the argument, you tend to soften your stance or change your mind. Have a subject deliver a speech in favor of the death penalty and her views shifted in favor of it; have her present a case against it, and her views shift against it. And when these subjects were tested before and after the manipulation, it became clear that their assessments of God's view of the particular position shifted, too. According to the subjects, God (and the subject) favored the death penalty more before the subject wrote and delivered a speech opposed to it, at which point God's view then shifted against it, along with the subject's.

What is more alarming is that this shift in our own views and in what we say about God's views tends to be invisible to us.[5] We don't notice that we are changing our minds. We will even deny that writing the essay against our original view had any impact on us. And then we don't notice that we are rewriting history by attributing our current view to our former self and to what we previously thought about God's views. What we think God's moral guidance is depends on what we are currently thinking; when our current thinking changes, God's views do, too, but we tend to see God's views and our own as monolithic and unchanging. "What I believe now, that's what I have always believed. And that's always been God's commandment, too."

Now we can get some insight into the seemingly inexhaustible capacity people have for studying their holy scriptures and arguing over their "real" meanings. (Consider that 37 percent of Americans say they study the Bible at least once a week.[6]) The study of religious texts brings together four factors: there is a human disposition to have your views drift depending on what you are currently reading, thinking about, or writing. There is also a tendency to revise your account of your own views, hiding the changes from yourself. We have a stronger tendency to attribute our current views to God, whatever they are, than we would to other people. And we have a large book filled with seemingly profound aphorisms, metaphors, poetry, psalms, parables, spiritual vagaries, and other ambiguities that has been endowed with mystical significance.

The believer who feels drawn toward textual exegesis as a means of settling substantial questions about God or reality would do well to step back and consider these phenomena from a distance. It is an easy and common mistake to be swept up in the heartfelt conviction that some deep, profound truth can be revealed through careful study and interpretive work on your scriptures. But there have been too many people doing it for too long with too many disagreements for the rest of us to share your optimism. What is going on here is more of an artifact of human psychology and the nature of religious texts and culture.

Several biases and fallacies emerge when we listen to advocates for different interpretations of a holy text. Confirmation bias, cherry picking, motivated reasoning, and confusions between obscurity and profundity can run amok against the rich field of stories, characters, spiritual lessons, vague philosophy.

Instead of asking, "What does the text say?" we need to consider what reasons we might have for thinking that the book contains the words of God. A temptation would be to point to the book itself and the claims that it contains about its coming from God. But we can all see the flagrant circularity of that view: Why do I believe that the Bible is the word of God? Because the Bible says it is. And why do I believe that the Bible can be trusted? Because God wrote it.

Now, if we are going to attach some supernatural significance to the words, then we need to find some source other than the text itself that provides us with justification for thinking that it's a communiqué straight from the creator of the universe. Of course, that is what we were doing in the early chapters of this book, and the results did not come out in favor of Christian views. The problem of the Salem witch trials and the other arguments we considered erode the foundations of other ancient religions, like the ones on Mencken's list, just as much or more than they undermine Christianity. Ancient religious texts and doctrines have not proven to be reliable sources of information about the world.

Even atheists and nonbelievers are prone to get caught up in this ill-framed dispute over what some religious book *really* says. They will fall for questions about whether or not the Bible really says X, or whether or not Catholics are really Christians, or whether or not *real* Muslims are intolerant of nonbelief. Then discussions between believers and nonbelievers that had promise of getting to the heart of the matter—whether or not any of the claims are reasonable to believe—morph into disagreements about what the correct interpretation of the book is. Far too much time and energy has already been invested in studying the Bible. Before anyone devotes her attention to it as a religious source of truth, she should have a clear answer to this question in her head first: Do we have evidence that makes it reasonable to believe that any of the supernatural claims in this book are true? If we do not, then that should profoundly affect the attitude we take about its worthiness for study and the sort of study it deserves.

One of the many troubling things about the prevalence of doctrinal disputes is the way it frames the discourse we are having about religion and God. Instead of actually talking about the reasons we might have for believing the text, followers have disputes about the correct way to understand it.

Therefore, it's difficult not to conclude that discussions about what some religious text says are largely pointless. The notion that some ancient textual source can somehow magically provide us with deep metaphysical truths about reality is a myth. The real question of whether you should accept a claim as true involves the evidence, the reasons, and how well it fits in with the rest of what we've been able to figure out about reality through science. When we consider a claim and whether it fits with the rest of what we believe to be true about the world, the criteria should be logical consistency, probabilistic consistency, corroboration by other known claims, predictive value, sensitivity to observations, and integration into the rest of what we know.

MY PRIVATE EXPERIENCE GIVES ME THE TRUTH

Another answer to the dead-gods problem might involve an appeal to some internal, private experience. "I can feel it in my mind," or "I have had a special revelation that my God is real," or "I have some religious experiences that inform me that my God is the one true God," or "I know Jesus through the witness of the Holy Spirit in my heart." Or something to that effect. Personal religious experience of some sort has led many believers to feel assured that their particular type of relationship with God is authentic. These experiences range from subtle feelings of resolution arising from time spent praying, to full-blown altered states of consciousness. And they are not uncommon. A recent PEW research poll on religious belief reported that "nearly half of the public (49 percent) says they have had a religious or mystical experience."[7]

Even if a person has had an intense religious experience, heard voices, or had what he thought was a supernatural communication with God, he will have very hard time presenting that personal experience as a satisfying answer to the problem that has been posed. It's difficult to see how his special revelations give someone else a reason to believe that the Christian God is the one true God any more than someone's having a special religious experience is adequate justification for thinking there are weapons of mass destruction in Iraq. A private experience, no matter how compelling, doesn't give anyone else any grounds for thinking that the Christian God is different from the others. Or at least his evidence, having had the experience himself, will be different from someone else's evidence which is confined to "he says he had a compelling and powerful private experience of God." From the outside, what the testimony about the experience tells us is that he is convinced on the basis of some inaccessible and internal experience that his God is the only God. The challenge is finding some independent corroboration that what he thinks he experienced is real. We need some reasons that we can access. Imagine having a trial for a murderer and using the accused man's own avowals of his innocence as the ultimate or only test of guilt.

Defendant: I am sure in my mind that I am not guilty, Your Honor.

Judge: Oh, well, in that case, take the handcuffs off him and
let him go.

The reason his word isn't good enough is that so many believers in other traditions report the same intense, personal, private feelings that their god is the one true God. The experiences are too common for us to take seriously any claim of religious exclusivity on their basis. Suppose some atheists also insist that they have some special a-religious experiences in their thoughts that give them a special revelation that there are no gods whatsoever? Should the Christian mystic think that these conflicting accounts are sufficient grounds to reject Christianity?

By their private nature, these experiences will be weaker evidence for someone else. But they aren't much better for the subject. The subject should be highly suspicious even of their adequacy to provide him with justification for the exclusivity of his religion or the reality of his god. The appeal to private experience generates a severe error-checking problem. If this is all you've got, how do you distinguish between authentic and inauthentic feelings? We know that inauthentic, nonsupernatural religious experiences are common. And it's not difficult to artificially induce them with sleep deprivation, chemistry, or other physical causes. Therefore, special feelings in his mind, even if they are poignant and apparently authentic, aren't adequate grounds for belief by themselves, especially when the matters in question are so important. The question is: Why is the Christian God any more likely to be real than all of the others that supposedly are not? Philosopher Nick Zangwill has even argued that given God's nature, having religious experiences of him are impossible.[8] None of us should accept "Because it really feels like that is true in my mind" as an answer.

Dan Barker, who was an evangelical, fundamentalist preacher from his teens until his thirties, describes in great detail the mystical experiences of God he had during this period. On a daily basis, he said he could sense a presence, a voice, and a guiding force in his thoughts. Barker, like a significant percentage of humans, has a strong tendency toward auditory and mental hallucinations. He says that we could think of the distribution of people across a bell curve of the propensity for religious experience.[9] For people like him out at the edge of the curve, the feelings of transcendence, elation, and a non-sensory awareness of a divine presence are powerful and undeniable. If you couple that propensity with some of the cultural expectations of charismatic, evangelical Christianity, the result is people who are utterly convinced that God is a real presence in the world and that their sect is the authentic means of access to him. The innate neurological dispositions of lots of human beings are going to predispose them to find this notion of the "testimony of the Holy Spirit in your heart" to be completely plausible and familiar. Of course, if they had been raised in a Buddhist, Sikh, or Zoroastrian cultural tradition, they would have attached a different significance and a different set of ulti-mate "truths" to those same feelings. And we must assume that if someone like this received a robust scientific education that included some neurobio-logical basics about human dispositions toward altered conscious states, then her conclusions about the likely cause of the experience would have been quite different. Given that we know that the human nervous system is capable of falsely producing a wide range of quirky, strange experiences, it's unfortunate that so many people remain in the dark about what they are going through.

NATURAL VERSUS SUPERNATURAL RELIGIONS

Many believers will be inclined to agree that the five hundred dead gods are, in fact, not real. For Christians, the existence of the God of Christianity and the resurrection of Jesus rule out these other gods. Or we could put it another way. Given the choice between continuing to practice and believe the tenets of their variety of Christianity and becoming a follower of Sobek or Gefjun, Christians would opt for continuing to practice Christianity. So, for the Christian, the religions that are incompatible with Christianity are "false" religions.

Some believers are not inclined to be so literal about the Christian God, Jesus, or the others, and the terms *false* or *mistaken* here will feel too strong in reference to other people's religious convictions. They will not want to take a hard view about the wrongness of those other religions; they may take a more inclusive, metaphorical view that is accepting of many paths and many concep-tions. We will consider problems with this approach in chapter 12. But notice that even the most liberal and inclusive people will have to acknowledge that many of the claims made by many human religions are mistaken. Consider the statistics we considered earlier about widespread beliefs in ghosts, clairvoyance, magic, healings, and spiritual matters. Even if some of these are correct, the evidence shows that humans get these sorts of ideas wrong far more often than they get it right. It may seem rude or intolerant, but in the end, we have to conclude that many of the transcendent explanations that people have for reality are mistaken.

For now, let's consider the situation of anyone who believes that some particular God or religious reality is real but that many or most of the gods on the list are not—or, more simply, the position of someone who acknowledges that many human religions are mistaken in their claims about the nature of reality. These religions, she will have to conclude, must have had a natural origin rather than a supernatural one. No matter what your particular religious convictions are, it should be clear that many religious ideas arise from human imagination, mistakes, psychological failings, or some other natural causes. So there are hundreds, thousands, or even tens of thousands of natural religions in contrast to the one or the few supernatural ones. Several points are implied by all of these dead gods. First, the believer has to acknowledge that the human-religious error rate is very high. For whatever reasons, humans generate a lot of religions without a real god. Second, the believer has to acknowledge that when we look at the natural religions and an allegedly real, supernatural one from a distance, there is considerable similarity: many of them arise from ancient people; miracle stories abound; God is the creator; he has a plan; he is the path to salvation, moral guidance, personal fulfillment, and so on. Third, the believer will have to acknowledge that some of the causes of these erroneous, natural religions must be some of the long list of psychological phenomena, epistemological problems, filters, or mistakes discussed earlier (particularly in chapters 4 through 8).

Here, then, is the dilemma for the believer. If she acknowledges that there are so many more erroneous religions with natural explanations that have at least some nominal similarity to her own, then on what grounds can she think that hers is different? On the basis of what differences can she assert both that "the majority of human religions spring from mistakes," and that "mine is not a mistake"?

False religious ideas flourish in human cultures. They are so prolific that the false ones far outnumber the "acceptable" ones, whatever your particular view of an acceptable one may be. All of these false or dead religions suggest that there is something else going on in their origination besides real contact with a supernatural, divine being. The dead gods suggest that it is people, not Sobek or Puluga, that are responsible for creating the majority of religious ideas. If someone is exclusivist and thinks that Islam, or Catholicism, or Mormonism is the one true religion that worships the one true God, it is clear that humans produce an abundance of imaginary or unreal religious traditions, doctrines, and practices. In some cases, historical contingencies, religious institutions, and other factors have sustained them across the centuries. Unreal gods and false religions proliferate in human cultures.

And it is this last point on which the atheists are (or should be) focusing. We know that humans frequently make up religions. The abundance of these false gods should make us highly suspicious of any particular one that also claims to be the one true path to a real God. It is possible that there is a God and that Christianity is the religion that he sanctions, or Mormonism, or some variety of Islam. But the failures of so many human religions have shifted the burden of proof considerably. Given the abundance of false religions, our presumption should be that a natural origin is the best explanation. Any religious view claiming an authentic supernatural origin needs to defeat this presumption. Christianity, as we saw in earlier chapters, falls far short of meeting this challenge.

In the five-hundred-dead-gods argument and in the "I'm just an atheist about one more God than you are," argument, authors like Richard Dawkins are suggesting that the believer should have a broader perspective on his own position in this larger pattern of human religious behavior. Separate from the truth question, religions clearly satisfy a number of human needs. For a large percentage of the population, if they are raised in a particular religious environment or exposed to a religious tradition as children, they will adopt it, and it will become deeply enmeshed in their belief structure, and they will come to have passionate feelings surrounding it, *even when it is false*. About three-quarters of Americans adopt the religious faith of their parents.[10] Even if there are reasons, as the Christian sees it, to think that her religious tradition is special, to have a clear-headed and objective view about it, believers need to acknowledge the real psychological, emotional, and personal pull that it has on people. The five hundred dead gods shift the burden of proof onto the believer: she must be honest with herself and acknowledge the extent to which her beliefs may be the product of the same sorts of mistakes that have produced so many other false religious beliefs. If she hopes to be reasonable, she must have grounds that distinguish Christianity from all the others that do not amount to special pleading. Any claim of exclusivity or authenticity has to be put against the backdrop of billions of other people all saying the same thing about their chosen beliefs. When viewed in the context of religious history, we have to wonder about the other factors that might have helped get those ideas into the believer's life.

There's no doubt that when the followers of those distant religions think about their own doctrines and beliefs, they seem obvious and true—just like the Christian's feel to her. And as we saw with Dan Barker, hearing or feeling an inner voice accompanied by intense feelings of religious poignancy and assurance aren't sufficient to vindicate your own religion over all the others. Lots of people in those other traditions are having those feelings, too, with the specific details of their traditions being similarly filled in. One can't simply rely on an internal corroboration to conclude that all of the other approaches to God are faulty.

KNOWING YOUR OWN MIND

From the inside, it can still be very hard to see how it could be possible that a belief about which one feels such deep conviction can be the result of these psychological forces and not anchored in the truth. When you believe, it doesn't feel like belief was installed in you by external causes or innate psychological tendencies. When someone like Mencken and the others liken your belief to the beliefs in the dead gods, they must be overlooking what your belief feels like for you or the reasons that you know you have for believing.

The empirical research suggests a different picture about our access to our own beliefs. We've been operating with some unspoken assumptions. You know whether you believe in God, and determining that you know what you believe is merely a matter of introspecting your own thoughts. Knowing what your reasons are for believing in God (or not) is also merely a matter of introspecting, and in so doing it will be clear to you what your reasons are for believing. The problem is that it's often the case that what you believe is not actually available to introspection, and either the grounds or reasons for your beliefs are not available to introspection, or introspection is not a reliable or accurate means of determining the grounds of your belief.

Decades of psychological research shows,

1. People often cannot report accurately on the effects of particular stimuli on higher order, inference-based responses. Indeed, sometimes they cannot report on the existence of critical stimuli, sometimes cannot report on the existence of their responses, and sometimes cannot even report that an inferential process of any kind has occurred. The accuracy of subjective reports is so poor as to suggest that any introspective access that may exist is not sufficient to produce generally correct or reliable reports.

2. When reporting on the effects of stimuli, people may not interrogate a memory of the cognitive process that operated on the stimuli; instead, they may base their reports on implicit, a priori theories about the causal connection between stimulus and response. If the stimulus psychologically implies the response in some way . . . or seems "representative" of the sorts of stimuli that influence the response in question . . . the stimulus is reported to have influenced the response. If the stimulus does not seem to be a plausible cause of a response, it is reported to be noninfluential.

3. Subjective reports about higher mental processes are sometimes correct, but even the instances of correct report are not due to direct introspective awareness. Instead, they are due to the incidentally correct employment of a priori causal theories.[11]

In short, there are many stimuli that influence or produce specific cognitive responses in us that we do not notice and we cannot report on. Rather than actually consulting some memory of the mental processes that contributed to a belief, our explanations of our own beliefs often resort to third-person, causal theories about people's minds. The cognitive processes that produce my beliefs are often just as opaque to me as the processes that produced someone else's beliefs, and I am reduced to theorizing from the outside about both of us. Similarly, I don't typically compose a sentence or rehearse it before I say it; I hear it at the same time you do. Rather than being privy to some behind-the-scenes processing, I more or less discover myself reacting to things I've heard, headlines, or people. Long experience and familiarity make it possible for me to produce explanations for why I believe the things I do, but that immediacy shouldn't be mistaken for incorrigibility. When I explain my beliefs, it's often because the folk psychological theory I employ incorporates a lot of information, not because of some privileged access I have to my own mind.

Furthermore, it turns out that what people will report they believe is highly influenceable by environmental factors, priming, context, and expectations. Flashing subjects particular pictures or words influences their performance on cognitive tasks that follow. Cue them or prime them one way, and they will report one set of beliefs. Change the stimulus and their reports change. Which belief or cognitive report a subject gives can be manipulated by changing a range of variables. And many of the changes in belief or the causes that produced them are invisible to the subject. What the research suggests is that there are cognitive gears set in motion below the conscious threshold that affect what we experience or are conscious of, but we are often unaware of these mechanisms at the conscious level. It follows then, that your introspections of what you believe or what you experience are relatively late-stage results of many processes that occur without your control, supervision, awareness, or access. And your reports about what you believe and why you believe it may or may not align with what is really going on in your head.

Our common-sense views about being able to know what we believe and being able to know the reasons or causes that lead us to believe it do not map cleanly onto the biological realities of the human cognitive system. Our own minds are simply not as transparent or accessible to us as we often think they are.

The point is particularly important for the question of believing in God.

Most people will readily admit that the existence of God is a matter of incredible emotional, psychological, and personal importance. Even without neuroscience researchers to test and examine our reports about our beliefs, we all know that when it comes to God, there are powerful subconscious or nonrational aspects of our cognitive constitutions at work. Let's call the powerful forces that drive us to believe in God *the urge*. Since we are not very good at knowing our own minds, and since we all seem to have the urge, and since there are all of those dead gods lying around, our religious beliefs should be prima facie suspect. Given the psychological evidence we have seen, a person's religious beliefs should be suspect to her, even if she has thought hard about it and it still seems to her that she has good reasons for believing and that those reasons are why she believes. Strange things happen in the recesses of the human mind/brain. And a growing body of very careful research and arguments suggest that there is an evolutionary, biological foundation of religious belief.[12]

By itself, the near-universal subscription, across cultures and time, to beliefs about some sort of afterlife and some sort of higher, supernatural power are highly suggestive of some sort of biological, evolutionary, or neurological explanation. In human history, we don't find so many people in so many cultures or eras in such deep agreement about anything. That they all believe in some kind of God or gods and that they spend so much time disagreeing about religious truths suggest that the rudiments of belief belong to something much more basic than our higher, rational intellects.

When news reporters interview the serial killer's mother, she defends him and insists that he was a good boy, no matter how many bodies were found in the basement. People are far more sensitive to allegedly mistaken calls made by referees in sports events when the call works against the interests of their own teams. Republicans are convinced that the news media is too liberal; Democrats are convinced that it is too conservative. Our prior dispositions, commitments, psychological needs, and other cognitive forces of which we are unaware exert a powerful effect on the conclusions we come to regarding what is true. That so many people have been so passionately religious for so long and that so many of them were mistaken should make us very reluctant to accept at face value any claims about God.

When May 21, 2011, came and went without the Rapture, Harold Camping and his followers expressed complete bafflement. Countless hours of study of the book of Revelations and other apocalyptic passages in the Bible had revealed what they thought was the exact date of the Second Coming of Jesus. They would have done well to do some homework about the thousands of other failed end-of-the-world dates set by eager believers over the centuries. Those mistakes should have raised doubts in the minds of Camping and his followers and shown them some underlying human dispositions that we would do well to guard against. There is something else going on here, given the history of similar religious beliefs, and the believer has an extra burden of proof that must be met for himself as much as for the rest of us if he wishes to assert that he's got a line on the only real God that has ever existed.

The five hundred dead gods should introduce doubt into the mind of the believer. The argument is not that our psychological dispositions make rational autonomy impossible—although for many people, conjoining a particular religious ideology with their psychological constitutions does seem to have robbed them of the capacity to think clearly and freely. What is becoming clear as science allows us to understand ourselves better, including the deepest, most private parts of our minds, is that achieving rational autonomy is much, much harder than we have assumed. And one of the lessons here is that achieving intellectual freedom and rationality has to be a higher priority in your mental life than adherence to an ideology. Being a Christian or a non-believer has to come second in line to being a clear, objective, careful, and diligent thinker. Otherwise, the ideology is believing you; it's not you making a reasoned choice to believe. In this way, we are a bit like alcoholics: once we know the truth about how strong our prior disposition to religiousness is, it takes discipline, vigilance, and habituation to resist the urge. Ironically, "you shall know the truth, and the truth shall make you free" (John 8:32).

Chapter 11

THE F-WORD

Blessed are those who have not seen and yet have believed.

—John 20:26

WHAT ABOUT FAITH?

For many believers (if they have made it this far), the most serious failing of this book will be its omission of the role of faith in believing in the resurrection and other religious doctrines. The arguments have been that there is inadequate evidence to justify believing, but when a person believes by faith, it may seem that the problem is circumvented. And many—perhaps most—believers think that faith is more central to their belief in the resurrection than the historical, evidential position that has been critiqued here. The problem, I will argue in this chapter, is that while faith may seem to avoid the problems associated with poor historical evidence, the costs of ignoring the need for evidential justifications are much worse.

For our purposes, faith is best understood as a description of how someone believes. To take something on faith or to believe by faith is to believe it despite contrary or inadequate evidence. It is to believe anyway when there's not enough support from evidence and reason to clear the way. Consider some nonreligious examples. A husband goes out of town on a business trip with an attractive coworker. Back home, the subject of infidelity comes up when his wife is talking to a friend. She says, "I have faith in him." A Detroit Lions fan sees yet another score made by the opponents that seems to seal the fate of his favorite team. But he still insists that he has faith that they can come through. A wife says, "I have faith that my husband will come home safely from Afghanistan." A mistrustful friend says, "She has lied to me so many times before, it would take a huge leap of faith for me to believe her now." Or, "Loaning the money to him to start his own business was an act of faith." People often say that it is important to have faith in yourself. To have faith in humanity is to overcome doubts, particularly in the light of some of people's bad behaviors, and believe that people are essentially good natured.

The overcoming of doubts or counterevidence is the essential feature of faith:

> *Let's have faith that right makes might, and in that faith let us, to the end, dare to do our duty was we understand it.*
> —Abraham Lincoln, 1860*

> *To follow by faith alone is to follow blindly.*
> —Widely attributed to Benjamin Franklin

> *Faith is taking the first step even when you don't see the whole staircase.*
> —Widely attributed to Martin Luther King

> *Faith . . . is the art of holding on to things your reason has once accepted in spite of your changing moods.*
> —C. S. Lewis, circa 1952†

> *Reason is the greatest enemy that faith has: it never comes to the aid of spiritual things, but—more frequently than not—struggles against the divine Word, treating with contempt all that emanates from God.*
> —Martin Luther, 1596‡

In all of these cases, believing by faith is overcoming some shortcoming in the evidence. In some cases, the evidence is lacking—the businessman's wife won't be able to confirm exactly what her husband is doing, or the soldier's wife doesn't know what is happening in Afghanistan. Or there is outright evidence contrary to the hoped-for outcome—the football team is losing and it is becoming increasingly unlikely that the players can turn the game around, or the fighting intensifies in Afghanistan, killing more soldiers. The consummate crisis moment for faith might be when someone is in a hospital waiting room waiting to hear the outcome after someone dear to them has been in a horrible accident. If the hospital chaplain says, "You have to have faith in times like these," the suggestion is to believe despite some powerful reasons to doubt.

The other side of faith is that we don't invoke it or feel like it is necessary in situations where there is sufficient evidence in support of the desired outcome. If your basketball team has been dominating every other team in the conference, and they are thirty points ahead in the fourth quarter of the final game, and two of the best players on the opposing team are injured, it would be peculiar to say, "I have faith that they will win." That the team will win is obvious and justified by the evidence. Faith would be superfluous.

We do not invoke faith in order to believe in some undesirable and unlikely outcome. If we don't want it to happen, we never justify believing it by faith. No healthy person would say he has faith that he has cancer, even though there are no indicators of it. No husband would say that he has faith that his otherwise committed wife is having an affair. And we don't hear atheists asserting that they have faith that there is no God. People only invoke faith in cases where they have a strong desire for a particular outcome or claim to be true and the evidence in favor of it is lacking in some regard.

So for someone who believes in the central doctrines of Christianity or some other religious doctrine as a matter of faith, the arguments of this book may have seemed beside the point. As philosopher Ludwig Wittgenstein said, "if there were evidence, this would in fact destroy the whole business."[1] Of course there are substantial reasons to doubt. But the value, purpose, beauty, and fulfillment of Christian belief is in overcoming these with faith.

SHOULD WE HAVE FAITH?

If someone's reaction to my arguments against the resurrection and other religious beliefs is that she has faith, then she is conceding the central point. In effect, she is acknowledging that in order to believe those religious doctrines, one must ignore the insufficiencies in the evidence and believe anyway. My argument has been that there is insufficient evidence in favor of the resurrection of Jesus to make it reasonable for us to believe. My presumption has been that if the evidence is insufficient, then one should not believe, although I have said little to defend this principle direct until now. If the critic responds that she is just going to have faith that it happened anyway, then we appear to agree on the insufficiency, and what remains is to critically evaluate the prospects of believing by faith. If it then turns out that there are serious problems with taking the faith path to belief (and there are) then the foundations of Christian belief and any other religious view that takes the same path have been utterly undermined.

REASON IS PRESCRIPTIVE, FAITH IS NOT

Does the faith response present any sort of challenge to the arguments that have been presented here so far? The answer is no, but the explanation is a complicated matter having to do with the difference between something being *prescriptive* versus *descriptive*.

The way they are typically treated, reason and evidence are prescriptive. When there is compelling evidence in front of someone and he understands it, and it is clear that it implies a certain conclusion, then he *ought* to believe that conclusion. Suppose that Anderson is a defendant in a trial. The prosecutors have shown video of Anderson holding up a liquor store; they found that the gun used is registered in his name with his fingerprints on it; multiple, reliable witnesses all testified that he did it; the store owner identified him as the robber; other witnesses heard him promising to rob the store the day before; and his alibi has been shown to be false. The jurors, if they are reasonable people, *should* convict him on the basis of the evidence. If they don't, they are being irrational or unreasonable, and they are failing to fulfill their epistemic (and moral) duties. So when the right conditions have been met, the evidence prescribes belief (there can be lots of mitigating circumstances that we will ignore for the moment). When someone doesn't believe under those conditions, then she is epistemically culpable or at fault. By not believing, she makes a mistake that she should rectify. This is what gave the historical argument for the resurrection its force, after all. The proponent of that argument could say, "You should believe it because here is compelling historical evidence that Jesus was real and that he arose from the dead. To refuse to believe would be like rejecting the existence of Caesar or the assassination of Lincoln."

If Smith has faith about some matter, can Smith then recommend that Jones likewise have faith? If Smith believes it on the basis of what he takes to be compelling evidence, then she can recommend that Jones should draw the same conclusion. But is faith prescriptive the way evidence is? When someone opts to believe despite the fact that the evidence underdetermines or even contradicts the conclusion, how could he maintain that others who haven't done the same are somehow at fault? Has he failed in his epistemic duties, or is he rationally culpable? In what way could the nonfaithful possibly be doing something wrong by not also having faith?

At the very least, having faith is a sort of indulgence or transgressing of the evidence on Smith's part, and Smith cannot have recourse to claim that failing to have faith is a mistake, irrational, or part of some failure to fulfill Jones's epistemic duties. Smith can't make the leap of faith and then insist that Jones is somehow blameworthy for not likewise having faith. A believer by faith simply has no grounds from which she can argue that others who don't have faith *ought to*. She can't criticize the nonfaithful for doing something contrary to reason or ignoring the evidence by not believing. By refusing to believe by faith, the nonbeliever may be only seeking to accept that which is supported by the evidence. The faithful believer cannot argue: "You're not listening to reason. You need to accept the obvious implication of the evidence! All of the evidence indicates that you should believe on faith." Faith carries no leverage against nonbelief.

Many believers have suggested to me that it is the combination of faith and evidence that justifies their belief. This is a mistake and a conflation. We have seen that faith is invoked and it is only necessary when there is some shortcoming in the evidence. If there is sufficient evidence to justify the conclusion, then faith isn't needed. So to suggest that faith and evidence jointly justify is to acknowledge that the evidence by itself isn't enough and to say, "I will ignore that gap and believe anyway." This notion of the joint work of faith and evidence won't recommend belief to Jones, and it shouldn't satisfy

Smith. Suppose a prosecuting attorney tells the jury, "You have all seen the full evidential case against the defendant, and you have seen that it is inconclusive about his guilt. However, if we invoke faith to overcome those doubts, we can convict him nevertheless. I urge you to have faith that he is guilty."

The arguments of this book so far have been that there is insufficient evidence to justify believing that Jesus returned from the dead. We have seen this illustrated both in reasons to suspect the reliability of the people who have given us the story and through examples of comparable claims that we would not accept. We have also considered a number of alternative natural hypotheses to the resurrection that, given what we know about human cognitive systems, are far more likely to be true about Jesus. To make matters worse for the resurrection view, we have seen why God would not perform miracles.

For the critic to assert that she has faith that the resurrection happened, or for some other religious view, in no way undermines the arguments that there is insufficient evidence to make that reasonable. In fact, the need to invoke faith to bridge the gap affirms the inadequacy of the evidence. Furthermore, having faith does nothing to make the alternative naturalistic explanations of the resurrection and other religious views any less likely. Faith, then, gives us no recommendation to believe something that we don't have justification for, and it certainly does not give us grounds to reject conclusions that are better supported by the evidence. At best, it amounts to a description of how some people will believe anyway. I have given a number of reasons for why we should not believe. In effect, the faith response amounts to, "I'm going to believe anyway, despite those objections." That's just dogmatic irrationality, not a serious consideration that the critic must give some further objection to. Nevertheless, there are serious internal problems with having faith that ought to lead the believer to reject it, too.

MORE PROBLEMS FOR FAITH

The faithful have implicitly revealed a principle that seems to be guiding their choices. Perhaps it is something like this, "in matters of great importance and emotional commitment, it is permissible to believe even though the evidence, on the whole, is neutral or contrary to the claim." Having faith is epistemically inculpable.

There are a number of disastrous effects of adopting this sort of principle, however. To see them, consider what we know about reasoning and the ill effects of doing it poorly. We now have a more comprehensive empirical picture of how humans form beliefs than we have ever had in history. There are countless pitfalls and errors into which we fall, and detecting them can be very difficult, particularly since we are using our cognitive faculties to evaluate the reliability of our faculties. Despite the difficulties, there are a number of procedural questions that we can ask about a particular case where we search for evidence, evaluate it, and draw a conclusion about it. Applying these questions to the evidence-gathering and evaluation phase in belief formation can dramatically improve the accuracy of the resulting conclusion. Cultivating these concerns into habits can develop the epistemic virtues that will make a person a far better thinker and decision maker.

- Are there data?
- What exactly are the data?
- Have I conducted an exhaustive search?
- If there were significant counterevidence, would my search have found it?
- What else could explain the data?
- What would disprove the hypothesis?
- Has my enthusiasm for any particular hypothesis affected the evidence I have searched for or emphasized?
- Have I adequately considered other alternatives?
- Has search satisfaction led me to stop looking prematurely?
- Have I thought about it long enough?
- Has my enthusiasm for a hypothesis led me to relax evidential standards for it or increase them for competing hypotheses?
- Am I prepared to change my mind in light of new or different evidence?
- Hypothetically, what information would change my mind?
- If there are personal, psychological, or social factors that tilt my evaluation of the evidence, would I be aware of it? What are they?

- If there are factors that are filtering my access to information, would I be aware of them? What are they?
- Have I given more or less important pieces of information their appropriate amount of weight?
- Has the order of my consideration of the evidence affected my evaluation when it shouldn't have?
- Has the recency or remoteness of some evidence in time affected my evaluation when it shouldn't have?
- Is my memory supplying me with a representative picture of the relevant experiences?
- Am I applying principles of justification here that are consistent with the ones I use normally?
- Did I sustain a high level of open-mindedness during the search and evaluation phase?
- Are the estimates of likelihoods or probabilities that I am employing accurate or realistic?
- Would the conclusion drawn withstand a reasonable level of skepticism?

There is no question that the systematic application of the standards of evidence that are reflected by these questions produces better justifications and better conclusions. If the circumstances where these sorts of concerns would be helpful are not clear, consider some cases of belief formation that would benefit:

- A doctor gathers and evaluates diagnostic evidence in order to identify and treat a life-threatening disease.
- A jury member tries to decide whether or not a defendant is guilty of a capital offense.
- A mechanic considers a potentially costly problem in the engine of a car.
- A student reflects on what college to attend.
- An investor decides how best to spend investment capital on the stock market.
- A couple tries to buy a house that best suits their various needs.

- A boyfriend considers what appears to be evidence that his girlfriend is cheating.
- A historian attempts to determine the sequence of events surrounding an important battle in an ancient war.
- A journalist gathers evidence about a corporation's involvement in the bribery of a corrupt politician.
- A plumber tries to figure out what's wrong with the sink.
- A voter tries to decide whether to vote for a bond measure that would fund stem-cell research.
- A philosopher considers a metaphysical question about what sorts of things are real.
- A teenager in a Sunday-school class tries to sort out the debate over evolution versus creation.

This all may appear to be belaboring the obvious, but there's a larger point here concerning religious belief. In every ordinary circumstance, it is obvious that the questions concerning evidence gathering and belief formation just listed make the difference between a good and bad decision. It is also obvious, I'm afraid, that in too many cases, a person's belief in Jesus, the resurrection, God, or other religious matters—particularly when it arises from faith— would fail horribly by the same measures.

That is, for too many of our religious views, the belief and the procedure that produced it would not pass muster for the minimally acceptable standards that we employ in almost every other case in our lives. The double standard is even more conspicuous when we consider that believing in God, arguably, is the single most important decision that a person can make in his or her life. For the most profound question, we employ the worst procedure for finding an answer. If your doctor, mechanic, investment broker, or plumber drew conclusions in the fashion that many people justify their religious conclusions, we would be horrified, and you would fire them without hesitation. If a jury member, wife, doctor or journalist made decisions that way, they would do irreparable harm. Even if it was the plumber drawing parallel conclusions, the results would be disastrous.

At a minimum, the believer needs to correct the gross double standard here. If the believer wants the rest of us to take him seriously, he needs to subject his belief to the same general standards of justification that are vital everywhere else. Not only is it a double standard with matters of faith, but we've created a peculiar and dangerous set of exclusions to protect the inconsistency. In a speech at Cambridge University, novelist Douglas Adams said,

> Religion doesn't seem to work like that. It has certain ideas at the heart of it which we call sacred or holy. What it means is, here is an idea or a notion that you are not allowed to say anything bad about. You're just not. Why not? Because you're not. Why should it be that it is perfectly legitimate to support the Republicans or Democrats, this model of economics verses that, Macintosh instead of Windows, but to have an opinion about how the universe began, about who created the universe, no, that's holy. So we're used to not challenging religious ideas. And it's very interesting how much of a furor Richard [Dawkins] creates when he does it. Everybody gets absolutely frantic about it because you're not allowed to say these things. Yet when you look at it rationally, there is no reason why those shouldn't be as open to debate as another. Except that we've agreed somehow between us that they shouldn't be.[2]

HAVING FAITH IS A VIOLATION OF ONE'S SOCIAL AND MORAL RESPONSIBILITIES

Having faith might appear to be innocuous. A person's religious convictions are private. And a person is within her rights to pursue these religious convictions as she sees fit. But the obvious issue is that a religious ideology exerts an enormous influence on a person's other beliefs, her moral and political judgments, her decisions, and her activities. And those other beliefs and decisions have a substantial effect on the rest of us. Because of their faith, believers go to worship, pray, and engage in significant ceremonies and lifestyle choices. The doctrines exert influence on a full range of the believers' worldviews. For example, their faith informs them whom they will vote for and what views they have about sex, marriage, women, abortion, medical research, and social policies. Believers claim that their religious commitments give them guidance in their moral decisions. Their faith influences whom they will go to war with and whom they will be at peace with. It influences whom they think is guilty or innocent. It guides the believer's goals about the sort of person she wants to become, and her hopes about the sort of people she wants others to be. Believers actively cultivate their views in their children, where their views can take hold in young, impressionable minds before the children are capable of thinking clearly about the topic for themselves. Then the cycle repeats when the children grow up and have children. The short point is that your beliefs matter to the rest of us.

If believing by faith is the lynchpin to this whole edifice of socially, politically, and morally vital views, there is something terribly wrong. It would be immoral and socially irresponsible to ignore what is indicated by the evidence and to simply believe what you want for the matters that are of the most significance to you and everyone around you. There is a widespread view that being religious is the best or only route to moral behavior. But if the foundation of being religious is having faith, then, in effect, one is adopting a set of beliefs and moral standards for which there are no evidential standards. To believe by faith amounts to believing what suits you with no responsibility to what is true or evidentially justified. And how can believing some sought-after idea without any accountability to the evidence be moral? How can it be moral to adopt moral principles that are not subjected to rational scrutiny through the evidence? Your religious views matter to the rest of us, but if they arise from faith, then they are groundless.

FAITH DOESN'T JUSTIFY

There is an equivocation going on with the way we use the words *faith* and *belief*. In ordinary circumstances, to believe something is simply to take it to be true. I believe that classes are cancelled on Veterans Day. I believe that President Obama is an American citizen. But sometimes people use the word *belief* in a peculiar way. They use it to mean something like "hope" or "principle they live by" or "fundamental outlook." So they say, "I believe my husband will be home safely from his military deployment by Christmas," or

"I have to keep believing that I will pull through this terminal illness," or "I believe that everything happens for a reason." Or, most importantly, "I believe and have faith that there is a God." For this sort of belief, just as with faith, you have good reasons to believe it is not true. To watch the news, it doesn't seem like many soldiers are coming home from soon. Or the prognosis for the disease is bad. Or you are trying to hold on to hope that everything happens for a reason because some inexplicably bad things just happened to you and you can't see what good could come of them.

We praise and encourage people to "believe" this way. We reward people for standing up for their principles, and we have reverence for unshakeable faith. It is interesting that these beliefs are ones that we stubbornly hold onto no matter what. In fact, we consider it a sign of weakness of will and defeat if someone relents and gives one of these up. These beliefs are a sort of pledging or promising to keep acting like something is true or that it will become true, even if it looks like it is not.

So when we believe this way, let's call it believe$_H$ (with a subscripted H for *hope*), the claim isn't evidently justified to take as true, but we talk and act as if it is. We may even convince ourselves that it is or manage to obscure the doubts enough so that it feels true.

Now here's an odd question: Are people entitled to believe this way? That might amount to asking if people are entitled to hope. Certainly people can and should have hope. But let's be clear—when we believe$_E$ (for *evidence*), we have grounds that justify or indicate that the claim is true. And the justification is what epistemically entitles us to claim that it is true. Under ordinary circumstances, gathering and evaluating evidence has proven to be the effective means of ascertaining the truth. Good justifications track truth more reliably than poor ones; we would rather have the doctor diagnosis us by consulting blood tests than by reading tea leaves. Compiling a good justification gives one confidence that the indicated conclusion is true. You are justified in accepting your justification. But hoping that something is true, particularly when the bulk of the evidence seems to count against it, does not similarly entitle one to actually claim or think that it is true. In many cases, we wouldn't fault or blame someone for having hope. But we must be careful about crossing the line. To believe generally means to take some described state of affairs to be true. Ordinarily a claim asserts that there is some state of affairs that obtains out there, independent of my ideas. When I say that my car is parked in the driveway, I mean that it is not parked in the street and it has not been towed away. If in fact the car is in the driveway, then my belief turns out to be true. If I based that belief on good justification, then I am entitled, in proportion to the reliability of the method that produced the justification, to conclude that it is true. But a belief$_H$, while nominally appearing to be about the facts in the external world, is really more about one's own cognitive or emotional states. And that equivocation is probably the best reason we should resist using "belief" in these believe$_H$ circumstances altogether. Hoping to win the lottery is one thing, but actually having the cash is another.

So the disbeliever$_E$ and the believer$_H$ are really talking at cross purposes to one another. The disbeliever$_E$ sees the questions as, "Does God exist?" or "Was there a man named Jesus who was a divine being who returned from the dead in 35 CE?" There is a fact of the matter about these questions—either there is a God or there isn't one, and either Jesus came back from the dead or he did not. And we've been trying our best to gather and analyze the evidence that would answer these questions. But the believer$_H$, who says that the answers to the questions are "yes," is often doing something different. The believer$_H$ is taking something to be true in the world without the evidence that would ordinarily justify it. But the impetus behind it is hope, or desire, or faith. But hoping, desiring, or having faith are irrelevant to truth. Believing, hoping, and acting like you will win the lottery does not make it true. What is the case in the world is independent of what we believe or hope to be true.

The problem arises when we equivocate between the two senses of belief. Calling a belief$_H$ a belief doesn't address the question of its truth at all. It's not actually true in virtue of someone's treating it like it is. Evidence is the only sort of thing that gives reliable indicators of truth. A belief that springs from faith is an idea that a person actually has good reasons not to believe or at least suspend judgment about—believing does not bring it about. And, oddly, a person's believing it, by itself, doesn't entitle him to actually think of it or treat it as true. As we have seen, calling it a belief doesn't entitle him to recommend that other people should believe it. Given that beliefs offer descriptions of reality, having them does not entitle a person to have that particular "belief" be immune from critical scrutiny or denial from the rest of us. And it doesn't sanction that belief to play a vital role in his other social, moral, personal, and spiritual convictions, especially when what he thinks about all of these things has such a significant impact on the rest of us.

That means that we have to reject the notion that "taking a belief on faith" somehow justifies or entitles the believer to adopt it, treat it as true, and assert it to others as a truth. To take it on faith is to pilfer something that you hope for but you have not earned. To then make a wide range of decisions that significantly impact the lives of others heaps insult on injury. You have failed in your social, moral, and epistemic duties to yourself and to the rest of us who have to live with you and suffer the results of your beliefs and actions. W. K. Clifford said,

> If I let myself believe anything on insufficient evidence, there may be no great harm done by the mere belief; it may be true after all. . . . But I cannot help doing this great wrong toward Man, that I make myself credulous. The danger to society is not merely that it should believe wrong things, thought that is great enough; but that it should become credulous, and lose the habit of testing things and inquiring into them; for then it must sink back into savagery.[3]

Having faith is a bit like stealing something and then claiming to own it. It's not yours, and it never was. "I have faith that God is real," says that you are going to take a particular state of affairs to be real, and act accordingly. But by attaching the F-word to it, there's an asterisk: you are admitting that you don't really have any justification for taking it to be true, you are just going to anyway.

THE FLOODGATES

The impact of a believer's faith on the rest of us is external, but by far, the more serious problem for faith is internal. It opens a torrent of possibilities that undermine the believer's whole belief structure from the inside. Think of reason as the set of cognitive capacities that make it possible for us to seek out evidence, sift through it, and draw conclusions. Our reasoning capacities are the only tools we have for separating reality from fantasy, fact from fiction, justified belief from nonsense. Once a person abandons them, she has opened the floodgates; there are no principled, coherent, or nonaccidental grounds on which to prefer one god over another.

By opting for faith, the believer disregards the need for evidential or rational justification of a belief. But if that choice is isolated, and as long as she is thinking just about the god with which she's most familiar or the one in which everyone around him believes, then making the leap of faith sans reason doesn't seem so problematic.

But how many supernatural hypotheses are out there for her consideration? How many gods are vying for her faith? Is the only game in town the God whom she had in mind from the start? Obviously not. There is a very long list of other beings lurking over there, waiting to get in.

When evidence and reasons mattered, the believer had some principled means of discerning among competing hypotheses. But if he writes off the role of reasons and evidence in making decisions about a divine being, he has a dilemma. On what basis will he decide to opt for one and not the others? Since he is allowing that it's okay to abandon reason and believe what he likes without regard for the evidence, then why not Baal, Acchupta, Ryangombe, Pu'gu, Pen Annwen, Orcus, Orunmila, Nintinugga, Ningirama, Montu, Mahamanasika, Kamrusepa, Haumiatiketike, or Hatdastsisi? Faith in one is just as good as faith in another, right? It has to be, because faith is believing despite the evidence. So now all the gods are on the same footing. The faithful believer has opened the floodgates to any and all gods and has left himself without the means to choose or hold any of them back.

Reason and the evidence were the only tools he had to hold back mistakes. We know that people are highly prone to err with regard to supernatural, spiritual, and religious matters. Reasoning carefully about the evidence is the only method we have for error checking. That is, there's not a sufficient case to be made in favor of believing any one of these and rejecting the others on the basis of evidence, so what are the criteria for preference? The faithful Christian might not think there's as much to recommend Haumiatiketike as there is to recommend Jesus. But he will only be able to defend his choice on the basis of personal preference, the way he picks from a menu at a restaurant. But decisions about reality, like, "God is the real creator of the universe," "Jesus was resurrected from the dead," or "there is an afterlife," are not equivalent to preferring Peking duck over General Tso's chicken. There is a fact of the matter in religious matters that goes beyond personal taste. And one's views about them have a vast impact on the lives of the rest of us.

The faithful believer often wants to have it both ways. He treats God, God's moral guidance, Jesus, the creation story, heaven, and hell as real things in the world that the rest of us should acknowledge. But when the believer's reality is challenged, he retreats to a defense of his beliefs as a matter of personal, private choice. What's to keep one of the devout followers of Hatdastsisi from pulling the same move: "The only way to true belief in Hatdastsisi is through faith," after all, "and those of you who don't believe will suffer with eternal torment." The internal problem is that without reasoning about what is justified by the evidence, the adoption of a religious belief and the whole system of related views to which it is connected becomes arbitrary. Nothing remains to separate it from madness.

The faith route can set the Christian believer up for an irreconcilable problem. On the one hand, when the evidence and reasoning turned out to be insufficient, then the belief was deemed acceptable anyway by means of faith. On the other hand, he may be tempted to *argue* or *reason* that there are some grounds for thinking that his God or Jesus is real and the other gods are not. But he can't have it both ways without being flagrantly irrational. It is incoherent to gerrymander some defense of believing in Jesus by faith while rejecting all the other entities with a reasoned argument that appeals to evidence. We cannot invoke the concern for truth and justification only to attack those views we do not prefer. We cannot selectively treat our ideas as true until they are challenged and then claim that they are exempt from critical analysis.

The problem becomes obvious when we reverse the situations. Suppose the atheist pulls the same move:

> *Atheist:* I know that there are no gods whatsoever.
> *Believer:* But how can we ever know something like that for
>   sure?
> *Atheist:* I have *faith* that there are no gods. And, by faith, I
>   know that your God isn't real.

Believer: That doesn't make sense. How can you have faith in something that isn't real? You can only have faith that there is a God.

Atheist: I don't have to be concerned with what makes sense. The beauty and virtue of faith is that I'm taking a leap into the unknown. Faith is being sure of what we hope for and certain of what we do not see.

Believer: But we don't have enough evidence to justify atheism.

Atheist: As an atheist, I live by faith, not by sight. Reason and evidence are not my concern. My faith in the vast *godlessness* of the universe is beyond human comprehension—it transcends our puny understanding.

Believer: But that's all insane. Your faith can't make my God not real. God is real, and your simply believing that he is not can't change that. How can you think that the evidence is irrelevant to what you believe or that you can just dismiss the importance of rationality or what is true?

Atheist: Actually, I find it all surprisingly comforting. As soon as I let faith into my heart, all my worries and rational needs about figuring out the truth and being reasonable dissolved. Faith brings great peace of mind. Now I've realized that I can believe anything I like without any responsibility for justifying it.

Believer: What about your responsibilities as a citizen and a moral agent in a society with the rest of us?

Atheist: You know, I don't like your tone. You're angry and strident. You're being intolerant and critical of my faith. I'm exercising my religious freedom with my faith in atheism, and you have to respect that or you're not respecting my personal religious choices.

DESIRE UNDERMINES TRUTH

We noted earlier that our use of the word *faith* shows that we don't have faith that something bad or undesirable will happen. Faith typically aligns with what we want to be true. No one has faith that she will be crushed by a meteorite or that he will be a complete failure in life.

The coincidence of faith with those things that we most want to be true should make us suspicious. The human cognitive system is an exceedingly complicated amalgam of neurological functions that have been redeployed from many of their original survival functions. Many aspects of the system appear to be byproducts, glitches, or atavisms. Natural selection kludges together solutions to problems with whatever genetic features happen to become available in a population. The results only need to be good enough to bestow some small survival advantage. The composition of the organisms that result is not as optimized, efficient, or elegant as it might be if there had been some advanced planning about its end state and ultimate purpose. The results of the operation of its cognitive systems are messy, particularly when the various subsystems work at cross-purposes to each other. It appears that motivated reasoning, the gambler's fallacy, or confirmation bias is to the brain what wisdom teeth are to the jaw, or the appendix is to the digestive system. We must be vigilant about some of the things we think because particular categories of misbeliefs appear to be the products of the way we are built.

One of the many things we know about the functioning of the human cognitive system is that the error rates for judgments go up significantly when people have strong emotional investments in particular outcomes. Gamblers, for instance, are prone to treat some loses as "near wins," thus inflating their estimates of how close they are to winning or their odds of winning. For instance, if a gambler is trying to roll a seven, with two six-sided dice and gets a six instead, he is more prone to take that as being close to winning than he would be if he had rolled a two, even though a two is as much of a loss as the six.[4] So the gambler gets a skewed idea of what is actually happening and an inflated sense of the odds of his winning. And it is the powerful desire to win that smears the picture of reality.

Our wanting makes it harder for us to think clearly about what is true. Research on motivated reasoning shows, for instance, that men will judge the risk of a sexually transmitted disease to be lower with women they find attractive.[5]

When you are attached to a certain outcome, you can't think as straight. Behavioral economists have long known that a when a person owns an item, she will attach a price to it that is higher than the value she would give it if it weren't hers. When we want something to be true it skews our judgment for the worse. Therefore, giving free reign to desire in the form of faith gives some license to fallacious judgment. With faith, as with other matters, if you follow those feelings, you will do a worse job overall of developing an accurate, real picture of the world.

The empirical evidence for the biasing effects of self-deception and desire in judgment is substantial.[6] When people want something to be true, they are more likely to draw the wrong conclusion. And what's also alarming about these studies is not just the increased error rates but also the extent to which subjects either are unaware of or manage to hide the real motivations that gave rise to the conclusion they drew. When experiments are devised that give subjects a personal or emotional investment in a particular outcome, their answers will expose their biases. But additional probing reveals that subjects are largely unaware of the bias introduced by their desires, and they go to great lengths in refusing to acknowledge it. Believing by faith and then treating the result as true potentially involves a complicated sort of self-deception. Self-deception is more likely to happen with "the presence of a desire to have a certain belief; an action or inaction designed to create or strengthen that belief; and an unawareness of the relation between the ultimate belief and the motivated action that gave rise to it. If you neglect to mention disturbing symptoms to your doctor, you must forget that you have done this, if you want to be cheered up when she pronounces you to be in excellent health."[7]

Far from indulging our desires through faith, we should take extra care to reign in, scrutinize, and be cautious in matters where we have a strong personal and emotional stake in the outcome. Our judgments about those matters are especially suspect.

RELIGIOUS BELIEF AND THE GOALS OF INQUIRY

There is a kind of reasoning about Jesus and other religious matters that is a seductive mistake. Our inquiries into some matter can be oriented toward defending a prior-held belief, or they can be evidence driven and receptive to whatever conclusion is best justified by what we discover. The difference is that we often approach the world with a preformed conclusion already in mind. Then, as we consider new information that is relevant to that cherished doctrine, we are receptive to the arguments, evidence, and reasoning that corroborate it and are hostile to arguments that run counter to it. Sometimes we are not aware of it, but our real purpose is to defend the preferred belief. Our faculties of reasoning get put into service protecting a belief instead of seeking the truth. Consider the example of a lawyer with great rhetorical and analytical skills whose goal is to defend the client without regard to the client's guilt. The lawyer's intellectual powers for reasoning, constructing arguments, and answering objections have been detached from the goal of drawing the correct or true conclusion.

By contrast, we can attempt to make an objective, balanced, and nonprejudicial approach to the relevant body of information, keeping the truth as our goal. We do not let our preference for one outcome skew our gathering and evaluation of the evidence. And we are resolved to accept whatever outcome that evaluation supports. The investigation determines the conclusion instead of the prior belief constructing the investigation.

In practice, it is hard to sustain the truth orientation. In matters of importance, there is always some outcome that we would prefer. And our propensity to be more critical and less receptive of evidence that is contrary to those preferences runs deep and strong. The biased acquisition and assimilation of evidence can be subtle and hard to detect, particularly when we are engaged in what appears to be careful and thoughtful reasoning about the matter.

In religious matters, the problem is much more pronounced. People often acquire their religious beliefs when they are young and receptive to supernatural thinking. They hold deep emotional, social, and psychological appeal. For many, the promise of eternal life hangs in the balance. To make matters more difficult, there is a growing scientific consensus that evolution has wired us to be religious. Religious beliefs are at the center of a perfect storm of neurobiological, evolutionary, emotional, social, and psychological forces that make them some of the hardest matters in our lives about which we can reason clearly.

DEFENSE LAWYERS FOR JESUS

There are believers in many religious traditions who have dedicated themselves to constructing rationalistic defenses of their doctrines. The doctrine itself is the unquestionable starting point or the presupposition. The purpose of the apologetic or polemic exercise is then to expose flaws of or to generate objections to any worldview that differs from that doctrine. Reasoning has been subordinated to religious belief; its use is confined to constructing defenses and corroborations of the belief. But the acceptability of the belief itself is not responsive to reasoning. No reasoning is permitted to raise legitimate doubts about a belief's fundamental legitimacy. The domain of reasoning is restricted just as the lawyer's application of her rhetorical and argumentative skills have been wholly subordinated to getting her client off the hook. The question of guilt is left aside. Philosopher Nicholas Wolterstorff embraces the subjugation of reasoning to religious believing more openly than many:

> The religious beliefs of the Christian scholar ought to function as control beliefs within his devising and weighing of theories. . . . Since his fundamental commitment to following Christ ought to be decisively ultimate in his life, the rest of his life ought to be brought into harmony with it. As control, the belief-content of his authentic commitment ought to function both negatively and positively. Negatively, the Christian scholar ought to reject certain theories on the ground that they conflict or do not comport well with the belief content of his authentic commitment.[7]

A complication in our trying to deal with this inversion is that it is sometimes difficult to tell which is the approach of one who would defend religious views. People are rarely as forthright about it as Wolterstorff. It can even be unclear from one's own perspective, whether you are engaging in casuistry or are on a genuine search for truth. The arguments produced by the rhetorician can be sophisticated and masterful. When they are viewed from up close, their logic can seem compelling. The causes and effects of bias are often invisible. And the need for the belief is strong. It is also part of our general predicament that with enough ingenuity, cleverness, and time, people can construct rationalizations for anything and then raise doubts and figure out objections to any contrary view. September 11 conspiracy theorists, global-warming deniers, Holocaust deniers, "birthers" (those who doubt President Obama's US citizenship), Illuminati theorists, and countless other examples show how far ill-founded rationalizing can take people from the truth.

As I have developed the arguments of this book, I have encountered many critics who I can only describe as defense attorneys for Jesus. From their perspective, it is a given that I am mistaken and that an apologetic refutation and a defense of the resurrection must be constructed. Disbelief in God, Jesus, or the resurrection is rejected without reflection. In some cases, I have been challenged to debates, confronted with vigorous objections, and had my theses flatly rejected even before the critic has read, heard, or thought about the arguments. Believing in the resurrection has been given a higher priority than worries about being mistaken or reasonable.

Those of us who are concerned with being reasonable should refuse to engage with these pseudovindications of the resurrection or, more generally, of religious belief. One of the projects of this book has been to explore the limits and structure of human reasoning, particularly regarding religious matters. We have seen a hundred ways in which religious beliefs can compromise our rational autonomy. It's a testimony to the power of the religious urge that so many people are willing to dedicate themselves to a religious ideology completely and even openly acknowledge that they will evaluate and subordinate everything else to it, even their capacity to reason itself. These ideologues can offer complex arguments in defense of their views, but the watershed question that separates the two approaches is this: Are there any considerations, even hypothetically, that would dissuade you of the existence of God or the divinity of Jesus? For many, under any circumstances, there really is no alternative to believing. So their arguments alleging to support belief under the guise of a rational exchange of ideas are presented under a false pretense. Only those considerations that corroborate their beliefs will be looked on with any favor, as Wolterstorff has made clear. All others will be rejected because of their incompatibility with the dogma.

Ultimately, I think we must treat this sort of choice to enslave oneself to religious belief as arbitrary and verging on delusional. If all reasoning is subordinated to the goal of defending the doctrine, then it cannot really be that sound reasoning supports and justifies the doctrine. The defender has constructed a polemical castle in the sky that is invulnerable to clear thinking. Ultimately there can be no reasoned preference for the belief that justifies preferring it over some other ideology that happened to co-opt one's thinking. If he was motivated, a clever apologist could construct a comparable framework of justifications and rebuttals with a belief in the Great Pumpkin or fairies at its center that is just as impressive. Despite the fact that they seem to employ sophisticated and careful reasoning to defend their beliefs, we have to conclude that believers have left the playing field of rationality. There will be many who are critical of the arguments in this book. I ask only that the critics be clear with themselves and the rest of us about which approach is theirs.

CONCLUSION

Taking the resurrection or other religious claims on faith is not an acceptable answer for a number of reasons. It concedes the point to arguments that show that the evidence is insufficient. At best, it describes how someone believes, but it gives us no reasons to think that the resurrection claims are true. Faithful believing embodies a dangerous policy that would wreak havoc in all of the other important decisions in our lives; we wouldn't accept a cancer diagnosis by faith, so we shouldn't give away our spiritual lives by it. Having faith in a religious ideology that affects one's social, political, moral, and personal decisions shirks one's responsibilities to the rest of humanity, whose lives are impacted. Having faith doesn't entitle a person to claim that it is true. Having faith in one's favored religious doctrines opens the floodgates to an endless stream of kooky possibilities; without reason, we have got no grounds to reject all of these possibilities. And the biasing effects of our desires on belief formation show that faith is something that should be reined in, not indulged.

Chapter 12

WHY SO SERIOUS?

What about nonliteral or more liberal varieties of religious belief? So far, the arguments in this book have focused on the weakness of the evidence for the resurrection and problems with historical arguments for religious claims, God, miracles, and faith. But there are many who identify themselves as believers who do not insist on such a strong, literal view about the resurrection or God or religious doctrines. Many believers adopt a "many paths, one God" view of different religious doctrines. They are religiously inclined but don't agree with the standard orthodoxies, so they adopt a general concept of God that might transcend sectarian disagreements. According to this view, Baptists, Catholics, Jews, Muslims, and Hindus all have different variants on a basic idea that make them appear to be different. But when we view them all from a sufficient distance, we can see that really they are all worshipping or believing in essentially the same thing. On this view, all of these believers subscribe to the general notion of a higher power—a guiding force—and their religions all do more or less the same thing for them.

Recent surveys seem to confirm that this form of inclusive theism is by far the most common in the United States:

> A strong majority of those who are affiliated with a religion, including majorities of nearly every religious tradition, do not believe their religion is the only way to salvation. . . . More than two-thirds of adults affiliated with a religious tradition agree that there is more than one true way to interpret the teachings of their faith, a pattern that occurs in nearly all traditions.[1]

Whether the same people who adopt the "many paths, one God" view also take a nonliteral view of the resurrection of Jesus (thus possibly avoiding the problems we saw in earlier chapters) will depend on the individual. We are interested here in the broad class of people who identify themselves as Christian or religious but who take a more liberal view about what that means in terms of required beliefs, and the people who are less concerned about the real events in first-century Palestine.

These more liberal believers are less troubled by the ambiguities and lack of evidence for Jesus' divinity because they may not take many of the specific doctrinal claims of Christianity to be literally true. It may seem like an oxymoron to describe someone as a Christian who does not believe in the actual resurrection of Christ. And I confess that it strikes me as a deeply conflicted view, to say the least. But for many, Christianity contains deeply moving and valuable sentiments. If pressed, they might not claim to believe that there actually was a person who returned from the dead, but they find the ideals, the tradition, the culture, the art, and the community of the Christian religion to be deeply fulfilling.

The common view is that there cannot really be anything objectionable about this sort of engagement in religious activities, ceremonies, and services as long as these liberal believers don't take some of the more outrageous, harmful, or erroneous claims seriously. In fact, this may be the most common position out there. "I enjoy going to church. I find the community edifying. The ceremonies are beautiful and inspiring. The art and music are wonderful. It gives me moral guidance," and so on. Even among famous religious skeptics, we find a soft spot for the cultural, emotive, and dramatic aspects of participating in religion. Richard Dawkins, perhaps to the dismay of believers, raves about the beauty of church hymns and music. Paul Kurtz describes this confined but rosy set of roles for religion: "The domain of the religious, I submit, is evocative, expressive, emotive. It presents moral poetry, aesthetic inspiration, performative ceremonial rituals, which act out and dramatize the human condition and human interests, and seek to slake the thirst for meaning and purpose. . . . Religious language in this sense is eschatological. Its primary function is to express hope."[2]

Kurtz is a nonbeliever who, like a great many religious believers, endorses a kind of compatibilism regarding science and religion. There is no tension, no conflict, and no disagreement between the two because religion, as Kurtz describes it, has been scrubbed clean of the factual claims, of all pretenses to knowledge, and of all the assertions. For people in this camp, the cognitive dissonance of compartmentalizing their religious activities from their scientific, empirical, and factual views is diminished because the religious moderate is just in it for the culture—the bells and smells, if you will. The religious moderate can't really take the claim seriously that all life on earth was created in its present form ten thousand years ago, or that the juice and crackers actually turn into flesh and blood in your mouth, or that Adam and Eve were the first humans, or that snakes and burning bushes can talk. She might say, "We don't actually, literally believe that stuff. But participating is edifying and wonderful, it's morally valuable, or at the very least, it is utterly harmless."

I must agree with some of these sentiments. If we were to consider a spectrum of religious people, with those who make the strongest assertions of fact about the Christian God, Adam and Eve, the resurrection, and so on at one end, and those who treat these ideas as mere metaphors or mythology that should not be taken as assertions of historical events at the other, there is much less to take issue with at the metaphorical end. My primary concern has been with assertions of fact and evidence. I have sought answers to the questions: Did the resurrection happen? What is our historical evidence concerning it? Are the miracle claims that support many religious institutions plausible? Would God perform miracles? Those questions strike me as being of vital importance, and I have argued that deeply mistaken views about them are at the foundations of modern religions. The implications of my arguments for questions about human religiousness ought to be of concern to all those who call themselves religious.

The liberal believer should find valuable lessons of self-discovery and critical thinking in what we have learned about human cognitive systems and the mistakes into which they are prone to fall. The larger lesson from these exercises can be seen this way. For the nonliteral believer, what exactly is it that you are asserting about the world? What do you think is true about God, spirituality, and an afterlife? Once we are clear on which claims he does think are true and not merely edifying stories, we can and should ask the same questions: Do we have good evidence to think that such a claim is accurate? How good is that evidence? What is the method for gathering or selecting evidence that leads to these conclusions? Is it reasonable? Is believing that claim consistent with the standards we employ elsewhere for justified, reasonable beliefs? In what ways are those beliefs contributing to your other views, your decisions, your social and moral views? As I have indicated before, I share the evangelicals' concern about the gravity of these issues. The truth here is of vital importance. And I suspect that when we start to explore those assertions of truth that the liberal believer is willing to make, these questions will reveal problems.

FAKING IT

Aside from the question of the liberal believer's assertions of truth, we should be concerned about his behaviors and participation in an institution that we can agree is built upon mistakes. One problem is with the suggestion that one can participate while "not really" believing. Do we think that we can prostrate ourselves before God (even if it is only metaphorical), repeat the claims, and generally mimic the more literal religious believers without any effect on our belief structures? Can we read the story of Adam and Eve again and again in a social context where it is taken seriously and literally, or fill our minds repeatedly with images of Jesus performing feats of magic and still comfortably and readily acknowledge that they are "just stories," not to be taken too literally? Before you answer, here is the Apostle's Creed, routinely avowed by millions of Christians:

> I believe in God, the Father Almighty, Maker of heaven and earth. And in Jesus Christ, His only Son, our Lord; who was conceived by the Holy Ghost, born of the Virgin Mary; suffered under Pontius Pilate, was crucified, died and was buried. He descended into hell. The third day He rose again from the dead; He ascended into heaven and sitteth on the right hand of God the Father Almighty; From thence He shall come to judge the quick and dead. I believe in the Holy Ghost, the Holy Christian Church, the Communion of Saints, the Forgiveness of sins, the Resurrection of the Body, and the Life everlasting. Amen.

Can a person repeat this thousands or tens of thousands of times, while surrounding herself with people who all claim to genuinely believe it, and have it be evocative and aesthetic, but not contribute to any sort of attitude in your mind about what is real and what is true? We have seen the relevant research on attitude change: when subjects who hold a particular position write essays in favor of the opposing view, their conviction about their original view diminishes. If a person's considered conclusion is that many of the claims that are essential to a religious doctrine shouldn't be taken literally, what will be the effects of repeatedly acting like and saying that they are true? A problem, as I see it, is the peculiar situation of self-conflict and self-deception in which the liberal believer has put herself. She knows, and perhaps she would admit if pressed, that many of these religious claims can't be true or reasonable. Yet on some matters of enormous importance and value, she is prepared to act like they are and misrepresent her real views to herself and to others.

Of course, for many, the question of lasting effects will be pointless because as they see it, there are positive effects to be experienced by believing. So even if it isn't true, it's good to act like it is. And if acting has the effect of altering our beliefs or even making us believe, then so much the better.

Keep in mind that the case here only concerns the religious moderate who does not take religious pronouncements literally. Ironically, many evangelicals and more literal believers will agree with me: the things you say in church are serious and should not be taken lightly. There is cognitive dissonance and a degree of intellectual dishonesty in going through the motions without addressing the grounds and authenticity of the things you are saying and doing. Saying it and not meaning it is duplicitous.

The many more literal believers and I will agree that either we should all believe and have good grounds for belief, or we should not pretend. The disagreement we would then have would be about whether there are rationally justifying grounds available to us to support these claims. But all that is a different disagreement.

The religious moderate, in conceding that she does not take many of the ideas to be literally true or reasonable, is not guilty of the outright irrationalities that literal belief would mire her in, perhaps. But she is trying to have her cake and eat it, too, as it were. She wants to go through the motions and participate without the epistemic responsibility for the words coming out of her mouth or acknowledging the significance of her kneeling, hand waving, singing, praying, or prostrating.

Another problem is that our actions and words cannot be fully compartmentalized this way, and that should concern us because what we say and do, what we believe, and why we believe it *matters*. The cognitive dissonance and the contradictions cannot be sidestepped because it is not really possible to strip out all of the metaphysical or assertion content from those actions. Trying to do so involves the religious moderate in an intellectual dissonance that none of us should be so willing to dismiss lightly.

The truth and being reasonable are of vital importance. And words and actions count. We all know that. A couple of examples make it painfully clear.

> Suppose that a boy is raised in the Deep South as a member of the Ku Klux Klan. All his life, on a regular basis, his family, friends, and other from the community put on their white robes and hoods and hold highly ritualized Klan meetings. They sing songs, burn crosses, hear devotionals about the evils of the inferior mongrel races, and so on.
>
> Now he's grown up. He's become enlightened in his life and come to realize that, contrary to what he was taught all his life, black people and Jews are not genetically inferior; the same goes for lots of the other things he had always heard in those Klan ceremonies. Suppose he's gotten so far past his upbringing that he's fallen in love with and married a Jewish, African American woman.
>
> After all those years, however, he's held onto his robe and hood. And on Sundays, he still enjoys putting it on and going to Klan rallies. He finds the songs and rituals evocative and aesthetically inspiring. The ceremonies, he tells his outraged wife, dramatize the human condition and "seek to slake the thirst for meaning and purpose," and so on. He doesn't really believe any of that stuff, he tells her. All that talk and ritual shouldn't be taken so seriously and literally. And as long as the values of the Klan rallies are solely cultural and eschatological, there can't be anything wrong with his going along.

The objection to this analogy, of course, will be that the ceremonies and words of religious services are not comparable to the malice and error of Klan rallies.

The religious moderate will insist that, while much of what people do and say in church isn't literally true, it isn't evil or racist or intolerant or so misguided.

But the accurate aspects of the analogy are telling. First, in fact, a great deal of what goes on in churches and mosques and other religious establishments is intolerant, disrespectful, erroneous, and even racist or malicious. The rantings against white America from President Obama's former preacher, Reverend Jeremiah Wright, do not represent a tiny, obscure splinter sect. The recent mobilization from religious groups in favor of California's Proposition 8 to ban gay marriage was massive. When we accommodate all of that, we are morally culpable to some extent. If we participate by sitting the pews, singing, donating money, and generally going along, then we have played a role at least in perpetuating the institution's agenda and misguided doctrines.

For example, many moderate believers have become dissatisfied with their church's policies toward homosexuality to the extent that it has caused great rifts within religious culture. Some of the sects have been more inclusive and tolerant. Their motivation was that discrimination against homosexuality is intolerant and morally wrong. That is to say, they insist that it is just not true that homosexuals should be excluded spiritually. But if the truth matters, then how is it any less misguided or irresponsible to continue propagating the ideas that all life was created all at once ten thousand years ago, or that disbelief will be punished for eternity in hell, or that Jesus was resurrected from the dead. Why continue to say it, teach it, and sing it if you don't really mean it?

This sort of participation directly contributes to sustaining and promoting hurtful, mistaken, and misguided beliefs in others, if not in yourself as well. It is no accident that 51 percent of Americans still refuse to believe that life on earth evolved. Fifty-five percent of Americans subscribe to some form of rapture theology; 36 percent maintain that the book of Revelations, with its apocalyptic imagery of seven-horned goats and an anti-Christ who lays waste to all the nonbelievers, is "true prophecy."[3] It would appear that a lot of people aren't just going along for nostalgia's sake—they mean it. So is the moderate believer one of those or is he of the group that sits quietly while the rest of them pump out these outrageous ideas? When he sings, does he keep careful track of which lyrics are metaphorical and which should be taken literally? Does he pray and keep the distinction clear? When he says the Apostle's Creed, does he, in his mind, attach an asterisk to the doubtful clauses? What does he do when his children learn their Bible lessons well and talk as if the stories are real?

Furthermore, when considered from some distance, the Klan example doesn't appear disanalogous because of their outrageous ideas. Is the Klan theory about the bastardized, mongrel, nonwhite races being descended from animals that much more outrageous than the view that an evil superbeing sends invisible, malicious demons to infect the bodies and minds of unsuspecting believers? Or that virgins can give birth? Or that dead people can come back from the grave?

Even if there is a significant difference between going to Klan rallies for nostalgia's sake and the moderates' engagement with religion, I fear that it is a difference in degree not in kind. We have all got to agree that it is highly implausible that a person could sanitize or compartmentalize his participation in such ceremonies enough to eliminate its cognitive and social effects and always keep the distinctions between truth and falsehood, reality and fantasy clear. If the religious moderate is really convinced that her participation can be isolated and that the Klan example is too outrageous, then she should try these experiments:

- Stand up in a room full of people you know and loudly announce, "I pledge my eternal soul to Satan, my master." Those are just words, after all, that need not be taken literally. Could you say it several times every day for years without its having any effect on you? Wouldn't you worry at least a little bit that making the pledge might actually give your soul to Satan?
- Imagine fully participating and performing all of the prayers, recitations, and physical ceremonies in an Islamic religious service or some other unfamiliar tradition.
- Suppose that President Obama had chosen to say, "So help me Allah," at the end of his presidential oath of office.
- Suppose that instead of "In God we trust," US currency said, "In Allah we trust," or "In Satan we pledge our trust."
- For Catholics, instead of pledging yourself to the Nicene Creed, imagine pledging to a religious creed that explicitly denies Catholicism.

If we are being honest, we will acknowledge that at the very least, some of these experiments give us a twinge of hesitation. Perhaps a person would be so uncomfortable she would simply refuse to do it. That is because words and actions matter. We can't really detach ourselves from religious behaviors to such an extent that their metaphysical and factual import vanishes. And that means that you cannot be epistemically disengaged from rational responsibility for your words and ceremonial activities.

The Christian would be correct to reject the analogy between what he does and what someone in the Klan is doing. By and large, most Christian organizations do not engage in hateful, intolerant, or misinformed practices that are comparable to the Klan. But it is not the moral offenses implied by the association that I find troubling as much as the disregard for the truth. If it's not true—if the earth was not created ten thousand years ago, if Adam and Eve were not the first humans, if there was no original sin, if there was life on the planet for billions of years before humans came onto the scene, if there was no great flood, if Jesus did not come back from the dead, if blood sacrifices are not required to absolve human beings of their moral misdeeds, if a fetus is not magically endowed with an immaterial soul during pregnancy—then why do we continue to talk, act, sing, pray, and worship as if all of that is true? Why lend your support to an organization and to people who believe those claims and who are actively trying to propagate them? Why don't we have a greater passion for reality, evidence, knowledge, and truth?

There are other unintended side effects from faking it, of course. By saying it and acting it out over and over again, we encourage more sloppiness, magical thinking, confusion, and duplicity in ourselves and in those around us.

If you know better but fake it anyway, what are you doing to others who are genuinely trying to understand whether there is a God, or whether he talks to us through burning bushes? What about children who trust and mimic the words and actions of the adults they see? What precedent do you set or fortify by letting false, misleading, intolerant, or harmful ideas and practices slide? If it is negligent or abusive for me to refuse to get medical care for my children when they need it, or to fail to feed them, then how much better is it to fill their heads with patently false ideas about the world that I don't really believe and that we have good reasons to reject? The nonliteral believer finds himself in the midst of a movement where a great many people do not take these religious claims as mere metaphors. They really believe, and in many cases their participation fortifies their more extreme views. So if there are non-literal Christians scattered in the pews among the literal believers, the beliefs and practices with which the nonliteral Christian is not comfortable are actually encouraged and proliferate in the community. Even if you don't believe it, acting like you do contributes to others actually believing it.

Arguably, faking it encourages sympathy or at least complacency about the more strident and dangerous views of the more literal believers, too. William Lobdell, the former religion writer for the *Los Angeles Times*, wrote the book *Losing My Religion*. Lobdell investigated numerous so-called prosperity gospel ministries, like Benny Hinn's program on the Trinity Broadcasting Network. He found charlatan and con-artist preachers who were making hundreds of millions of dollars by demanding that their poor and disadvantaged followers give what little money they had to the ministries. Followers were even exhorted to max out their credit cards or stop their medical treatments for the promise that God would provide for them later. Lobdell didn't find his faith challenged by these outright frauds, but he was more disillusioned by the more mainstream Christian leaders on the network who failed to say anything critical about the fraudulent activities of their peers. When he pressed Billy Graham, Franklin Graham, Joel Osteen, Robert Schuller, and other heavyweight leaders in the moderate Christian movement to respond, none of them were willing to be critical of the charlatans.[4]

There is a more chilling effect of faking it that we may not appreciate. In a recent study about the effects of scriptural violence on aggression, researchers set out to measure the effects of reading passages that said that God sanctioned some case of violence. After reading the passages, subjects more readily punish losers in assigned tasks, suggesting that scriptural violence that is sanctioned by God or that comes from the Bible increases aggression. The effect was stronger in believers, but it was also present in those who did not claim to believe in God or the Bible.[5]

BRACKETED BELIEF

The religious moderate may want to paint religion in the glowing light of cultural and metaphorical edification. He may insist that he can bracket off the false, offending, extreme, or misleading assertions and implications of the words and actions. But it is implausible that you can talk the talk and walk the walk over and over again with complete detachment. The ideas sink in. The influences are there, whether or not we acknowledge them. And the duplicity is bad for the moderate as well as for those around him. We know enough now about human brain function to see the hazards of putting ourselves in such an environment and going through the motions (recall the source-amnesia phenomena from chapter 3). Sam Wang, a neuroscientist at Princeton University, and Sandra Aamodt, former editor of *Nature Neuroscience*, say,

> The brain does not simply gather and stockpile information as a computer's hard drive does. Facts are stored first in the hippocampus, a structure deep in the brain about the size and shape of a fat man's curled pinkie finger. But the information does not rest there. Every time we recall it, our brain writes it down again, and during this re-storage, it is also reprocessed. In time, the fact is gradually transferred to the cerebral cortex and is separated from the context in which it was originally learned. For example, you know that the capital of California is Sacramento, but you probably don't remember how you learned it. This phenomenon, known as source amnesia, can also lead people to forget whether a statement is true. Even when a lie is presented with a disclaimer, people often later remember it as true.
>
> With time, this misremembering gets worse. A false statement from a noncredible source that is at first not believed can gain credibility during the months it takes to reprocess memories from short-term hippocampal storage to longer-term cortical storage. As the source is forgotten, the message and its implications gain strength. This could explain why, during the 2004 presidential campaign, it took weeks for the Swift Boat Veterans for Truth campaign against Senator John Kerry to have an effect on his standing in the polls.[6]

The source-amnesia problem suggests that we must be diligent about where we put ourselves, who we listen to, and what sorts of things we repeat. And we must be cognizant of the effects that our words and actions have on others given that the same separations between sources and truth will be happening in their minds. Given the effects on the human brain, repeatedly making claims and taking actions that you would deny are true is an active program of self-deception.

Immersing yourself in an environment that discourages curiosity and skepticism stifles the intellectual dissent that is essential to scientific and human advancement. The fundamental relationship of humanity to the world within many religious traditions is subservience to God, obedience, and an acknowledgement of God's truths above everything else. In Christian religious institutions, the ultimate source of all knowledge is a fixed eternal authority. Whatever else we learn or discover must be reconciled with the immovable doctrinal claims of the religion or it will be rejected. That puts the religious ideology at odds with the Enlightenment view that all ideas can and should be critically analyzed by reason, and those that cannot be made to fit with our empirical observations are not justified. In fact, since access to new information is vital to our making informed political, social, and moral decisions, we may legitimately worry that religious environments, particularly those with a more evangelical or fundamentalist bent, are antithetical to the foundations of a democratic society.[7]

There is evidence that the problem is much worse than just forgetting the sources of our knowledge. Once some beliefs get in there, nothing can get them out, not even directly contrary, discrediting evidence. A number of studies have shown that people will go on believing something even after their reasons have been shown to be faulty.[8]

DIGGING IN

Research shows how tenacious religious beliefs are, even when they generates acute cognitive dissonance. Researchers used a questionnaire and a measurement scale to assign a value to the strength of religious belief for a group of test subjects.[9] Then the subjects were asked to publicly declare (in front of a group of believers) whether they answered "yes" to the question: Do you believe that Jesus was the Son of God? Next, they were all given an article to read and discuss. The article, they were told, was written anonymously and was "denied publication in *The New York Times* at the request of the World Council of Churches because of the obvious crushing effect it would have on the entire Christian world."[10]

The article reports that, using a collection of recently found scrolls, scholars in Jordan had conclusively proven that the major writings in the New Testament are fraudulent. The scrolls, which are judged to be authentic by reliable scholars and radiocarbon dating, reveal that the composers of the New Testament conspired to fake reports of Jesus' resurrection because, "our great teacher, Jesus of Nazareth, was killed by the Romans, I am sure we were justified in stealing away his body and claiming that he rose from the dead. For, although his death clearly proves he was not the Son of God as we had hoped, if we did not claim that he was, both his great teaching and our lives as his disciples would be wasted!"[11] The article goes on to report that the lead scholar on the project had found "no alternative but to renounce my former belief that Jesus Christ was the Son of God. I can no longer be a Christian." It also said that the World Council of Churches sought to repress the story because it would undermine the foundations of Christianity.

After reading the fake article, 24 percent of the subjects indicated that they accepted the article as true (they were not told it was fake until after the study). The rest of them were unsure or clearly rejected it. Then researchers remeasured the strength of the subjects' religious beliefs. The results are remarkable. The subjects who had identified themselves as non-believers at the outset had their levels of religious belief drop after reading the article. The believers in the group who indicated that they doubted the belief-disconfirming story had their levels of religious belief diminish. But the most interesting result was that the believers who also said that they believed the news story that refuted Christianity had their religious beliefs strengthened. That is, even when faced with outright disconfirming evidence that they accepted as true, rather than come to doubt that Jesus is the Son of God, the believers indicated having an even stronger belief.

C. Daniel Batson, the lead author in the study, comments,

> It has been said, "You will know the Truth and the Truth will make you free"
> [John 8:32]. The present research seems to question this assertion. The more
> one publicly proclaims one's conviction about personally significant truths,
> the more one seems bound to these truths. One is less free to modify one's
> position, to take account of new, discrepant information. But perhaps this is
> not what is meant by freedom in the above statement. If it means that one
> will be free from the rational process of taking account of all relevant infor-
> mation in the formulation of one's beliefs, than the present research seems
> clearly supportive."[12]

It is difficult to conceive of a clearer, more objective demonstration of
outright irrationality. But let me offer some additional speculations about
the recalcitrance of religious belief. The presumption throughout this volume
has been that through discussion of the relevant evidence, we can achieve
some rational progress on which conclusions are epistemically responsible to
believe, and as a result the thoughtful person will proportion the strength
of her conviction about different claims to the strength of the evidence for
those claims. We are all concerned (or at least we should be) with having
sensible beliefs that fit with the facts, as best as we can ascertain them. If
not, then there is really no point to the exchange of views other than vain
pronouncements of dogmatism.

What the evidence in Batson's study shows is that there are a great many
religious adherents who are simply and obviously unconcerned with the facts,
or at least they are more concerned with other matters, like defending a view
to which they have publicly committed themselves, than with believing what
is true or justified by the evidence. They are resolved to maintain their views
not just by denying contrary evidence, but they will also hold onto them
even in cases where they acknowledge that the contrary evidence proves their
beliefs to be false.

Without stretching it too much, I think we can see the implications for
the nonliteral believer. Spend a lot of time in Sunday school entertaining
stories about Adam and Eve, Noah, and people rising from the dead, and you
may well end up believing it; even if you discover that the evidence for those

beliefs is suspect, the belief has a way of persisting. Once it's in there, it's very hard to get it out. And through your participation, you're fostering a set of dangerous and irrational cognitive practices that exploit our neurobiological foibles. Even without taking the neurological angle, we can think of religious faking it as reinforcing cognitive vices in ourselves and others that can undermine intellectual integrity and growth.

NONCOGNITIVISM AND RELIGIOUS BELIEF

Philosophers have made a distinction in human speech acts between those that are *cognitive* and those that are *noncognitive*. Cognitive speech acts amount to assertions. They are claims that the world is one way and not another. So if Jeremiah Wright claims that "AIDS is the product of a US government conspiracy to kill black people," he is asserting that something is true. He intends that AIDS originated in one way and not another. If a prosecuting attorney argues that a defendant is guilty of murdering a liquor store owner in a holdup, she means that the death of the store owner was due to the defendant's actions and not caused by something else; it is not the case that the defendant did not do it. To assert that P is the case is to assert that it is not the case that not-P is true. The world is one way and not another.

This is not to say, however, that cognitive speech acts are all true. What this means is that the speech act expresses a proposition that is either true or false, and determining whether it is true is another matter. But by labeling it "cognitive," we mean that the sentence conveys a description that reflects or represents some state of affairs that is either in the world or isn't.

But noncognitive speech acts are common, particularly in our religious practices, and they don't admit of evaluation in terms of true or false. Many of our utterances are not intended as claims about what is true. They cannot be usefully construed as denials that their opposites are the case. Consider a cheerleader leading a crowd of football fans through a chant. Or imagine a crowd booing a bad performer on a stage. The best way to understand what they are doing is not as assertions. Other noncognitive speech acts include crying out in pain when you hit your thumb with a hammer or mindlessly singing the lyrics to a song from the radio. These sorts of utterances are better understood as emotive or expressive of feelings. They may even be done with the intention of inducing similar feelings in their audiences. The cheerleader is certainly trying to achieve a certain sort of mental state in her audience. She wants to stir up feelings of excitement, enthusiasm, and support for her team. The poet may want to evoke similar subtle aspects of mood in his audience as he was experiencing when he had an experience. Some noncognitive speech acts could be understood as something like, "I am feeling this way, and I want you to feel it, too. Share my emotional state." (But it certainly kills the mood to describe it this way.)

Lots of religious speech acts and behaviors appear to be noncognitive. Reciting chants and litanies; motioning ritualized actions, such as making the sign of the cross; saying "Amen" in response to someone else's words; singing songs; and saying some prayers should all be considered noncognitive. The best way to understand the function of these acts and behaviors in the lives and minds of the people performing them is often not as bold assertions of some fact they take to reflect the world. There are mixed cases and borderline cases, of course, but we would be missing something if we took a cheerleader to be literally asserting that, "We will, we will, rock you." Singing psalms in church or sprinkling water on a newborn baby shouldn't be understood as assertions of facts. They are speech and behavior gestures that play a different role in humans' lives.[13]

Noncognitive speech acts often succeed. That is, they often do produce the desired emotional and mental states in the speaker and audience. Consider the effects of playing the American national anthem and looking at the flag (even if you aren't American). That music makes us feel a certain way. Cheers often make us have pronounced feelings. Poetry does evoke strong visceral, intellectual, and emotional reactions in us.

Here is the hazard with repeatedly engaging in noncognitive religious utterances. Many noncognitive speech acts induce beliefs in us. That is, many speech acts that are not themselves assertions about the world nevertheless create in their audiences the mental state of thinking that something is true. No reasons or reasoning have been given. No evidence has been cited. And no argument has been presented. But in many cases, people still end up believing that certain things are true about the world. What started as a subjective expression of emotion, or maybe as an act intended only to induce some shared feelings in the listener, actually yields a conviction that something else is true in the world (e.g., "the United States is the greatest country on earth"). Certainly people are roused to political action by poetry and song. They become motivated to act on their beliefs and bring about change, whereas they weren't before they read or heard these moving words. Or the intense passion of the moment generated by the speech act leaves them with a deep sense of conviction. Psychologist Jonathan Haidt has coined the term "moral elevation," for the sentiment these situations stir in us.[14] National anthems and patriotic songs have been used in countless cases to rouse people to go to war. And a willingness to go to war is predicated on beliefs that something is true of the enemy and that its contrary is not. Intense public rallies stirring up fervent German nationalism made it much easier to believe that Jews were the wicked source of Germany's economic problems.

Priming experiments in psychology, as we have seen, show that our cognitive systems are measurably and predictably affected by stimuli of which we are unaware. The significance for religious belief is that a person's beliefs at the conscious level are often affected by stimuli and cognitive systems within his own brain about which he is utterly unaware. What feels like a voluntary mental and physical act that seems to be transparent to introspection, in fact, is significantly influenced by forces and aspects of the nervous system that for us are intellectually behind the scenes. We don't have access to and don't know about the forces that produce beliefs that appear in consciousness. But they are there, and they are affecting the way we think.

So we can begin to see the ways in which noncognitive speech acts and behaviors might be working on us to produce or affect beliefs. If priming experiments in psychology show that the contents of their conscious awareness can be causally affected or changed without the subjects' awareness, then the same mechanisms will be at work on us in religious contexts. Noncognitive speech acts affect us, sometimes strongly. Furthermore, we are often unaware of the causal factors and stimuli that contribute to the production of the beliefs we find in our minds. And the line between noncognitive and cognitive speech acts is often blurry.

The hazards of forming convictions about what is true on the basis of non-cognitive utterances and behaviors should be obvious. A belief that something is the case in the world should not be based upon visceral, emotional, and unconscious processes, if we can help it. It's dangerous to vote, fight, argue, march, pull triggers, and pass laws on the basis of emotion instead of reason. Passion is a highly unreliable guide to the truth. In fact, for many of us and many of our beliefs, they are inversely correlated.

Many people defend religion as being a source of personal fulfillment and meaning. They make remarks such as, "We don't take those stories literally. We don't actually think that the earth was created six thousand years ago or that people's physical bodies will literally ascend to heaven after death. Those are just metaphorical, poetic ways of speaking. Those words aren't literally true."

The problem is that the lines between reality and imagination, truth and fiction, accurate description and metaphor, are frequently blurred and crossed. The difference in feeling between mere metaphor and actual assertion, as we have seen, can be slight. The fierce feelings of pride, aggression, and enthusiasm produced by rousing cheers from the cheerleaders or by playing the national anthem as a flag ascends aren't compartmentalized in our minds. Witness the fights, riots, and even murders that frequently occur at sporting events. Egypt and Algeria have recently come to the brink of serious international conflict for the sake of a soccer game.[15]

The feelings that noncognitive speech acts induce aren't controlled and isolated from the rest of our convictions and our beliefs about what is true. Those feelings produce *actions*, and actions feed beliefs, then those beliefs feed more actions, and the beliefs and actions catalyze more noncognitive speech acts that rouse us further. We can't sing or chant that "Jesus is our Lord and savior," or that "there is only one true God," over and over for years while having strong emotional reactions to the music, while being surrounded by a throng of pious believers, and while listening to a passionate sermon and not be significantly affected at the cognitive level.

When we engage in noncognitive speech acts without being very clear about the lines between truth, feeling, and assertion versus nonassertions, we run risks. If you don't really believe in God, if you don't take all the ontological claims in religious doctrine seriously, and if you don't really think that humans need salvation from an invisible, magical being that reads minds, then how can it be acceptable to repeatedly act and talk as if you do? Those speech acts affect us—they change us. In religious contexts, they blur the line between reality and wishing. They affect other people who do frequently take the claims as serious assertions and then act accordingly. They train us to believe and act emotively instead of on the basis of good evidence. Religious speech acts foster visceral, intuitive, emotive believing. They train and reinforce bad intellectual habits instead of acute critical-thinking skills.

"GOD IS ENERGY" AND OTHER NEW AGE CONCEPTIONS OF GOD

There is an even more liberal variety of beliefs that stretches the notion of God so much that they cannot really be identified with a particular religious movement. It's quite common for people to have some of the following views about the nature of God and the diversity of religions: "Isn't God just the energy in the universe?" Or, "the God I believe in is all the matter and energy in the universe. Einstein showed that all matter is energy, after all." And, "Science has shown that energy cannot be destroyed." "Aren't all the different religions really just different ways of expressing interest in the same underlying force or ultimate reality or energy in the world?" Or, "The concept of God that people use is another way of describing all the love, power, and spiritualism that we all experience. Worshipping God should be coming to feel that love and energy and spreading it in the world. The notion of God as a person who listens to prayers and passes judgments is too anthropomorphic."

These attempts to redefine God in a way that would allow us to reconcile what appear to be irreconcilable differences between religions and to square what we know in science with religion have a great deal of appeal. A New Age interpretation of God appeals to those with a strong spiritual inclination, and it might let them avoid the uglier side of organized religions and their histories. It might also make it possible to avoid a number of the paradoxes and philosophical difficulties, like those detailed in this book, that plague more traditional notions of God.

So why shouldn't we redefine God to suit our modern needs and avoid the problems with the old one? First, doing so will not suit many believers, particularly those who take seriously the resurrection of Jesus or the authenticity of Muhammad's prophecies. But as we've seen, there is not much to recommend their accounts of God either. There is a long list of problems with the New Age God notion that are more substantial than its inability to fit with the Bible, however.

The energy that spiritualists, psychic healers, chi masters, and New Age believers are describing is not the same energy that modern physicists study (or that Einstein studied, for that matter). Energy in physics is electromagnetic (EM) radiation. At lower wavelength energies, we find gamma radiation and x-rays. A small range of the electromagnetic spectrum is visible light (about four hundred to seven hundred nanometers). And at the high wavelength end of the spectrum we find microwaves and radio waves. We have centuries of exhaustive scientific investigation that has established the existence of EM radiation. If the energy to which these believers refer is different than EM radiation, we do not have evidence, aside from their word, that any such thing exists. If they mean that EM radiation is God, then they are simply mistaken on several counts. Electromagnetic radiation is not what is typically meant by "God" for the billions of believers on the planet. Electromagnetic radiation is not all-powerful; it is not all-knowing; it is not all-good; it is not the designing agent that planned and brought about the creation of the universe; it is not something that we should pray to, or something with which we should form a personal relationship.

One of the reasons that the classic, monotheistic God, who is omnipotent, omniscient, and omnibenevolent, has been so influential in the history of religion is that such a being—if one exists—would be worthy of worship. If there was such a being, the implications for your life, your consciousness, your future, your relationships, and your conduct would be profound. Such a being would be worthy of study, emulation, profound respect, awe, dedication, obedience, and complete devotion. The physical force that warms up burritos in your microwave oven, or the energy the dentist uses to take pictures of your wisdom teeth, is none of these things.

Furthermore, the adherents to the various human religions in history do not appear to think that what they are doing is compatible with or the same thing as what all the other religions' adherents are doing. Many Catholics do not believe that what the Muslims are doing is just as good. Pentecostals do not believe that they are worshipping the same God as the Buddhists. And many believers have dedicated vast amounts of time and energy to making very clear the ways in which they think they are different and the ways in which they think all the other practitioners are wrong. Many of the individual religious sects are quite explicit that the other sects are mistaken; their gods aren't real, they worship false gods, and my god forbids that sort of idolatry. As noted in the Christian Bible, "You shall have no other gods before me" (Exodus 20:3). From a very high altitude, it may be possible to make vacuous claims such as, "they are all really just doing the same thing." But we have to blur the details here so much that *same* scarcely means anything at all. We can assert that bacteria and humans both "eat," for example. But the differences are obviously more important than the similarities if we want to get beyond sixth-grade science class.

While it is tempting to redefine *God* simply to mean *love*, or *spirituality*, or some other word that few people find offensive, there are more powerful reasons not to. The term *God* has a very clear set of connotations and denotations in our cultures. What the three major monotheistic religious traditions—Christianity, Islam, and Judaism—agree upon and mean by the term is the all-powerful, all-knowing, and all-good creator of the universe who dispenses justice on human-kind. Deciding to use the term in a new way doesn't make those associations go away. It doesn't clarify the concept or edify anyone who is trying to understand what God is. The billions of people in those traditions don't understand the term in this New Age form. Many of them explicitly reject it. That's not what they mean. And that's not what they want the term to stand for.

Skeptics, agnostics, and atheists want to call it what it is. If we can find some solace in thinking about love or spirituality, or if we think it is an admirable goal to spread love and spirituality in the world, then let's call it that. If we mean the laws of nature or electromagnetic radiation, then we have clear terms for those phenomena. The *God* term has baggage. It's been the rallying cry behind pogroms, crusades, inquisitions, religious tribunals, theocracies, brutal oppression, genocide, and wars, among other things. And the goals there were not to spread fuzzy ideals of love and spirituality.

No one will deny that love is a good thing. If more people loved each other, it would be good for all of us. But truisms about love, God, and energy won't help any of us deal with the very real menace of supernatural thinking, religious fundamentalism, and theocratic political agendas that pose serious threats to our lives, our freedom, and our future. By refusing to take the question of God seriously, the New Age believer ignores the people who think that God told them to strap on a bomb and blow up a bus. He ignores the ones who think that evangelical Christianity needs to be imposed upon everyone on the globe. And he ignores the ones who are trying to exacerbate the hostilities in Israel between Jews and Palestinians in order to hasten the coming of the Apocalypse and Judgment Day.

In the end, there is no avoiding making some claims about what is real and what is not. There's no way to avoid the truth problem. Either what is being claimed about the world, its origins, and humankind's place in it is accurate or it is not. And either we have good reasons to think it is true or we don't. What are those claims and what is the evidence for them? Does all life emanate from some spiritual force? Is some supernatural, conscious, or personal force responsible for the creation of the universe or not? Do we entirely cease to exist when we die or not? What are our reasons for thinking so?

At first glance it may appear that this open-minded approach to other faiths can solve a lot of problems. But there are more questions that it raises. Where does this liberality end? Is it confined to Christians, or to Protestants? Can Hindus get into heaven, too? What about Muslims? Zoroastrians? Judging from other polls about how much Americans revile atheists, we will assume that they won't allow atheists, too. The point is that there will be lines to draw, and in the end these lines will be sectarian or doctrinal. And now we are back to the same problem. The believer has arrived at the conclusion that there is a God and that God has certain features in virtue of which he rewards or blesses some and punishes or rejects others. So the looming questions will be the following: What are our grounds for thinking that such a being exists and that he has these properties and not some others? Why is this account of God correct in believers' minds rather than some other account? These believers often respond to criticisms of religion with comments like, "Well, that's not real Christianity," or "The real Islam isn't like that."

The "many paths, one God" mentality is a form of intellectual laziness. It reflects a refusal to ponder the implications of one's actions, one's words, one's behaviors and appreciate their meanings. The skeptic wants to get the details about this being onto the table to see what it is and what grounds there might be for believing in it. If they don't hold up to scrutiny, then this notion of god needs to go on the scrap heap of bad ideas from history.

IS THE NONLITERAL BELIEVER EQUIVOCATING?

When people are prompted to give an account of what God is and they know that what they say is under scrutiny, they are inclined to describe a "theologically correct" being. That is, after centuries of debate and scholarly inquiry, philosophers and theologians have developed a highly abstract description of a being who possesses a set of carefully defined properties. Questions and challenges about the notion of God that the Old Testament Hebrews touted, for instance, have led us to explain God in ways that are less easily rejected as implausible. The general direction of these accounts has been away from anthropomorphism. And the New Age account of God can be seen to be doing the same thing. It moves away from a male authoritarian figure who passes judgment with punishments or rewards, and it moves toward a nebulous, impersonal, universal force.

The most simple, and objectionable, accounts of God are also the most anthropomorphic. God is conceived of as a person who occupies specific times and places, perhaps the way we do. He goes walking in the Garden of Eden, he argues with contrary humans, he impregnates women, he has desires and beliefs, he learns about events, he reacts to human actions as if he didn't see them coming, and so on. Characterizing God in personal terms such as these is at odds with the more abstract and infinite properties of infinite energy, power, and transcendence. The abstract God is not easily reconciled with the personal God. If God is the infinitely powerful creator of the universe, why would he resort to such terrestrial and human means to achieve his ends as messengers, floods, sermons, and petty miracles? If God is transcendent and outside of time and space, how and why is it that he forms a personal, loving, intimate relationship with you when you pray on Tuesday night at 10:32 p.m. in Pittsburgh?

In practice, many believers appeal to whichever description is necessary to address the questions at hand. If someone is enduring some hardships, then God is a personal, loving presence who will help her through her difficult time. If the skeptic raises hard questions about how to reconcile the existence of God with what we know about the origins of the universe and life, then God is transcendent, he is energy, he is pure spirit. The personal-God talk, the nonliteral believer may insist, is really just metaphorical and shouldn't be taken that seriously. Excessively anthropomorphic accounts of God are slightly embarrassing to the believer, or the nonbeliever who focuses on these types of accounts has failed to see the real nature of God.

Some recent evidence from cognitive psychology sheds some important light on our equivocations about God's nature. It appears that when prompted, or when they are being careful, people will typically give a theologically correct, abstract, and less personal account of God. But when they are tested in ways that reveal their unspoken assumptions and their default ideas about God, they have an individual person in mind who lives in space and time, who acts like a human, who hears (God has ears?!), who literally watches (God has eyes?!), and who goes first to one place to answer a prayer and then to another to perform a minor miracle.

Psychologists Justin L. Barrett and Frank C. Keil investigated the extent to which people anthropomorphize in their characterizations of God depending on the context. They played audio recordings of brief stories to a number of subjects and then asked them questions about the events of the story. Barrett and Keil's hypothesis was that if the subjects had strong anthropomorphic ideas about God, then they would unknowingly fill in details of the stories to answer the questions that were more anthropomorphic than the stories' details. So they were given this story, for example:

> It was a clear, sunny day. Two birds were singing back and forth to each other. They were perched in a large oak tree next to an airport. God was listening to the birds. One would sing and then the other would sing. One bird had blue, white, and silver feathers. The other bird had dull gray feathers.

While God was listening to the birds, a large jet landed. It was extremely loud: the birds couldn't even hear each other. The air was full of fumes. God listened to the jet until it turned off its engines. God finished listening to the birds.

And here's the amazing part. When questioned about the story, subjects made comments such as these:

> "God was listening to two birds singing in a tall tree next to an airport. When a large jet landed, God listened to it because he could no longer hear the birds. Then he listened to the birds again."
> "A jet came and began destroying the beauty and even took God's attention away."
> "The noise was so loud God couldn't hear the birds."
> "God could only hear the jet until it turned off its engines."

They were also given this story:

A boy was swimming alone in a swift and rocky river. The boy got his left leg caught between two large, gray rocks and couldn't get out. Branches of trees kept bumping into him as they hurried past. He thought he was going to drown and so he began to struggle and pray. Though God was answering another prayer in another part of the world when the boy started praying, before long God responded by pushing one of the rocks so the boy could get his leg out. The boy struggled to the river bank and fell over exhausted.

And when questioned about the story, they gave highly anthropomorphic answers such as this one: "This story suggests that God cannot listen to more than one prayer at a time, however, he will get to each prayer and answer it in time. Much like Santa Claus delivers toys to all houses in one night."[16]

For all of our fancy, philosophical, and theologically abstract descriptions of God as the transcendent source of reality, what's really lurking in many believers' heads is an idea of God who is pretty much the bearded guy in the robe, a human with magical powers. The evidence indicates that the image they have in mind isn't far off from Santa Claus. If they were pressed on the point—does God really have ears? Does he have to go first to one part of the earth to help one person and then to another?—they would probably tell a very different story.

We know that the urge to be religious and believe in God is very strong. What the study suggests is that we morph our image or description of God to suit the particular needs of the situation, even when those images conflict. It is difficult to know for sure, as not even the moderate believer may be able to tell this about himself, but it may be that the moderate believer is equivocating when it comes to the God he believes in. In some contexts, God is a real, personal being with power, knowledge, and goodness; in other contexts, God is a mere abstraction of spiritual energy. And if something like this is going on in the believer's head, then he is confused and equivocating. Either God exists or he does not. And either he has a specific set of features or he does not. And we cannot form a coherent or plausible account of the truth or what's real by playing so fast and loose with our descriptions.

ATHEIST PREACHERS

We have been considering what many nonliteral believers would characterize as the positive side of their engagement with religion. But there are other, darker aspects for people in this peculiar intersection of views. Many people feel the tremendous social and familial pressure to keep up religious appearances long after they have ceased to believe. For them, the situation can amount to a kind of entrapment. Surrounded by believers—spouses, children, family, friends, and community—and knowing the enormous disapproval that not practicing religion would garner them, they settle into a kind of resigned cooperation. In its most acute form, this conflict manifests as preachers, priests, or clergy who have ceased to believe.

Philosopher Daniel Dennett and Linda LaScola, a clinical social worker, have done something quite remarkable in "Preachers Who Are Not Believers."[17] Through private channels, Dennett and LaScola have found a number of practicing clergy in American Christian churches who do not believe in God. They have compiled several extensive interviews with these clergy members about the curious lives they are living. These are preachers and ministers who give sermons, sing God's praises, lead prayers, offer counsel, and advise—all within the Christian community—but for all intents and purposes, they are atheists. Dennett and LaScola have gotten them to talk openly about how they came to doubt their convictions, what their lives are like, what their futures hold, their relationships with their families and other believers, and what it's like to be "in the closet."

The revelations are telling. All of them have struggled to find ways to deal with the intense cognitive dissonance of their situations.

> Here's how I'm handling my job on Sunday mornings: I see it as play acting. I kind of see myself as taking on a role of a believer in a worship service, and performing. Because I know what to say. I know how to pray publicly. I can lead singing. I love singing. I don't believe what I'm saying anymore in some of these songs. But I see it as taking on the role and performing. Maybe that's what it takes for me to get myself through this, but that's what I'm doing.[18]

It is also evident that the comfort and security of an ecumenical job has a lot to do with their staying with the church.

> So maybe there'll be a divorce between myself and the Presbyterian Church. I need to feel fulfilled, and I need to provide for myself and my family. I can go back and get new education and training, but I've got to do something.[19]

> I'm where I am because I need the job still. If I had an alternative, a comfortable paying job, something I was interested in doing, and a move that wouldn't destroy my family, that's where I'd go. Because I do feel kind of hypocritical.[20]

> If somebody said, "Here's $200,000," I'd be turning my notice in this week, saying, "A month from now is my last Sunday." Because then I can pay off everything.[21]

And all of them cite the difficulties in reconciling what the Bible really says with what they learned in Sunday school. Actually sitting down and reading

the Bible carefully and looking at the textual-criticism literature generated a
crisis of faith for all of them. They came to realize that they couldn't actually
believe that Adam and Eve were the first humans, or that a guy lived in the
belly of a whale, or that Jesus was born from a virgin. They also acknowledge
the profound problems with literal interpretations of the Bible or with putting
too much stock in anything the Bible states, given its convoluted history.

> Well, I think most Christians have to be in a state of denial to read the
> Bible and believe it. Because there are so many contradicting stories. You're
> encouraged to be violent on one page, and you're encouraged to give sacri-
> ficial love on another page. You're encouraged to bash a baby's head on one
> page, and there's other pages that say, you know, give your brother your fair
> share of everything you have if they ask for it.[22]

> Most clergy take beliefs metaphorically, not as literally true. Given that
> assumption, there is quite a lot of creative wiggle room.[23]

All of the respondents report that doubts like their own are widespread among
others in their trade. But there is an unwritten code of silence, a secret that
each one acquires individually, and each one knows that the others know it,
but no one dares acknowledge it publicly.

The confessions here give us some new insights into some of the most
mystifying behaviors of the clergy that nonbelievers have observed with incre-
dulity. The nonbelievers can't fathom how smart, educated, thoughtful people
can possibly believe the things that they seem to earnestly report believing.
Skeptics grow frustrated with what appear to be endless, convoluted rationalizations, evasions, and logical gymnastics from believers. And skeptics cannot
see how the believers can really mean what they are saying. The simple answer
suggested by the Dennett and LaScola study is that many of them don't.

What several of the atheist clergy acknowledge is the legitimacy and
seriousness of the challenges and arguments that atheists have been raising
against the received views within their sects. For some of them, the atheistic
arguments changed their views about God. They acknowledge that many scientific claims cannot be reconciled with religious doctrines; God cannot be an
anthropomorphic, personal being. We don't have sufficient evidence to prove

a virgin birth or a resurrection. Pointless suffering cannot be reconciled with a loving creator. God doesn't fulfill some necessary explanatory function in the world, and so on.

The accurate and not uncharitable way to characterize them is that they are systematic liars. Admittedly, they think that they can continue to preach, sing, pray, and counsel toward some greater, positive, humanitarian goals. But the simple fact is that in order to continue doing what they see as good work, atheist clergy members must flatly lie to people who trust them and who do not have the benefit of their education to know better. They exploit the ignorance and fears of the masses. They leverage their extensive training and experience in apologetics, casuistry, psychology, and counseling to manipulate their congregations into believing things that they acknowledge are false. Even worse, these atheists continue to implant stories that they don't believe into the heads of children where the stories will take hold and create a new lifelong struggle to reconcile deep-seated and emotional convictions from childhood with the reality they discover as adults. Ironically, despite the staggering conflict and anguish in their own minds, the atheist clergy members persist in propagating the ideology that will duplicate that inner turmoil in the minds of thousands of others. They conceal their struggle in order to inflict it on others.

If they weren't responsible for such a harmful misrepresentation, their stories would be more heartbreaking. They have been trapped in a prison where they cannot say publicly any of what they think is true. They will lose their jobs, their support networks, and their families. And they have been made to suffer tremendous psychological tensions in order to keep up appearances while sealing off their doubts.

> I didn't plan to become an atheist. I didn't even want to become an atheist. It's just that I had no choice. If I'm being honest with myself . . . I want to understand Christianity, and that's what I've tried to do. And I've wanted to be a Christian. I've tried to be a Christian, and all the ways they say to do it. It just didn't add up.[24]

> The love stuff is good. And you can still believe in that, and live a life like that. But the whole grand scheme of Christianity, for me, is just a bunch of bunk.[25]

When we see the conflict of these preachers' inner lives, an obvious truth confronts us. It must be better for all of us to live a coherent, consistent, and honest life than to misrepresent our beliefs by aping religious conviction. And the lapsed preachers also make it clear how extensive the effects of one person's mimicking belief can be on those around him. Their continued participation in Christianity cultivates real belief, not just nonliteral participation, in many of those around them. And each new generation of believers that is created by this false propagation becomes part of the rolling expansion of a set of ideas that its promoters have admitted are false.

BAD FAITH

We can assume that there are many more preachers, priests, and religious leaders with serious doubts about what they are saying and doing than just the small group brave enough or fed up enough to speak to Dennett and LaScola. And in many congregations, there are many more people who would acknowledge that they are what we have been calling nonliteral believers. There will be many more in a congregation who do not really believe but because of social pressure, family concerns, habit, and personal investment, they would not openly admit to their real feelings.

So here is a large group of people engaged in sermons, teaching, songs, prayers, psalms, liturgies, ceremonies, and rituals where a significant proportion of them would actually reject the truth that is alleged to underlie what they are doing. Imagine the surreal and absurd situation of a whole church where all the adults, including the priests or preachers, are actually atheists. The only people who have genuine beliefs are the children who have listened earnestly and have taken to heart the Sunday-school lessons taught to them by the (disbelieving) adults. There may never have been a whole church like this, but Dennett and LaScola's study suggests that it is a possibility and that a significant portion of some of the most important and influential movements in human history may have this strange and specious character. Psychologists Daniel Katz and Floyd Allport coined the term *pluralistic ignorance* for a situation where the majority of a group privately reject some norm, but they assume that most of the others accept it when in fact they don't. The norm gets perpetuated, sometimes with great harm.[26]

Jean Paul Sartre coined the term *living in bad faith* to describe the situation of a person who lives inauthentically, who engages in self-deception in his or her outward presentation of what he or she is in contrast to what he or she knows intellectually to be true. For Sartre, living in bad faith generates the worst sort of dishonesty and philosophical paradox. The description could not be more apt and ironic for the duplicitous nonbelievers.

CONCLUSION

This chapter has answered several questions about what nonliteral belief is and what the motivations are that may lead people to adopt it. More importantly, our discussion has presented a long list of problems with this weaker variety of belief. It fosters bad cognitive practice. It contributes to a set of counterproductive and dangerous belief standards. It amounts to a sort of bad faith, an active self-misdirection. It exacerbates some negative cognitive dispositions that would be better rectified by training and discipline in critical thinking and problem solving. Engaging in this form of practice puts you at odds with yourself as though saying, "I don't actually believe (most?) of this stuff, and I can't reconcile it with the other things I know, but I'm going to talk, behave, worship, sing, pray, and interact with others as if I do." There is no way to avoid adopting some criteria of evaluation about which conceptions of God are acceptable and which are objectionable. By settling for or participating in the religious traditions we know, we endorse and propagate them. And by endorsing and propagating, we create more of the same in the world. The decision to do so shouldn't be haphazard or unconscious. We must take responsibility for our actions, their impacts on others, and their implications. If we hope to develop a coherent picture of reality, we must demand more from ourselves and others in our personal and cognitive practices.

Chapter 13

ATHEISM AND THE
CASE AGAINST CHRIST

Hundreds of millions of humans on the planet profess to be Christians, hundreds of millions more claim to believe in God, and many more believe in some more nebulous form of divinity. In the United States alone, 100 to 150 million people claim to believe that Jesus was the son of God and he was resurrected from the dead; three in ten Americans believe that the Bible is the actual word of God and is to be taken literally.[1]

The essential doctrine of Christianity is that after three days of being dead in a tomb, Jesus miraculously returned from the dead. His return has been taken to be an unequivocal demonstration of his divine powers and a corroboration of his claims to be the son of God. It is symbolic of God's love for humanity, and Jesus' self-sacrifice on the cross is thought to afford us some moral and metaphysical absolution for our misdeeds.

We have seen how deeply mistaken and unjustified these beliefs are, given the problems with the evidence. We cannot be thoughtful, reasonable people with intellectual integrity and accept that Jesus was resurrected from the dead. We have seen that for the Christian, believing in the resurrection is inconsistent with the epistemic standards that we employ for other comparable supernatural or extraordinary propositions. The case for Jesus' performing magical acts is even weaker than the evidence we have for witchcraft at Salem, for example, yet reasonable people refuse to accept the latter. We would not accept a comparable alien-abduction story if the evidence was as poor in its favor as it is for Jesus' return. The problem would also be vividly clear if someone were wrongly accused of a murder on the basis of comparably bad evidence. Convicting them on grounds that resemble the evidence we have for the resurrection would be a gross injustice. The incongruity makes it clear that if it were not for the considerable cultural and psychological traction that the tradition has, we would lump Christianity in with the rest of the superstitions, dead gods, spiritual tales, alien-abduction stories, and mythologies that we routinely reject as silly.

We have also elaborated on the specific problems that make the historical case so weak. The information is sketchy at best. It comes to us through a highly convoluted, selective, and unreliable conduit. A variety of factors have compromised the fidelity of transmission across the many links of the chain. We have seen that there are numerous reasons to doubt the alleged eyewitnesses, the repeaters, the authors, the copiers, and the canonizers. Problems with the transmission of the stories accumulate and compound over the centuries, amplifying the probability that the information we received cannot be trusted. So we have seen that Christianity is built upon a grand historical and epistemological mistake.

We've also concluded more generally that an all-powerful, all-knowing, all-good God would not perform miracles. The miracles that form the essential foundation of so many human religions cannot be reconciled with the sort of acts that a being like God would do. God would not employ such indirect, ineffectual, or impotent means to accomplish his ends. Miracles make perfect sense, however, as the products of human imagination and error.

Furthermore, the quantity and quality of evidence about miracles and God that we have should have been much better if God had wanted us to form a reasonable, justified belief about his existence. Making the resurrection believable for reasonable people would have been a trivial act for God.

Nor will appeals to faith vindicate religious belief. Helping yourself to a belief that can't be justified with adequate evidential grounds violates the believer's epistemic, social, and moral duties to himself and to the rest of us. Taking the faith route opens the floodgates to an endless list of other supernatural beings and leaves the believer with no principled or reasoned grounds of preference for Christianity. If faith is permissible, then anything goes. And finally, we have seen that more liberal, metaphorical, or New Age varieties of belief in God mire the believer in cognitive bad practice, inauthenticity, and, ironically, bad faith.

THE CASE FOR ATHEISM

The term *atheist* describes a person who does not believe that God or a divine being exists. It has come to be widely accepted that to be an atheist is to affirm the nonexistence of God. British philosopher Antony Flew called this *positive atheism*, whereas to merely lack a belief that God or gods exist is called *negative atheism*.[2] Parallels for this use of the term are *amoral, atypical*, or *asymmetrical*. So negative atheism would include someone who has never reflected on the question of whether God exists and who has no opinion about the matter. It would also include someone who had thought about the matter a great deal and has concluded either that she has insufficient evidence to decide the question, or that the question cannot be resolved in principle. *Agnosticism* is traditionally characterized as neither believing that God exists nor believing that God does not exist. Agnostics, because they lack a belief in God, are negative atheists.

Atheism can also be narrow or wide in scope. The narrow atheist does not believe in the existence of a particular description of a divine being, such as the omni-God, or the Muslims' Allah, for example. Christians are typically narrow atheists about Allah. A wide atheist does not believe that any gods exist, including the traditional omni-God, Jehovah, Allah, and so on. The wide positive atheist denies that God exists, and she also denies that Zeus, Gefjun, Thor, Sobek, Bakunawa, and others exist. The narrow atheist might reject the existence of the Christian God but need not take a stronger view about the existence or nonexistence of other supernatural beings.[3]

So what sort of atheism is justified now that the case for Christ has been so thoroughly undermined? At the very least, we should be narrow positive atheists about the Christian God. Without the resurrection, without miracles, and with so many internal paradoxes, we must reject too many essential aspects of Christianity.

What about other gods? Can any notion of a supernatural being be salvaged? Much of what we have said specifically about Christianity and the resurrection story applies to a wide range of other religious beliefs and traditions. When ancient sources propagate stories about fantastic supernatural events, special human encounters with God, or other miraculous phenomena, we should have the same concerns: the Salem witch trials; the Lourdes, France, problem; failed prayers; mistaken paranormal beliefs; ignorance; receptiveness to supernatural claims; confirmation bias; bereavement hallucinations; co-opted memories; false memories; embellished memories; source amnesia; social conformity; the Asche effect; groupthink; the IQ problem; the Flynn effect; the Dunning-Kruger effect; the invisible-gorilla problem; anti-introspectionism research; the money-bag problem; the canonization problem; the counterevidence problem; the disconfirmation problem; the problem of miracles for God; the faith problem; problems with nonliteral interpretations; the New Age God problem; the problem of other religions; and so on. The analysis of Christianity has made it possible for us to build a rough model for the critical examination of the foundations of all human religions. Our model is based on well-founded research about how religious (and other) ideas emerge and then flourish in populations of human cognitive systems. We understand how these ideas originate and then spread by natural—not supernatural—causes in human minds. My model of religious analysis should lead us to reject the many gods of human religions because it offers a much more plausible account of their origins. My model shows how high the burden of proof for a real supernatural being is, and it shows how miserably human efforts to justify their gods have failed.

Islam shares some ancient sources with Judaism and the Christian Old Testament, but Muslims view the Koran as the literal revelations of the will of Allah. Muhammad is reported to have retreated to a cave where he began to have overpowering visions of the archangel Gabriel who instructed him in the will and the words of Allah. Muhammad, filled with a new, evangelical spirit to spread his revelations to others, reported these visions to his followers, who are alleged to have faithfully written them down. Reportedly, Muhammad refused to appeal to miracles to demonstrate the authenticity of his connection to God. Rather, the Koran itself and the massive growth of Islam are treated as standing miracle testimony to its own authenticity. Muhammad was alleged to be nearly illiterate, so his production of such a remarkable book of insight, poetry, and spiritual guidance is thought to demonstrate its supernatural origin. In the Koran, God is thought to be speaking in the first person. So Muslims are "therefore inclined to consider each individual sentence of the

Holy Book as a separate revelation and to experience the words themselves, ever their sounds, as a means of grace."[4]

We can see that Islam is not likely to fare any better against the long list of doubts that have been raised against Christianity. The argument against Islam will be the same in outline, even though the details of how my naturalized model of religious analysis will differ. A full treatment of Islam would take a volume of its own. But we can see that, as with Christianity, there are too many naturalistic explanations that make better sense of the origins, propagation, and appeal of the tenets of Islam. Ironically, I think that if the argument from the Salem witch trials (in chapter 3) or the problems with believing the believers (from chapter 4) were presented in their parallel forms against Islam, many believers in non-Islamic religions would readily acknowledge the refutation. Likewise, many Muslims may be sympathetic with my rejection of Christianity. That is, Christians might be inclined to accept that my arguments apply successfully to Islam, and Muslims might acknowledge that the arguments undermine Christianity. My point, and the only consistent position, is that both collapse when we apply my analysis. We also have substantial research showing a *bias bias* in humans; we acknowledge fallacies and errors in thinking in others more readily than we see them in ourselves.[5] The challenge, we have seen, is to achieve consistency and objectivity in evidential principles and rational analysis despite the pervasive and subtle effects of bias. Given the frequency of powerful visions of divinity in human populations, and the rest of what we have learned about how religious ideas gain traction and spread, we should assume provisionally that Islam springs from natural—not supernatural—origins.

Joseph Smith, the founder of Mormonism, reported being seized by visions of light and an angel who gave him directions to a set of golden plates buried by Native American prophets in Manchester, New York. Smith claimed to have translated the plates to create the Book of Mormon, but he refused to let anyone else see into the box that was alleged to hold them. After he translated them, Smith returned the plates to the angel and they were never seen again. Mormonism fares no better against the long list of doubts in this book.

Even in movements such as Buddhism, where the Buddha advocated against using miracles to substantiate his teachings, miracle reports abound.

He is reported to have created with his mind a golden bridge in the air and then walked on it. He tamed a wild elephant with only his touch. He flew in the air and performed other remarkable feats.

The Jewish Torah shares versions of a number of the stories from the Christian Old Testament about God's creation of the world, God's destruction of the enemies of Israel, and the miraculous benefits God bestowed on his chosen people.

There are more miracle stories that play integral parts in the religions of the world than we could hope to document. This book has constructed a template for taking those claims seriously and examining the evidence. The prospects for believing them depend upon addressing a long list of questions. We have seen that Christianity rests upon a mistake. In the broader picture, the analysis of the faulty processes that generate and sustain religious beliefs undermines a wide class of the theological claims with which we are confronted today. Our doubts about the origins of Christianity should extend to these other religions.

Just consider the role that visions of angels play in the origination and perpetuation of human religious belief. The angel Moroni appears to Joseph Smith and gives him God's revelation. The archangel Gabriel appears to Muhammad and gives him Allah's revelations. Angels in white appear to Mary in the tomb and tell her that Jesus has been resurrected. A burning bush appears to Moses and gives him God's laws. An angel appears to Daniel. An angel appears to Jesus. An angel appears to the Apostles. Angels appear to Joseph, Peter, Philip, Paul, John, and so on. Half of Americans believe they are protected by guardian angels.[6] Now consider a list of just a few of the physiological causes that we know to be responsible for these sorts of experiences: hypoxia, brain trauma, sleep deprivation, fasting, dehydration, starvation, altered states of consciousness, schizophrenia, mental illness, bipolar disorder, blood loss, sudden drops in blood pressure, shock, auditory and visual hallucinations, and so on. Give me a group of subjects (and relax those meddlesome ethical restrictions on human testing) and we can have them all raving about seeing angels in a few hours. There are predictable, well-documented physiological causes that produce these experiences on a regular basis in a significant percentage of the human population. Now we realize that we must approach those stories with the appropriate level of skepticism, and when we do, a huge portion of the edifice of belief in God, Christian and otherwise, collapses.

Our concerns are not just with miraculous, angel, or other supernatural religious claims. Religious traditions make assertions about alleged historical facts and present us with claims about the nature of reality. Our religious traditions assert that God or some gods are real, they portend to give us an accurate account of the origins of the universe and humanity, and they claim to accurately describe the place of humanity in a spiritual and metaphysical framework. They locate us in relationship to supernatural forces or some larger, unseen reality. Insofar as any religious tradition makes assertions about historical facts, miracles, or, simply put, *reality*, we have a long list of questions and doubts that should lead us to reject them. Given the arguments of this book that undermine so many important religious claims, we are justified in adopting a broad, pervasive skepticism about religious models of the world. Fool me once, shame on you; misrepresent matters of vast moral, personal, historical, and metaphysical significance the way human religions do, and I will demand that a very high burden of proof be met before I accept anything you say.

L. Ron Hubbard's Scientologists hold that seventy-five million years ago, the galactic tyrant Xenu ruled dozens of planets, including the Earth, which was then called Teegeeack. The planets were overpopulated so Xenu captured billions of people, froze them, and transported them by spacecraft to be dumped into volcanoes on Teegeeack. Nuclear bombs were set off in the volcanoes and the disembodied souls of the victims were liberated from their bodies. Now those souls, or thetans, attach themselves to living people and inflict psychic suffering on them. The cure can be found in Scientology's deprogramming or auditing procedures, which also, coincidentally, are quite expensive.

When viewed from a sufficient height, the Scientology story is no more initially implausible than people with special powers defying the laws of physics; corpses returning from the dead; visitations by transcendent, angelic beings; and magical ascents into an otherworldly existence.

If the essential foundations of the traditions that offer us these pictures of the world have been undermined, and if we doubt or reject the events that are alleged to give those traditions their authority and authenticity, then what grounds do we have for accepting anything else in their model of the world? They have proven to be highly unreliable sources of accurate information on too many other issues. The claims that a religious doctrine makes about the world should not be afforded special respect or authenticity because of our affection for religion or the mystique surrounding its origins. If it is justified to accept any religion's doctrinal claim about the world, then it will be because it fits the evidence, not because it is alleged to emanate from a supernatural source. We have too many legitimate doubts about the alleged supernatural sources of other human religions. We have seen that in many cases, religious pictures of reality have survived and spread because they exploit the defects of the human cognitive system. And what we know about the human propensity toward religiousness and our credulity about religious claims ought to figure largely in our evaluation of those claims, too. Our knowledge of human psychology justifies a substantial skepticism about religions.

Once we have conducted the broader critical analysis of religious claims begun by this book and removed those claims from play, what leg does believing in God have left to stand on? It's not reasonable to believe the major historical religious traditions' essential claims about reality. We are all atheists about the existence of hundreds or thousands of the gods from other human religions. And now we've seen compelling reasons to add the most influential gods in human religious history to the scrap heap. We have seen why it is reasonable to conclude that there is no Ahti, Baiame, Suiren, Damballa, Gunfled, Vaisravana, Hermes, Nzambi, Maahes, Nebo, Ogoun, Tagd, Ogma, Weneg, Perkele, or Zonget. Our reasons for rejecting Achtupa, Baal, and Puluga, are parallel to our reasons for rejecting the resurrection, Christianity, Islam, and the rest. Are we proving the negative yet? Do we not have enough reason to adopt wide positive atheism at this point?

I can imagine someone resisting wide positive atheism at this point in a couple of different ways. She might think that it is necessary to address every god before she can draw a reasonable conclusion in favor of a defeasible, wide positive atheism. In some cases, critics deny that wide positive atheism is justified because it is not possible to *prove the negative*. The assumption seems to be that in order for us to believe some claim reasonably, call it true, and treat it as a fact, we must give some sort of comprehensive and deductive demonstration of it. Or someone might resist wide positive atheism at this point in favor of agnosticism. He may have the sense that caution is warranted because arguments undermining the historical religions show only the failure of their supporting bodies of evidence; they do not show that there is no God or no gods. In what remains of this chapter, I will raise a number of considerations that should satisfy those who still have a quarrel with wide positive atheism.

THE GOD OF THE PHILOSOPHERS AND THE GODS OF RELIGIONS

Traditionally, there are three families of arguments from philosophical and theological circles that have been offered for the existence of God: ontological, cosmological, and teleological. Instead of addressing those, we've been analyzing God and gods from the ground up. We've been considering the miracles, religious texts, or accounts of the manifestations of religious beings in religious history. Philosophers and theologians have typically taken a top-down approach by seeing if there are conceptual considerations or inductive grounds for concluding that God is real. Then perhaps the religious accounts of God could be fortified or corroborated by those independent efforts to discover God.

Long ago, philosophers and theologians settled on the notion of an omnipotent, omniscient, and infinitely good being. A being of this sort would be worthy of the title "God." Many have taken an argument from J. N. Findlay to be pivotal. Findlay, like many others, argues that in order to be worthy of the label "God," and in order to be worthy of a worshipful attitude of reverence, emulation, and unrestrained admiration, the being that is the object of that attitude must be inescapable, necessary, and unsurpassably supreme.[7] A lesser being in any respect might warrant respect, emulation, or perhaps fear. But we should insist, with Findlay, that the title "God" be reserved for the ultimate omnicharacterization of God. To adopt a religious attitude of worship toward a lesser being would be idolatrous or misguided. We are also motivated to focus our attention on this conception of an omnibeing because it

280 ATHEISM AND THE CASE AGAINST CHRIST

would fit, roughly, with the divine beings portrayed in religious history. What the Christian, Jewish, and Islamic traditions seem to have in common is that, at some point or other, they all ascribe the ultimate amount of power to God. Furthermore, he knows everything, and he is morally perfect, or infinitely loving. So for millennia, when philosophers and theologians have directed their efforts at proof, it has been toward this sort of being because this is the only sort of being that is really worthy of our interest and the title. If this being isn't real, then the lesser beings are not worth bothering about. That is to say, narrow atheism about this sort of being is wide enough to address any religious being that matters.

In order to justify concluding that there is no God, does one have to address all the serious attempts at proving God? A number of philosophers have tackled this monumental project. They have systematically analyzed the best arguments that we have to date for the existence of God. Finding all of them wanting, they have rejected theism.[8]

But doubts about the existence of God are not limited to these philosophers. In a recent survey of over three thousand professional philosophers, a clear trend emerges: 73 percent of them accept or lean toward atheism with only about 15 percent accepting or leaning toward theism.[9] The vast majority of experts in the field, the ones who are most familiar with our most sophisticated efforts at finding some proof of God, are unconvinced. The proofs, as they see them, don't work. As Findlay said in 1948, "The general philosophical verdict is that none of these 'proofs' is truly compelling."[10]

Even if someone finds some version of one of the proofs to be more plausible than philosophers have, closing the circle between the God of the philosophers and the specific Christian, Islamic, or Jewish God proves to be insurmountable, particularly for teleological and cosmological arguments. That is, we cannot get to the Gods of the major historical religions from the arguments the philosophers are giving for God. Teleological arguments attempt to show that the best explanation of the complexity, organization, or order of the natural world is the existence of a designer with power and knowledge sufficient to the task. The problem is that these arguments, even if they succeed in giving us a being or beings of great power and great knowledge, don't give us a justification for the God that Christians, Muslims, Jews, and the rest of people actually believe in. The bigger problem for teleological arguments is that infinite goodness or moral perfection is not manifest in the order of nature such that we could attribute either of them to the designer. If there is a force behind the universe, it is far from evident that it is good willing at all. Indeed, in many of the discussions of the problem of evil, theists have been at great pains just to establish that the creator of the universe is *possibly* good willing, benevolent, or morally perfect. If the best that philosophical theism can do is argue that the cause of the universe is possibly good, then we cannot justify concluding that there is a god that is.

Cosmological arguments allege to prove the existence of some first cause that created the universe. Again, as a group, even if this sort of argument succeeds, the challenge has been to show that there must be one creator, and that it must have infinite power, infinite knowledge, and infinite goodness. While these might be sufficient to have created the universe, none of them is necessary. So, from the existence of the universe, we can't infer that the cause must have them.

Suppose that we could prove the existence of an omni-God by means of one of these philosophical arguments. Could that being be connected with the traditional object of human religious traditions? The Christian God differs in many details from the Islamic God. The Mormon God differs from the Jewish one, and so on.

The cosmological and teleological arguments are motivated by consideration of the first cause of the universe, the big bang, or the complicated structures of organisms. But none of these sorts of evidence motivate uniquely Christian, Muslim, or other religious doctrine. If a rational justification for any particular religion of human history is to be found, we must go to some other source than science or reasoning about necessity and absolute beings. Believers need a reasonable way to bridge the gap from the God of the philosophers to the divine subject of human religions. But we have seen that we cannot accept the religious traditions themselves as reliable sources about human encounters with divine beings. If the religions in human history that gave us our notions of gods have proven to be unwarranted to believe, then it appears that nothing remains to justify believing. The arguments for God's existence fail; even if one of them succeeded, it would not justify the particular God endorsed by historical religious movements; and the arguments of this book have undermined the reliability of the claims made about God by the historical religions. So it appears that there is nothing left to recommend believing in God.

So the prospects for theism of any significant sort look dim. I have presented and defended a model for the critical analysis of religious origins that undermines the biggest religious traditions. For centuries, there have been arguments that purported to show the existence of God. But the ontological arguments, teleological arguments, and cosmological arguments haven't panned out. The widespread view among philosophers is that these arguments fail to give us what they promised. Fallacies or contentious assumptions continue to undermine repeated efforts to restructure them. And even in their best forms, they don't support the notion of a being that would be worthy of the title "God." And the vast majority of trained experts who best know this topic have concluded that God isn't real. We have not salvaged some defensible and meaningful belief in God. Theism is not justified.

If theism is not justified, can we draw the wide positive atheist conclusion? Should we decide, at least provisionally, that there are no gods? We have seen all the best efforts to justify the biggest, most important religious traditions in human history collapse. In light of the arguments of this book, should a reasonable person conclude that none of the gods is real, or should she adopt the more conservative, agnostic view? Perhaps she should decide that she does not know one way or another, so she should suspend judgment. The failure of evidence or arguments in favor of God shows only that those attempts to justify God have failed, they do not show the stronger conclusion that there is no God, right? Our inability to find a cure for cancer thus far doesn't prove that there isn't a cure, after all.

Wide positive atheism is more reasonable than agnosticism. First, a clarification about the atheist conclusion is in order. The belief that no gods exist should be, as with everything else we believe, defeasible. A reasonable person believes that which is justified by her evidence, she proportions the strength of her convictions to the strength of that evidence, and she folds in new information and revises her belief structure accordingly. To continue to believe in the face of outweighing counterevidence or to believe despite a lack of evidence is irrational. The atheist (as well as the agnostic or theist) should be prepared to change her mind if the arguments justify it. With that in mind, I believe we are in a position to conclude on the basis of so many failures to justify our gods that there are no such things. Let's consider the status of our god hypotheses overall.

THE GOD THEORY

Consider the difference between the way the history of science has treated the concepts of *heat* and *demons*. The modern account of heat defines it as the kinetic energy or molecular motion. When one object heats up another, some of that energy is transferred from one object to the other, where the mean level of molecular motion increases. But in the 1700s, alchemists thought that the real nature of heat was a special substance known as phlogiston that moved between objects. After problems with the phlogiston theory developed, scientists postulated the transfer of an invisible fluid known as "caloric" between the objects. When we began to understand molecular energy levels and molecular motion, the term *heat* was retained, but the definition of heat as "caloric" was dropped. The label survived the expansion and change created by progress in scientific knowledge, but only by radically redefining the ultimate nature of the phenomena in question. We still talk about heat, but we mean something very different than they did three hundred years ago.

At one point, demons had their place in our explanations of the world, too. During the Middle Ages, erratic or bizarre behavior in some people was attributed to demon possession. But when our knowledge of the phenomena developed and we began to understand mental illness as a nervous-system pathology, we ultimately abandoned the concept of demons altogether. The idea was too embedded in an outmoded, nonfunctional, unhelpful ontology to make it usable in the better description of the world. Demons were eliminated in favor of a new concept; the term *mental illness* explained the symptoms in the context of a theory that conceived of the problem in terms of a physical illness and neuroscience rather than the elaborate metaphysics countenanced by the demon-possession explanation.

The naturalized model of the origin and growth of religious ideas developed in this book shows that we are at the same stage in history concerning God. The agnostic who resists wide positive atheism will acknowledge that many gods are not real. He might say, "There are people who still harbor a highly anthropomorphic conception of God that varies little from the concept as it was understood by the founders of the Judeo-Christian and Islamic religious traditions. And what you've shown is that holding onto this ancient notion of God is comparable to insisting that demons are the cause of erratic personal behavior or disease. Your arguments show that those supernatural beings aren't real. But that doesn't mean that we should conclude that there is not some other sort of divine being."

But like the question about heat and demons, the questions for this agnostic are: What room is there left for God in the natural order? What explanatory work will postulating God do for us? If God's advocates backpedal from the claims made by the traditional religions when we make advances in science, what sort of being do we have left? In what ways does the room left by the closing gaps leave us with something that is worthy of worship or worthy of the name? Whatever is left no longer resembles the God we started with. And we have seen good reasons for ruling out the divine beings of Christianity, Judaism, Islam, and many other religious traditions. So which god is it that the believer can continue to defend? What is the divine possibility that the agnostic is suspending judgment for the sake of? Why does the believer continue to defend the notion? And why does the agnostic stop at suspension instead of rejection? At some point, aren't we entitled to dismiss the God theory altogether unless some categorically better and new reasons for believing are forthcoming? Imagine that an agnostic confessed, "Yes, I have to acknowledge that Xenu in the Scientology account is preposterous with the souls being fed to volcanoes and all, but even if none of that stuff happened with the enslavement of galactic thetans, I am still agnostic that Xenu in some other form might still exist." At some point, as religious stories about the world unravel, continuing to be agnostic is foot dragging.

Dreams of a perpetual-motion machine have seduced inventors for centuries. A device that could produce more energy than the amount put into it could revolutionize technology, solve the major problems facing humanity, and make the discoverer rich and famous beyond his wildest dreams. For decades, the British and US Patent Offices analyzed diligently every patent application for a perpetual-motion machine that was submitted to them. Thousands of the paper schemes turned out to describe systems that were physically impossible or that didn't work. In the formal sense of deductive disproof, no one has shown that no perpetual motion exists or can exist. But enough failures warrant rejection, not merely agnosticism. Rather than continue to invest enormous portions of their budgets taking the applications seriously, patent offices officially declared an end to the submissions of plans for perpetual-motion machines. The new policy stipulated that if you want a patent on a perpetual-motion machine, you must produce a real, working example. That fixed the problem.

With regard to God, we are in a similar position to the patent offices. We have justifiable doubts that lead us to reject the claims made by a long list of human religions. Centuries of attempts to prove God have failed. And we have a much better natural explanation for where God ideas come from. Until some significant new evidence comes to light, we are entitled to conclude that no such beings exist. At this point, we should not be agnostic about God or gods any more than we should be agnostic about Santa Claus, the tooth fairy, or Xenu.

Typically, the agnostic is motivated to suspend judgment when the evidence we have is evenly split enough in favor of contrary conclusions to warrant caution, or when there isn't enough evidence to warrant concluding either way. But neither condition applies to God. Our evidence about God is not evenly split. It has failed across the board to substantiate the God conclusion. And the failed attempts to justify God themselves serve as evidence, like a stack of unworkable plans for perpetual-motion machines. The fact that our efforts have not produced the sought after proof itself suggests that no such proof is forthcoming. At some point in their inquiries, agnostics ought to reach a tipping point where continuing to suspend judgment doesn't make sense any more.

Given that centuries of effort to justify God have failed and that there is a much better, natural explanation for the origination of God ideas in the human psychology, does it make more sense to think that a God who defies or evades all our attempts might still be out there, or that there isn't one? As the heap of failed religious justifications grows, it should get harder and harder for the agnostic to conceive of how it could turn out that God or some god was real all along. Knowing what we know now about physics and chemistry, it is exceedingly hard (and growing harder) to conceive of how a working perpetual-motion machine could fit into the world. Given what we know about the Santa Claus hypothesis, it has become exceedingly hard to see how he could turn out to be real. And as that gap closes, the agnostic needs to shift over; the justification for suspending judgment will grow strained and convoluted. "Well, maybe Santa has a secret base buried under the ice at the North Pole and sophisticated cloaking technology that makes him invisible, and maybe he is brainwashing all the parents to think that they are actually the ones wrapping and giving presents to kids . . ." Yeah, maybe. But doesn't a-Santaism just make more sense overall?

The history of science shows us a conceptual revolution that fortifies the move to wide positive atheism. The Ptolemaic model that had the sun orbiting the earth began to disintegrate as careful thinkers made close observations and calculations. The sun rises and falls as if it was orbiting the earth, but the planets have retrograde paths across the sky—they inch forward then go back, then inch forward more, and then go back, and so on. As their observations grew more detailed and careful, astronomers postulated more orbits within orbits, and epicycles within orbits, to preserve the geocentric model of the universe. By the sixteenth century, the geocentric theory had become baroque to the point of uselessness.

Then Copernicus brought a conceptual revolution that resolved the discrepancies in the data. A fundamental assumption was wrong; the earth must be revolving around the sun. Belief in God has undergone the same accumulation of ad hoc provisions, speculations, and epicycles. It turns out that he didn't create humans six thousand years ago. Life evolved on its own for billions of years (but somehow that's still the result of his will). Centuries ago, God showed himself to humanity regularly, but now that no one sees him, we are told that he hides in order to preserve our freedom to believe by faith. Sickness was once the obvious manifestation of his disapproval, now there are viruses and bacteria. Prayer doesn't work, but that's only because it won't work for anyone who doubts and lacks faith, or because God's plans are mysterious. Our efforts to corroborate and understand just what God is are unsatisfied, but that is because in his wisdom he wishes us to grow. For every hard question, some elaborate provision, special pleading, or ad hoc revision is offered to try to salvage the idea of God. When an objection is offered to that rationalization, a new notion of God is engineered. Perhaps the ultimate trump card is the claim some believers make when they say, "We just can't know what God is really like or how everything makes sense, but we can be sure that it does from his perspective." A similarly recalcitrant geocentrist or demonologist could insist that we just can't understand how the sun *really* orbits the earth or how demons use viruses as their means of invasion, and it's beyond our capacity to understand how all the data could be wrong. A tenacious Scientologist might also argue that Xenu has managed to hide all of the evidence of his existence and Hubbard's account of the history of the galaxy.

Like demonology, it grows more and more implausible to continue patching up the account of God each time we discover some aspect of the old account that cannot be reconciled with new knowledge. What we know now makes it impossible to believe in or even make coherent sense of the God we worshiped during the infancy of humanity. It doesn't fit with physics. An infinite metaverse that contains countless variable universes in which ours is a single, insignificant speck cannot be reconciled with a picture of humanity and the earth as the purpose and pinnacle of God's creation. The young-earth creationism account of the origins of human life and the cosmos must be rejected. There was no Adam and Eve, no great flood, no resurrection. Evolution has rendered superfluous the God who was invoked to explain the complexity and appearance of design in nature. Molecular biology, genetics, and medical research have supplanted God, demon possession, and transcendent visions. The moral principles that guided Iron Age nomads to sacrifice goats for transgressions of ancient dietary laws are ill-equipped to accommodate the complexity and demands of modern ethical challenges like the best conduct of stem-cell research or international economic relations.

What psychology and epistemology have taught us about our cognitive natures undermines the foundations of ancient religions like Christianity. It is clear now how easily a false religious movement can develop, even one as vast and influential as Christianity. There are those who still have an affection for religion and religious ideas and who hold onto the notion that there still could be some higher power out there, watching over us. The religious urge dies slow and hard. But what is clear, and growing clearer, is that the God hypothesis has even less to recommend it than the Ptolemaic scheme of the sun orbiting the earth or demonology. It takes wilder and wilder gyrations and rationalizations in order to hold onto the view as we mature scientifically, socially, morally, and philosophically. An Iron Age mythology just can't be reconciled with what we now know about ourselves and the world we inhabit without straining that scheme to the breaking point or without imposing Procrustean limitations on what we are. And at some point, it should become evident that making a shift analogous to the one Copernicus did and rejecting theism for atheism makes a lot more sense of the information overall. Once we do, we will feel like the dumbfounded thinker in Plato's cave who emerges into the light after casting off the chains that bound him in ignorance.

NOTES

CHAPTER 1. SPEAKING ILL OF JESUS

1. In this text, I have adopted a convention of referring to the divine being in the Christian tradition or an omnipotent, omniscient, and infinitely good being as "God." I will use "god" or "gods" to refer to other, lesser-divine beings.

2. C. S. Lewis, *God in the Dock: Essays on Theology and Ethics* (Grand Rapids, MI: Wm. B. Eerdmans, 1994), p. 101.

3. I Cor. 15:14–15 (New International Version).

4. Gallup News Service, "Another Look at Evangelicals in America Today," Gallup, December 2, 2005, http://www.gallup.com/poll/20242/another-look-evan gelicals-america-today.aspx (accessed May 8, 2012).

5. The Harris Poll®, "More Americans Believe in the Devil, Hell and Angels Than in Darwin's Theory of Evolution," Harris Interactive®, no. 119, November 17, 2008, http://www.harrisinteractive.com/vault/Harris-Interactive-Poll-Research -Religious-Beliefs-2008-12.pdf (accessed July 6, 2011).

6. PEW Forum on Religion and Public Life, *U.S. Religious Landscape Survey: Chapter 1—Religious Beliefs and Practices* (Washington, DC: PEW Research Center, 2008), http://religions.pewforum.org/pdf/report2religious-landscape-study-chapter-1 .pdf (accessed July 6, 2011). For many, "the literal word of God" means that the book is infallible and internally consistent, and events depicted within occurred literally as they are described. In chapter 2, we will see a number of reasons why we cannot accept this view. We will be treating the Christian holy book in the same fashion as it is treated by the vast majority of historians and Bible scholars: as a document whose merits and problems can be ascertained the same way as any other historical document.

7. Ibid., p. 54.

8. Ibid., p. 34.

9. *Arational* is not a commonly recognized word, but it should be. *Irrational* means contrary to the dictates of reason. By *arational*, I mean outside or without reason, and I leave open, for the moment, whether believing arationally is also irrational.

10. Richard Carrier, "Why the Resurrection Is Unbelievable," in *The Christian Delusion*, ed. John Loftus (Amherst, NY: Prometheus Books, 2010), pp. 291–92.

11. Here's a tiny portion of the empirical evidence about the effects of desire on

evidence gathering and belief formation gathered from Jonathan Baron's *Thinking and Deciding*: E. Babad and Y. Katz, "Wishful Thinking—against All Odds," *Journal of Applied Social Psychology* 21 (1991): 1921–38; L. A. Brenner, D. J. Koehler, and A. Tversky, "On the Evaluation of One-Sided Evidence," *Journal of Behavioral Decision Making* 9 (1996): 59–70; D. Frey, "Recent Research on Selective Exposure to Information," in vol. 19 of *Advances in Experimental Social Psychology*, ed. L. Berkowitz (New York: Academic Press, 1986), pp. 41–80; A. Lowin, "Approach and Avoidance: Alternative Modes of Selective Exposure to Information," *Journal of Personality and Social Psychology* 6 (1967): 1–9; W. J. McGuire, "A Syllogistic Analysis of Cognitive Relationships," in *Attitude Organization and Change*, ed. M. J. Rosenberg et al., (New Haven, CT: Yale University Press, 1960), pp. 65–111; Emily Pronin, Thomas Gilovich, and L. Ross, "Objectivity in the Eye of the Beholder: Divergent Perceptions of Bias in Self versus Others," *Psychological Review* 111, no. 3 (2004): 781–99; N. Weinstein, "Unrealistic Optimism about Future Life Events," *Journal of Personality and Social Psychology* 39 (1980): 806–20; J. C. Weeks et al., "Relationship between Cancer Patients' Predictions of Prognosis and Their Treatment Preferences," *Journal of the American Medical Association* 279 (1998): 1709–14.

12. Woefully, four in ten Americans continue to be Young Earth Creationists. They affirm that "God created human beings pretty much in their present form at one time within the last 10,000 years or so." See Frank Newport, "Four in 10 Americans Believe in Strict Creationism," Gallup, December 17, 2010, http://www.gallup.com/poll/145286/Four-Americans-Believe-Strict-Creationism.aspx (accessed July 6, 2011).

13. "Rep. John Shimkus: God Decides When the 'Earth Will End,'" YouTube video, 2:25, from the US House of Representatives Subcommittee on Energy and the Environment, March 25, 2009, posted by "ProgressIllinois," March 27, 2009, http://www.youtube.com/watch?v=_7h08RDYA5E (accessed July 25, 2011).

14. The Baylor Religion Survey, *American Piety in the 21st Century: New Insights to the Depth and Complexity of Religion in the US* (Waco, TX: Baylor Institute for Studies in Religion, September 2006), http://www.baylor.edu/content/services/document.php/33304.pdf (accessed July 6, 2011), p. 39.

15. Sam Harris, *The End of Faith* (New York: W. W. Norton, 2004); Christopher Hitchens, *God Is Not Great: How Religion Poisons Everything* (New York: Twelve Books, 2007); Phil Zuckerman, *Atheism and Secularity* (Santa Barbara, CA: Praeger, 2009).

16. C. S. Lewis, "Man or Rabbit?" *God in the Dock: Essays on Theology and Ethics*, (Grand Rapids, MI: Wm. B. Eerdmans, 1994), p. 101.

17. According to modern physics textbooks, the laws of nature should be conceived of as statistical. So on this account, we can think of a miracle as an exceedingly unlikely event given the laws of nature, rather than a violation of them. But we should

understand "exceedingly unlikely" here as orders of magnitude more rare than, say, winning the lottery or being struck by lightning.

18. David Hume, *Dialogues concerning Natural Religion*, ed. Norman Kemp Smith, (Oxford: Clarendon Press, 1937).

19. Hume says, "That no testimony is sufficient to establish a miracle, unless the testimony be of such a kind, that its falsehood would be more miraculous, than the fact, which it endeavours [*sic*] to establish. . . . If the falsehood of his testimony would be more miraculous, than the event which he relates; then, and not till then, can he pretend to command my belief or opinion." David Hume, *Enquiry Concerning Human Understanding*, ed. L. A. Selby-Bigge (1902; repr., Oxford: Clarendon Press, 1975), p. 91.

20. Chapter 4 of this book presents a number of recent studies about psychological contributors to belief, but those arguments will bear on the reliability of the early Christians as transmitters of information, not directly on truth. I will argue more directly in chapter 9 that a being like God would not be responsible for miracles.

21. Jim Holt, "Beyond Belief," review of *The God Delusion*, by Richard Dawkins, *New York Times*, October 22, 2006, Sunday Book Review, http://www.nytimes.com/2006/10/22/books/review/Holt.t.html (accessed July 10, 2011).

22. Stephanie Merritt, "Faith No More," review of *The End of Faith*, by Sam Harris, *The Observer*, February 6, 2005, http://www.guardian.co.uk/theobserver/2005/feb/06/society (accessed July 10, 2011).

23. Leon Wieseltier, "The God Genome," review of *Breaking the Spell*, by Daniel Dennett, *New York Times*, February 19, 2006, http://www.nytimes.com/2006/02/19/books/review/19wieseltier.html (accessed July 10, 2011).

24. Penny Edgell, Joseph Gerteis, and Douglass Hartman, "Atheists as 'Other': Moral Boundaries and Cultural Membership in American Society," *American Sociological Review* 71, no. 2 (2006): 211–35.

25. Sam Harris, "10 Myths—And 10 Truths—About Atheism," *Los Angeles Times*, December 24, 2006, http://www.samharris.org/site/full_text/10-myths-and-10-truths-about-atheism1/ (accessed July 6, 2011).

26. W. K. Clifford, "The Ethics of Belief," in *The Ethics of Belief and Other Essays* (Amherst, NY: Prometheus Books, 1999), pp. 70–96.

27. PEW Forum on Religion and Public Life, *Many Americans Uneasy with Mix of Religion and Politics* (Washington, DC: PEW Research Center, August 24, 2006), http://pewforum.org/docs/?DocID=153 (accessed July 6, 2011).

28. See Sam Harris's appearance in the Brian Flemming film documentary *The God Who Wasn't There*, directed by Brian Flemming (Beyond Belief Media, 2005), DVD.

29. Sam Harris, "The Politics of Ignorance," *Huffington Post*, August 2, 2005,

http://www.huffingtonpost.com/sam-harris/the-politics-of-ignorance_b_5053.html (accessed July 10, 2011).

CHAPTER 2. THE HISTORY OF THE JESUS STORY

1. The general picture of the consensus about the Jesus story was gleaned, in part, from the following sources. If one enrolls in an Introduction to the New Testament course in almost any reputable university in the English-speaking world, the odds are very good that one or more of these will be assigned texts. Bart Ehrman, *The New Testament: A Historical Introduction to the Early Christian Writings* (New York: Oxford University Press, 2004) pp. 479–80; Bart Ehrman, *The Orthodox Corruption of Scripture: The Effect of Early Christological Controversies on the Text of the New Testament* (New York: Oxford University Press, 1993); Bruce Metzger, *The Canon of the New Testament: Its Origin, Development, and Significance* (New York: Clarendon Press, 1997); Bruce Metzger, *The Text of the New Testament: Its Transmission, Corruption, and Restoration* (New York: Oxford University Press, 1992); F. F. Bruce, *The New Testament Documents: Are They Reliable?* (Leicester, UK: InterVarsity, 1960); Helmut Koester, *Ancient Christian Gospels: Their History and Development* (Valley Forge, PA: Trinity, 1992); Helmut Koester, *Introduction to the New Testament*, 2 vols. (Berlin: Walter de Gruyter, 1983); Kurt Aland and Barbara Aland, *The Text of the New Testament: An Introduction to the Critical Editions and to the Theory and Practice of Modern Textual Criticism*, trans. Erroll F. Rhodes (Grand Rapids, MI: Wm. B. Eerdmans, 1989); Richard Heard, *An Introduction to the New Testament* (New York: Harper and Brothers, 1950); William Farmer, Denis M. Farkasfalvy, and O. Cist, *The Formation of the New Testament Canon: An Ecumenical Approach* (New York: Paulist Press, 1983).

2. Ehrman, *New Testament*, pp. 479–80.

3. Ibid., p. 480.

4. Aland and Aland, *Text of the New Testament*, p. 69.

5. Ehrman, *New Testament*, p. 219.

6. Ibid.

7. The issue here brings to mind the early female individual in the *Homo sapiens* line that anthropologists have dubbed Mitochondrial Eve. She is special among our ancestors in that she possesses mitochondrial DNA that subsequently can be found in all contemporary humans. She was not the only living woman in her time, and many of her contemporaries have living descendants today, but only through their sons. She is the matrilineal ancestor of all humans. Given her pivotal point in the history of human biology, like the pivotal point a few sources have in the history of the Jesus

information, if she had died before having female children, or if her biology had been different, the entire human race would be different.

CHAPTER 3. YOU ALREADY DON'T BELIEVE IN JESUS: THE SALEM WITCH TRIALS

1. An earlier version of the argument appears in Matthew S. McCormick, "The Salem Witch Trials and the Evidence for the Resurrection," in *The End of Christianity*, ed. John Loftus (Amherst, NY: Prometheus Books, 2011). I am indebted to Richard Carrier for many helpful comments on that contribution.

2. Some of the influential arguments for the historical resurrection can be found in C. Blomberg, *The Historical Reliability of the Gospels* (Downers Grove, IL: InterVarsity, 1987); William Lane Craig, *Assessing the New Testament Evidence for the Historicity of the Resurrection of Jesus* (Lewiston, NY: Edwin Mellen, 2002); William Lane Craig, "The Historicity of the Empty Tomb of Jesus," *New Testament Studies* 31 (1985): 39–67; William Lane Craig, "The Bodily Resurrection of Jesus," in *Gospel Perspectives I*, eds. R. T. France and D. Wenham (Sheffield, UK: JSOT, 1980), pp. 47–74; Gary Habermas, "Resurrection Research from 1975 to the Present: What Are Critical Scholars Saying?" *Journal for the Study of the Historical Jesus* 3, no. 2 (2005): 135–53; Gary Habermas, *The Historical Jesus: Ancient Evidence for the Life of Christ* (Joplin, MO: College Press, 1996); Tim McGrew and Lydia McGrew, "The Argument from Miracles: A Cumulative Case for the Resurrection of Jesus of Nazareth," in *The Blackwell Companion to Natural Theology*, eds. W. L. Craig and J. P. Moreland (Oxford: Wiley-Blackwell, 2009), pp. 593–662; Richard Swinburne, *The Resurrection of God Incarnate* (New York: Oxford University Press, 2003); N. T. Wright, *The Resurrection of the Son of God* (Minneapolis, MN: Fortress Press, 2003).

3. Gary Habermas, "The Case for Christ's Resurrection," in *To Everyone an Answer: A Case for the Christian World View*, eds. Francis Beckwith, William Lane Craig, and J. P. Moreland (Downers Grove, IL: InterVarsity, 2004), pp. 180–98. To view an online version of Habermas's contribution in *To Everyone an Answer* (chapter 11), visit http://www.garyhabermas.com/books/inbook_to-everyone-an-answer/habermas_case-for-xp-res.htm (accessed July 6, 2011).

4. Ibid., p. 194.

5. Ibid., p. 195.

6. For just a start, see Paul Boyer and Stephen Nissenbaum, eds., *Salem-Village Witchcraft: A Documentary Record of Local Conflict in Colonial New England* (Belmont, CA: Wadsworth, 1972); Paul Boyer and Stephen Nissenbaum, eds., *The Salem Witchcraft Papers*,

vols. 1–3, (New York: Da Capo, 1977); Richard Weisman, *Witchcraft, Magic, and Religion in 17th Century Massachusetts* (Amherst: University of Massachusetts Press, 1984).

7. "Did Jesus Christ Come to the City? Job Mutungi's Testimony," *Kenya Times*, June 22, 1988.

8. James Randi, *Flim Flam! Psychics, ESP, Unicorns and Other Delusions* (Buffalo, NY: Prometheus Books, 1982); Jonathan Baron, *Thinking and Deciding* (New York: Cambridge University Press, 2000); Martin Gardner, *Fads and Fallacies in the Name of Science* (New York: Dover, 1957); Thomas Gilovich, *How We Know What Isn't So* (New York: Free Press, 1991); Stephen Law, *Believing Bullshit: How Not to Get Sucked into an Intellectual Black Hole* (Amherst, NY: Prometheus Books, 2011); Elizabeth Loftus, *Eyewitness Testimony* (Cambridge, MA: Harvard University Press, 1996); James Randi, *Faith Healers* (Buffalo, NY: Prometheus Books, 1989); Carl Sagan, *The Demon-Haunted World: Science as a Candle in the Dark* (New York: Ballantine Books, 1996); Theodore Schick and Lewis Vaughn, *How to Think about Weird Things: Critical Thinking for a New Age* (Boston: McGraw-Hill, 2002); Michael Shermer, *Why People Believe Weird Things: Pseudoscience, Superstition, and Other Confusions of Our Time* (New York: Henry Holt, 2002).

9. *Stanford Encyclopedia of Philosophy*, s.v. "naturalism," February 22, 2007, http://plato.stanford.edu/entries/naturalism/ (accessed May 11, 2012).

10. N. T. Wright, "Jesus' Resurrection and Christian Origins," *Gregorianum* 83, no. 4 (2002): 615–35.

11. Nicholas Wolterstorff, *Reason within the Bounds of Religion* (Grand Rapids, MI: Wm. B. Eerdmans, 1994), p. 72.

12. William Lane Craig, "Interview with Dr. William Lane Craig: Handling Doubt," Google video, 5:38, 2006, http://video.google.com/videoplay?docid=453 8185102301600532&q=william+lane+craig# (accessed July 6, 2011).

13. William Lane Craig, "The Historicity of the Empty Tomb of Jesus," *New Testament Studies* 31 (1985): 39–67. Unfortunately, the meaning of "believing on the basis of the self-authenticating witness of the Holy Spirit" is beyond the scope of our study here. But I have discussed it, and several crippling problems with it, on my blog, *Proving the Negative* (www.provingthenegative.com). As I see it, the absence of error checking is the central problem with claims that some private feelings or inner sense gives the believer special incorrigible knowledge of God. We know that a wide variety of powerful subjective feelings are common, and we also know that many of them are mistaken, such as when they are the result of schizophrenia, epilepsy, or even a Justin Bieber concert. If the only way for you to check the accuracy of your feelings about the nature of the external world is to consult those feelings, then there is no way for you to discern the authentic ones from the mistaken ones.

CHAPTER 4. BELIEVING THE BELIEVERS

1. Interestingly, some Protestant readers will be reluctant to grant that even these miracles are real, particularly the ones that are attributed to Catholic saints. Such a bias will lower the Protestant's estimation of the numerator in what follows. And many Catholics will be skeptical about, say, the miracles surrounding the origins of Mormonism.

2. I'm being generous in not including all the cases where people used the term "miracle" to describe natural and even common events like having a baby or falling in love. If we included all these in the denominator, the reliability for real miracle claims would plummet even lower.

3. The point will be clearer shortly, but unless the total number of cases where people thought something miraculous happened is less than 134 (instead of four million), the end result of this argument will be that miracle testimony should be mistrusted more often than it is trusted.

4. PEW Forum on Religion and Public Life, *U.S. Religious Landscape Survey: Chapter 1—Religious Beliefs and Practices* (Washington, DC: PEW Research Center, 2008), http://religions.pewforum.org/pdf/report2religious-landscape-study-chapter-1.pdf (accessed July 6, 2011).

5. Herbert Benson et al., "Study of the Therapeutic Effects of Intercessory Prayer (STEP) in Cardiac Bypass Patients: A Multicenter Randomized Trial of Uncertainty and Certainty of Receiving Intercessory Prayer," *American Heart Journal* 151 (2006): 934–42; Randolph C. Byrd, "Positive Therapeutic Effects of Intercessory Prayer in a Coronary Care Unit Population," *Southern Medical Journal* 81, no. 7 (1988): 826–29; K. Y. Cha, D. P. Wirth, and R. A. Lobo, "Does Prayer Influence the Success of In Vitro Fertilization-Embryo Transfer? Report of a Masked, Randomized Trial," *Journal of Reproductive Medicine* 46, no. 9 (September 2001): 781–87.

6. The Baylor Religion Survey, *American Piety in the 21st Century: New Insights to the Depth and Complexity of Religion in the US* (Waco, TX: Baylor Institute for Studies in Religion, September 2006), http://www.baylor.edu/content/services/document.php/33304.pdf (accessed July 25, 2011), p. 47.

7. "One Million Dollar Paranormal Challenge," James Randi Educational Foundation, October 30, 2008, http://www.randi.org/site/index.php/1m-challenge .html (accessed July 7, 2011).

8. Matters are complicated by the fact that a person is typically more disposed to accept particular types of supernatural claims over others because of priming, ideology, background information, and expectations. You might find your horoscope in the newspaper fairly plausible, but you might be more skeptical about the sacrifice of a chicken in a Haitian voodoo ritual foretelling the same thing. We can simplify

this issue by asking what the general disposition of the first-century Christians would have been in order to accept supernatural claims regarding their spiritual leader, Jesus.

9. Their real rate is zero, I suspect. (Admittedly, my SBT is very high.) But the point is that whatever their real rate, Gloria errs on the side of accepting too many as true.

10. Some research suggests that one of the things that keeps gamblers gambling is that they tend to treat losses where the result is close to a win as near wins instead of simply as losses. Having the ball land in the slot next to the one on which you bet in roulette has no impact on the overall odds of winning, but the gambler presses on because a near win feels like he is on the verge of a win.

11. Frank Newport, "Belief in God Far Lower in Western U.S.," Gallup, July 28, 2008, http://www.gallup.com/poll/109108/Belief-God-Far-Lower-Western-US.aspx (accessed July 25, 2011); The Harris Poll®, "More Americans Believe in the Devil, Hell and Angels Than in Darwin's Theory of Evolution," Harris Interactive®, no. 119, November 17, 2008, http://www.harrisinteractive.com/vault/Harris-Interactive-Poll -Research-Religious-Beliefs-2008-12.pdf (accessed July 6, 2011).

12. Bart Ehrman, *The New Testament: A Historical Introduction to the Early Christian Writings* (New York: Oxford University Press, 2004), p. 226.

13. Baylor Religion Survey, *American Piety in the 21st Century*, p. 48.

14. The World Tribune, "Move over Tiger: N. Korea's Kim Shot 38 under Par His 1st Time Out," *World Tribune*, June 16, 2004, http://www.worldtribune.com/ worldtribune/WTARC/2004/ea_nkorea_06_16.html (accessed July 10, 2011).

15. We often compartmentalize our skepticism. Some modern Christians will display sophisticated critical-analysis skills in one case, to carefully dismantle the scientific evidence for global warming, for example, while accepting the underre-ported claim from a small group of first-century Iron Age religious adherents that their leader was magically brought back from the dead.

16. Vaughan Bell, "Ghost Stories: Visits from the Deceased," *Scientific American*, December 2, 2008, http://www.scientificamerican.com/article.cfm?id=ghost-stories -visits-from-the-deceased (accessed July 6, 2011); A. Grimby, "Bereavement among Elderly People: Grief Reactions, Post-bereavement Hallucinations and Quality of Life," *Acta Psychiatrica Scandinavica* 87, no. 1 (2007): 72–80; W. Dewi Rees, "The Hallucinations of Widowhood," *British Medical Journal* 4 (1971): 37–41.

17. You may have noticed this very sort of revision and convergence happen in your family or among a group of friends as they talk about and recall some important event.

18. C. Chabris and D. Simons, *The Invisible Gorilla, and Other Ways Our Intuitions Deceive Us* (New York: Crown, 2010), pp. 45–46.

19. In one study, a group of Stanford students was exposed repeatedly to an

unsubstantiated claim taken from a website purporting that Coca-Cola® is an effective paint thinner. Students who read the statement five times were nearly one-third more likely than those who read it only twice to attribute the claim to *Consumer Reports* (rather than the *National Enquirer*, their other choice), giving it a gloss of credibility. Sam Wang and Sandra Aamodt, "Your Brain Lies to You," *New York Times*, June 27, 2008, http://www.nytimes.com/2008/06/29/opinion/29iht-edwang.1.14069662.html (accessed June 2, 2011).

20. Elizabeth Loftus, *The Myth of Repressed Memory: False Memories and Allegations of Sexual Abuse*, (New York: St. Martin's Griffin, 1994); D. L. M. Sacchi, F. Agnoli, and Elizabeth Loftus, "Changing History: Doctored Photographs Affect Memory for Past Public Events," *Applied Cognitive Psychology* 21 (2007): 1005–22; K. A. Wade, M. Garry, J. D. Read, and S. Lindsay, "A Picture Is Worth a Thousand Lies: Using False Photographs to Create False Childhood Memories," *Psychonomic Bulletin and Review* 9 (2002): 597–603.

21. Thanks to Carla Mulford at Pennsylvania State University and Kate Sprawka for helping me see the point about Franklin and King.

22. Oral Roberts, *The Call: Oral Roberts' Autobiography* (New York: Avon, 1973).

23. Reinhard Bonnke, interview by Pat Robertson, "Reinhard Bonnke Tells of Nigerian Man Raised from the Dead," http://www.cbn.com/700club/features/bonnke_raisedpastor.aspx (accessed July 25, 2011).

24. "Did Jesus Christ Come to the City? Job Mutungi's Testimony," *Kenya Times*, June 22, 1988.

25. For example, Daniel Greenberg has found at least three different accounts from President Bush of what he was doing when he heard about the 9-11 attacks. "President Bush's False 'Flashbulb' Memory of 9/11/01," *Applied Cognitive Psychology* 18 (2004): 363–70.

26. Ulric Neisser and Nicole Harsch, "Phantom Flashbulbs: False Recollections of Hearing the News about *Challenger*" in *Affect and Accuracy in Recall: Studies of "Flashbulb" Memories*, eds. Eugene Winograd and Ulric Neisser (New York: Cambridge University Press, 1992), pp. 9–31.

27. J. M. Talarico and D. C. Rubin, "Confidence, Not Consistency, Characterizes Flashbulb Memories," *Psychological Science* 14 (2003): 455–61. Chabris and Simons gather many of these studies and give an excellent summary of the big picture of human memory research in *The Invisible Gorilla* (see chapter 4, note 18). They call this false confidence in the accuracy of our memories of important events the illusion of memory.

28. J. Kruger and D. Dunning, "Unskilled and Unaware of It: How Difficulties in Recognizing One's Own Incompetence Lead to Inflated Self-Assessments," *Journal of Personality and Social Psychology* 77 (1999): 1121–34.

29. L. Ross, M. R. Lepper, and M. Hubbard, "Perseverance in Self-Perception and Social Perception: Biased Attributional Processes in the Debriefing Paradigm," *Journal of Personality and Social Psychology* 32, no. 5 (1975): 880–92.

30. Daniel J. Simons and C. Chabris, "Gorillas in Our Midst: Sustained Inattentional Blindness for Dynamic Events," *Perception* 28 (1999): 1059–74. For more information, see also Daniel J. Simons, "Selective Attention Test," YouTube video, 1:22, from the Visual Cognition Lab, 1999, http://viscog.beckman.illinois.edu/flashmovie/15.php (accessed May 8, 2012).

31. Daniel Simons and Daniel T. Levin, "Failure to Detect Changes to People during a Real-World Interaction," *Psychonomic Bulletin and Review* 5, no. 4 (1998): 644–49.

32. Daniel Dennett, *Consciousness Explained* (New York: Little, Brown, 1991), pp. 111–13.

33. Solomon Asch, "Effects of Group Pressure upon the Modification and Distortion of Judgments," in *Groups, Leadership, and Men*, ed. H. Guetzkow (Pittsburgh: Carnegie, 1951).

34. Richard Nisbett, quoting Linda Gottfredson. *Intelligence and How to Get It* (New York: W. W. Norton, 2009), p. 4.

35. Ibid., p. 22.

36. "IQ Gains over Time: Toward Finding the Causes," in *The Rising Curve: Long Term Gains in IQ and Related Measures*, ed. U Neisser (Washington, DC: American Psychological Association, 1998), pp. 25–66.

37. Theodora Kroeber, *Ishi: In Two Worlds* (Berkeley: University of California Press, 1961), pp. 215, 225, 248.

CHAPTER 5. THE REPEATERS AND THE MONEY-BAG PROBLEM

1. A failure to recognize the inherent circularity of justifying appeals to the authority of the Bible by appealing to the Bible is one of the most common mistakes I find in my discussions, debates, lectures, and interviews with believers on this issue. An unfortunate habit has developed among many Christian apologists of referring to the "facts" of the Gospels that need to be explained. This rhetorical move presumes the very thing at issue. What we have is a manuscript containing reports of some event. There is a great deal of work to do, as we have seen, to successfully argue from that report to any claim of fact.

2. Bart Ehrman, *The New Testament: A Historical Introduction to the Early Christian Writings* (New York: Oxford University Press, 2004), p. 12.

3. Justin Kruger and David Dunning, "Unskilled and Unaware of It: How Difficulties in Recognizing One's Own Incompetence Lead to Inflated Self-Assessments," *Journal of Personality and Social Psychology* 77, no. 6 (1999): 121–34.

4. R. E. Nisbett and T. D. Wilson, "Telling More Than We Can Know: Verbal Reports on Mental Processes," *Psychological Review* 84, no. 3 (1977): 231–59.

5. P. Adams and J. K. Adams, "Confidence in the Recognition and Reproduction of Words Difficult to Spell," *American Journal of Psychology*, 73 (1960): 544–52; S. Lichtenstein and B. Fischoff, "Do Those Who Know More Also Know More About How Much They Know?" *Organizational Behavior and Human Performance* 20 (1970): 159–83; S. Lichtenstein, B. Fischoff, and B. Phillips, "Calibration of Probabilities: The State of the Art to 1980," in *Judgment under Uncertainty: Heuristics and Biases*, ed. D. Kahneman, P. Slovic, and A. Tversky (New York: Cambridge University Press, 1982), pp. 306–34; Nisbett and Wilson, "Telling More Than We Know."

6. Some recent efforts to make Pope John Paul II into a saint have focused on two cases: one where a boy with a 50 percent chance of surviving a disease recovered after his grandfather began praying to the deceased pope, the other involving allegations that a French nun recovered from Parkinson's after two fellow nuns alleged they began praying to John Paul II. The bar for miracles has been set very low. Francis Rocca, "Beatification Prompts Closer Look at John Paul's Miracles," *USA Today*, April 27, 2011, http://www.usatoday.com/news/religion/2011-04-27-Pope_miracles_26_ST_N.htm (accessed July 10, 2011).

7. Thomas Bayes (1702–1781) laid the foundation of modern conceptions of probability where it is determined subjectively as and with regard to a person's belief rather than a simple calculation of objective frequencies. One of the best Bayesian analysis in favor of the resurrection is Tim McGrew and Lydia McGrew, "The Argument from Miracles: A Cumulative Case for the Resurrection of Jesus of Nazareth," in *The Blackwell Companion to Natural Theology*, ed. William Lane Craig and J. P. Moreland (Hoboken, NJ: Blackwell, 2009), 593–662. Their aim is telling in its modesty (found on p. 594): "We shall argue that there is significant positive evidence for R, evidence that cannot be ignored and that must be taken into account in any evaluation of the total evidence for Christianity and for theism."

8. I frequently hear believers citing First Corinthians 15:5–8, where Paul reports that the resurrected Jesus appeared to more than five hundred people, as fortifying evidence. Consider Josh McDowell making the mistake here:

"Let's take the more than 500 witnesses who saw Jesus alive after His death and burial, and place them in a courtroom. Do you realize that if each of those 500 people were to testify for only six minutes, including cross-examination, you would have an amazing 50 hours of firsthand testimony?

Add to this the testimony of many other eyewitnesses and you would well have the largest and most lopsided trial in history."

Josh McDowell, "Evidence for the Resurrection," Leadership U, 1992, http://www.leaderu.com/everystudent/easter/articles/josh2.html (accessed July 26, 2011). The embarrassing conflation here is between one person's report that there were five hundred alleged eyewitnesses and five hundred eyewitness reports.

9. McGrew and McGrew, "The Argument from Miracles."

CHAPTER 6. ABDUCTED BY ALIENS AND A FALSE MURDER CONVICTION

1. As with many of the claims surrounding Jesus, I am suspending judgment about this claim. The previous chapters' considerations about the weakness of the evidence show that there's just too much we don't know about the sources and the events.

2. Daniel Dennett, *Breaking the Spell: Religion as a Natural Phenomenon* (New York: Viking Press, 2006), ch. 8.

CHAPTER 7. THE COUNTEREVIDENCE PROBLEM

1. Peter H. Ditto et al., "Motivated Sensitivity to Preference-Inconsistent Information," *Journal of Personality and Social Psychology* 75, no. 1 (1998): 55.

2. You might be inclined at this point to say that District Attorney Michaels, the jury, and Dr. Lee are *not* justified in drawing their mistaken conclusions: they should have done a more exhaustive job of gathering and analyzing all the evidence and drawn the right conclusion, and until they have done so, they are not justified. But consider that no matter how much homework Michaels, the jury, or Lee do, they could still get it wrong, and not for lack of trying to get it right. They could have exhausted every resource they have to find the truth, but Ortega or Chevalier could have still engineered the evidence toward their conclusions. Ptolemy was a brilliant astronomer who had mastered all of the current information and tools available to the ancient Greeks, but he still concluded that the sun orbits the earth. If Ptolemy was not justified in drawing his mistaken conclusion, then I think we would have to conclude that no one is ever justified or reasonable in the conclusions he or she draws. So I will adopt the view that it is possible to have a justified but false belief. This position is known as *fallibilism* in epistemology.

3. The principle here is similar to Stephen Wykstra's CORNEA principle that he brings against William Rowe's inductive argument from evil against the existence of God. Wykstra says, on the basis of cognized situation S, human H is entitled to claim, "It appears that P" only if it is reasonable for H to believe that, given her cognitive faculties and the use she has made of them, if P were not the case, S would likely be different than it is in some way discernible by her. See "The Humean Obstacle to Evidential Arguments from Suffering: On Avoiding the Evils of 'Appearance,'" *International Journal of the Philosophy of Religion* 116 (1984): 73–93. The details for a principle like this in epistemology can get very complicated. As it is stated, this principle will not withstand serious "Chisolm-ing" or efforts to generate some counterexamples. While this statement of the principle is rough and oversimplified, the idea behind it is a good one. My goal here is just to bring out the vital role that the search for counterevidence must play in our beliefs if they are to be well founded. It cannot be sufficient to justify a belief by only searching for or considering evidence that supports it.

4. The majority of Americans believe that they have prescient dreams or dreams that reveal important truths about their lives. When asked, they often cite some cases they remember where they had a dream that something would happen, then it came true the next day or the next week. Or they give a case where a dream revealed something they took to be significant to an important matter in their lives. Leaving aside the other problems here, let's do some math. If you live to an average age of seventy-five, you'll sleep through 27,375 nights (leaving out the wild parties), and if you have, say, ten dreams per night, you'll have 273,750 dreams. Many of them will incorporate some normal activities that are on your mind. Now if a person cites three cases where she recalls having a dream that X would occur and it did, but she does not reflect on the 273,747 dreams she has had that were not remarkable, should we be inclined to conclude that she has some magical power to see the future that manifests in her dreams?

5. Kurt Aland and Barbara Aland, *The Text of the New Testament: An Introduction to the Critical Editions and to the Theory and Practice of Modern Textual Criticism*, trans. Erroll F. Rhodes (Grand Rapids, MI: Wm. B. Eerdmans, 1989), p. 69.

6. Ditto et al., "Motivated Sensitivity to Preference-Inconsistent Information," p. 54.

7. I've been "out of the closet" as it were, for many years, and my publications, lectures, and university courses on atheism have been the subject of some attention and nervous interest. It has become quite common for people with attitudes ranging from minor doubts about God to full blown atheism to seek me out and speak to me in somewhat hushed tones or in my office with the door closed about ideas they frequently have but are unable talk about with anyone for fear of recrimination. Being

an atheist is now something like what being a homosexual used to be (and still is, in many communities).

8. See chapter 3, pp. 68–69.

9. There is now a substantial community of "Michael Jackson is alive" believers. See this amazing website: www.michaeljacksonsightings.com (accessed July 10, 2011).

10. Julie Holland, interview with Terri Gross, "Venturing inside Bellevue's Psychiatric ER," *Fresh Air*, National Public Radio, October 26, 2009, http://www .npr.org/templates/transcript/transcript.php?storyId=114095164 (accessed July 10, 2011). For more information, see Holland's book, *Weekends at Bellevue: Nine Years on the Night Shift at the Psych ER* (New York: Random House, 2009).

11. National Institute of Mental Health, "Any Disorder among Adults," http:// www.nimh.nih.gov/statistics/1ANYDIS_ADULT.shtml (accessed August 15, 2011).

12. Jeffrey L. Saver and John Rabin, "The Neural Substrate of Religious Experience," *Journal of Neuropsychiatry* 9, no. 3 (1997): 498–510. See Saver and Rabin's bibliography for a number of useful studies of religious experience and mental illness.

13. "Patterson Bigfoot Hoax," *Skeptic* 4, no. 2 (1996): 19; Kal Korff and Michaeila Kocis, "Exposing Roger Patterson's 1967 Bigfoot Film Hoax," *Skeptical Inquirer*, July/ August, 2004.

14. Lee Krystek, "The Surgeon's Hoax," http://www.unmuseum.org/nesshoax .htm (accessed July 10, 2011).

15. Carl Sagan, "Crop Circles and Aliens: What's The Evidence?" *Parade Magazine*, December 3, 1995, pp. 10–12, 17.

16. Carl Charlson, "Secrets of the Psychics," *Nova*, original broadcast October 19, 1993 (Boston: WGBH, 2000).

17. Jonathan Baron, *Thinking and Deciding* (New York: Cambridge University Press, 2000).

CHAPTER 8. WHY ARE ALL OF THE GODS HIDING?

1. Unfortunately, there is substantial evidence showing that when a belief is cherished or entrenched, powerful contrary evidence that should disprove it and change a person's mind actually has the opposite effect. The believer digs in deeper and expresses even greater conviction for the disproven belief. See these studies for a start: Bendan Nyhan and Jason Reier, "When Corrections Fail: The Persistence of Political Misperceptions," *Political Behavior* 32, no. 2 (2010): 303–30; Peter H. Ditto et al., "Motivated Sensitivity to Preference-Inconsistent Information," *Journal of Personality and Social Psychology* 75, no. 1 (1998): 54; Craig Anderson, Mark R.

Lepper, and Lee Ross, "Perseverance of Social Theories: The Role of Explanation in the Persistence of Discredited Information," *Journal of Personality and Social Psychology* 39, no. 6 (1980): 1037–49; C. Daniel Batson, "Rational Processing or Rationalization? The Effect of Discontinuing Information on a Stated Religious Belief," *Journal of Personality and Social Psychology* 32, no. 1 (1975): 176–84.

2. "Best Prayer Ever! Pastor Joe Nelms—Nascar Nationwide—Nashville, TN," YouTube video, 1:10, from the NASCAR Nationwide Series race in Nashville, Tennessee, on July 23, 2011, posted by "Paulk9pg," July 23, 2011, http://www.youtube.com/watch?v=J74y88YuSJ8&feature=player_detailpage (accessed July 26, 2011).

3. Daniel Howard-Snyder and Paul Moser, eds. *Divine Hiddenness: New Essays* (New York: Cambridge University Press, 2002), pp. 9–10.

4. Thanks to Eric Sotnak for making this point clearer to me.

5. Theodore Drange, *Nonbelief and Evil* (Amherst, NY: Prometheus Books, 1998); J. L. Schellenberg, *Divine Hiddenness and Human Reason* (Ithaca, NY: Cornell University Press, 1993); J. L. Schellenberg, "Divine Hiddenness Justifies Atheism," in *Contemporary Debates in the Philosophy of Religion*, eds. Michael Peterson and Raymond VanArragon (Oxford: Blackwell, 2006), pp. 30–41.

6. If someone is tempted to say now that some people, like skeptics and atheists, would reject God no matter what the evidence, resist that temptation. Now he is blaming the lack of belief on them and changing the subject from God, God's goals, and the evidence.

CHAPTER 9. WOULD GOD DO MIRACLES?

1. Evan Fales, "Successful Defense? A Review of *In Defense of Miracles*," *Philosophia Christi* 3, no. 1 (2001): 13.

2. See for instance J. L. Mackie, *The Miracle of Theism: Arguments for and against the Existence of God* (Oxford: Clarendon Press, 1982), p. 22; Steve Clarke, "When to Believe in Miracles," *American Philosophical Quarterly* 34, no. 1 (1997): 95–102; George Mavrodes, "David Hume and the Probability of Miracles," *International Journal for Philosophy of Religion* 43, no. 3 (1998): 167–82; Wesley Salmon, "Religion and Science: A New Look at Hume's Dialogues," reprinted in *The Improbability of God*, ed. Michael Martin and Ricki Monnier (Amherst, NY: Prometheus Books, 2006), pp. 167–93.

3. The bulk of philosophical discussions follow my notion, but there have been a number of arguments contesting the "violation of the laws of nature" definition. Collier says, for example, "The impossibility of a complete explanation in terms of

natural laws is not itself sufficient for an event to be a miracle, as the fundamental indeterminacy postulated by the standard interpretation of quantum theory shows." See John Collier, "Against Miracles," *Dialogue* 25 (1986): 349–52.

See also R. F. Holland, "The Miraculous," *American Philosophical Quarterly* 2 (1965): 43–51, reprinted and revised in *Logical Analysis and Contemporary Theism*, ed. J. Donnelly (New York: Fordham University Press, 1972), pp. 218–35; C. Hughes, "Miracles, Laws of Nature and Causation," *Proceedings of the Aristotelian Society* 66 (1992): 179–205; Robert Larmer, "Miracles, Evidence, and God," *Dialogue: Canadian Philosophical Review* 42, no. 1 (2003): 107–22; T. J. Mawson, "Miracles and Laws of Nature," *Religious Studies: An International Journal for the Philosophy of Religion* 37, no. 1 (2001): 33–58; George, Mavrodes, "Miracles and the Laws of Nature," *Faith and Philosophy* 2, no. 4 (1985): 33–46.

In cases where miracles are defined more broadly to include events that can be accounted for according to natural law (such as a bus driver falling asleep at the wheel and coming to a stop before hitting a child), the argument from the occurrence of a miracle of this sort to the existence of God will be much more difficult to make since an obvious natural explanation is readily available. And in cases where miracles are defined to be acts of God, then the debate over inferring the existence of God from the evidence becomes a debate about whether or not an event is a miracle. I am electing to frame that discussion in terms of whether naturally inexplicable events provide evidence for the existence of God.

On accounts where the laws of nature are conceived of fundamentally as statistical, like Swinburne's (and, indeed, according to modern physics textbooks) a miracle may be defined as an exceedingly unlikely event given the laws of nature, rather than a violation of them. I take it that as the likelihood of an event increases according to the laws of nature, the extent to which that event can be employed to prove the existence of God diminishes. I believe it will be possible to adapt the arguments I am making to accommodate many of these different accounts of what a miracle is.

4. Earlier, our main focus was the Christian God. Here, unless otherwise noted, I will use "God," and "omnibeing," interchangeably and to mean a being that is all-powerful, all-knowing, and all-good. There is significant literature concerning the best way to understand those terms and there are several rival definitions for each. As far as I can see, the points I will make can be applied with equal effect to the different definitions, so I will just use "omnipotent," "omniscient," and "omnibenevolent," without elaboration.

5. To be fair, there is potential for a better argument here: (1) it is reasonable under some circumstances to think that a miracle has occurred, and (2) the best explanation of that miracle is that an omni-God or the Christian God exists. But if it can be successfully argued that an omnibeing wouldn't do miracles, as I am going to do in the latter part of this chapter, then these arguments will be undermined, too.

6. Later, I will argue against this possibility as well. That is, I will argue that omnipotent beings would not exercise their power by means of miracles, so any miracle we encounter would not be an omnipotent being's act.

7. Recently, an Ontario man found a miraculous burn pattern on a fish stick he had cooked that resembles Jesus. "Virgin Mary Grilled Cheese vs. Jesus Fish Stick," *Chicago Tribune*, November 26, 2004, http://articles.chicagotribune.com/2004-11-26/news/0411270037_1_grilled-cheese-virgin-mary-sandwich (accessed May 24, 2012).

8. By some accounts (see T. J. Mawson, "Miracles and the Laws of Nature," *Religious Studies: An International Journal for the Philosophy of Religion* 37, no. 1 (2001): 33–58, and Robert Larmer, "Miracles, Evidence, and God," *Dialogue: Canadian Philosophical Review* 42, no. 1 (2003): 107–22, for example), a miracle is, by definition, a good thing. Mawson says, "There would be something odd about calling an event a miracle if one did not think it was for the good" ("Miracles and the Laws of Nature," p. 37). Perhaps so, although for our argument what is relevant is that supernatural interventions in the course of nature perpetrated by good agents and by evil agents are alike in this central respect; they both produce a violation of the laws of nature. Were we to encounter one of those, the question would be: What could we infer about its source? That the cause is good cannot be assumed a priori in an argument that seeks to show that an infinitely good supernatural being exists.

9. In the next section of this chapter, we will consider an argument that a being's performing miracles is incompatible with that same being possessing omnibenevolence.

10. Christine Overall, "Miracles, Evidence, Evil, and God: A Twenty-Year Debate," *Dialogue: Canadian Philosophical Review* 45, no. 2 (2006): 358.

11. Overall and I are essentially in agreement on this point. She says,

As those who would defend the argument from evil point out, there is a huge amount of evil in the world—psychological and physical suffering, malnutrition, starvation, pandemics, cruelty, torture, poverty, racism, lynching, sexism, child abuse, assault, war, sudden deaths from natural disasters—the list is appalling. . . . Instead of using miracles to feed a small number, to transform water into wine, or to convert a few people, God could very well be performing miracles that have a much larger effect, especially on the lives of the millions of children whose suffering is particularly incomprehensible to anyone with a sense of justice. The question is why a good God would be concerned with details like the need for wine at a wedding, and yet apparently not be concerned with huge tragedies like the holocaust of six million Jews.

Ibid., p. 360. My claim is that even if some force were to enact some vast repara-tion, like miraculously preventing the Holocaust, we would still not have sufficient evidence for omnibenevolence as long as any other events remain. An omnibenevolent being would not have allowed any such horrors to occur at all if they had been worthy of repair; so a miracle, *in principle*, would neither be consistent with nor be evidence for omnibenevolence.

12. Ibid., p. 359.

13. William Rowe, "Friendly Atheism, Skeptical Theism, and the Problem of Evil," *International Journal for Philosophy of Religion* 59 (2006): 79–92.

14. James Keller, "A Moral Argument against Miracles," *Faith and Philosophy* 12, no. 1 (1995): 54–78.

15. Philosophers and theologians make a distinction between natural and moral evil, or instances of seemingly pointless suffering that result from natural, nonhuman causes, like hurricanes, and cases like child abuse or genocide that humans cause. Religious culture gives us many examples of God's miraculously intervening in both cases.

16. For a more detailed version of this argument, see my chapter "The Paradox of Divine Agency," in *The Impossibility of God*, ed. Michael Martin and Ricki Monnier (Amherst, NY: Prometheus Books, 2003), pp. 313–22.

17. John Hick, *Philosophy of Religion* (Englewood Cliffs, NJ: Prentice-Hall, 1963), pp. 44–45. Hick says,

Suppose, contrary to fact, that this world were a paradise from which all possibility of pain and suffering were excluded. The consequences would be very far-reaching. . . . No one would ever be injured by accident: the mountain-climber, steeplejack, or playing child falling from a great height would float unharmed to the ground; the reckless driver would never meet with disaster. . . . There would be no call to be concerned for others in time of need or danger, for in such a world there could be no real needs or dangers.

To make possible this continual series of individual adjustments, nature would have to work by "special providences" instead of running according to general laws which men must learn to respect on penalty of pain or death. The laws of nature would have to be extremely flexible: sometimes gravity would operate, sometimes not; sometimes an object would be hard and solid, sometimes soft. There could be no sciences, for there would be no enduring world structure to investigate.

18. Theodore Drange, "The Argument from Nonbelief to Atheism," *Religious Studies: An International Journal for the Philosophy of Religion* 29 (1993): 417–32.

19. Christine Overall has an argument that God would not thwart our ability to understand the world by performing miracles. We will consider this argument in more detail shortly.

20. James Keller has argued that for God to put some people into a favorable situation with regard to having their faith fortified or their body of evidence improved while so many others are not provided with the same benefit is unfair. So bias or preferential treatment is yet another reason to conclude that God, if one exists, would not employ miracles in order to achieve some epistemic end. Keller, "Moral Argument against Miracles," p. 62.

CHAPTER 10. FIVE HUNDRED DEAD GODS AND THE PROBLEM OF OTHER RELIGIONS

1. Luke Muehlhauser, "Gods You Don't Believe In," *Common Sense Atheism* (blog), June 5, 2009, http://commonsenseatheism.com/?p=285.

2. H. L. Mencken, *A Mencken Chrestomathy: His Own Selection of His Choicest Writings* (New York: Vintage Books, 1982), pp. 97–98.

3. "Richard Dawkins on Militant Atheism," TED Talk video, 29:14, filmed February 2002, posted April 2007, http://www.ted.com/talks/richard_dawkins_on_militant_atheism.html (accessed July 15, 2011).

4. N. Epley et al., "Believers Estimates of God's Beliefs Are More Egocentric Than Estimates of Other People's Beliefs," *Proceedings of the National Academy of Sciences* 106, no. 51 (2009): 21533–38.

5. For some of the research about our revisionist histories of ourselves, see R. E. Nisbett and T. D. Wilson, "Telling More Than We Can Know: Verbal Reports on Mental Processes," *Psychological Review* 84, no. 3 (1977): 231–59.

6. PEW Forum on Religion and Public Life, *U.S. Religious Knowledge Survey* (Washington, DC: PEW Research Center, September 28, 2010), http://pewforum.org/Other-Beliefs-and-Practices/U-S-Religious-Knowledge-Survey.aspx (accessed July 17, 2011).

7. PEW Forum on Religion and Public Life, *Many Americans Mix Multiple Faiths: Eastern, New Age Beliefs Widespread* (Washington, DC: PEW Research Center, December 9, 2009), http://pewforum.org/docs/?DocID=490#1 (accessed July 17, 2011).

8. Nick Zangwill, "The Myth of Religious Experience," *Religious Studies: An International Journal for the Philosophy of Religion* 40 (2004): 1–2.

9. Dan Barker, *Godless: How an Evangelical Preacher Became One of American's Leading Atheists* (Berkeley, CA: Ulysses Press, 2008). And personal conversations.

10. PEW Forum on Religion and Public Life, *U.S. Religious Landscape Survey: Religious Affiliation—Summary of Key Findings* (Washington, DC: PEW Research Center, 2008), http://religions.pewforum.org/reports (accessed May 24, 2012).

11. Nisbett and Wilson, "Telling More Than We Can Know," pp. 231–59.

12. A short list: Scott Atran, *In Gods We Trust: The Evolutionary Landscape of Religion* (New York: Oxford University Press, 2002); J. L. Barrett, "Exploring the Natural Foundations of Religion," *Trends in Cognitive Sciences* 4, no. 1 (2000): 29–34; Pascal Boyer, *Religion Explained: A Cognitive Theory of Religion* (New York: Basic Books, 2001); Daniel Dennett and Ryan McKay, "The Evolution of Misbelief," *Behavioral and Brain Sciences* 32 (2009): 493–561, especially section 11; Daniel Dennett, *Breaking the Spell* (New York: Viking Press, 2006).

CHAPTER 11. THE F-WORD

* Spoken by Abraham Lincoln during a speech at Plymouth Church in Brooklyn, New York, February 27, 1860.

† From C. S. Lewis, *Mere Christianity*, 1952; based on Lewis's previous works *The Case for Christianity* (a.k.a. *Broadcast Talks*) (1942), *Christian Behavior* (1943), and *Beyond Personality* (1944).

‡ Taken from *The Table Talk of Martin Luther*, trans. William Hazlitt (Philadelphia: The Lutheran Publication Society), p.353.

1. Ludwig Wittgenstein, *Lectures and Conversations: On Aesthetics, Psychology, and Religious Belief*, ed. Cyril Barrett (Berkeley: University of California Press, 1966), p. 55.

2. Douglas Adams, "Is There an Artificial God?" (speech, Digital Biota 2, Cambridge UK, September 1998), http://www.biota.org/people/douglasadams/ (accessed July 15, 2011). Richard Dawkins uses this passage in *The Devil's Chaplain* and in public lectures.

3. W. K. Clifford, "The Ethics of Belief," in *Lectures and Essays*, ed. Leslie Stephen and Frederick Pollock (London: Macmillan, 1886), p. 5.

4. Thomas Gilovich, "Biased Evaluation and Persistence in Gambling," *Journal of Personality and Social Psychology* 44, no. 6 (1983): 1110–26.

5. Hart Blanton and M. Gerrard, "Effect of Sexual Motivation on Men's Risk Perception for Sexually Transmitted Disease: There Must Be Fifty Ways to Justify a Lover," *Health Psychology* 16 (1997): 374–79.

6. Elisha Babad and Y. Katz, "Wishful Thinking—against All Odds" *Journal of Applied Social Psychology* 21 (1991): 1921–38; J. Elster, *Ulysses and the Sirens: Studies*

in Rationality and Irrationality (New York: Cambridge University Press, 1979); J. Elster, *Sour Grapes: Studies of the Subversion of Rationality* (New York: Cambridge University Press, 1981); G. A. Quattrone and A. Tversky, "Causal versus Diagnostic Contingencies: On Self-Deception and the Voter's Illusion," *Journal of Personality and Social Psychology*, 46 (1984): 237–48; O. Svenson, "Are We All Less Risky and More Skillful Than Our Fellow Drivers?" *Acta Psychologica* 47 (1981): 143–48; N. D. Weinstein, "Unrealistic Optimism about Future Life Events," *Journal of Personality and Social Psychology* 39 (1980): 806–20.

7. Jonathan Baron, *Thinking and Deciding* (New York: Cambridge University Press, 2008), p. 216.

8. Nicholas Wolterstorff, *Reason within the Bounds of Religion* (Grand Rapids, MI: Wm. B. Eerdmans, 1984), p. 72.

CHAPTER 12. WHY SO SERIOUS?

1. PEW Forum on Religion and Public Life, *U.S. Religious Landscape Survey: Summary of Key Findings* (Washington, DC: PEW Research Center, 2007), http://religions .pewforum.org/pdf/report-religious-landscape-study-key-findings.pdf (accessed July 17, 2011).

2. Paul Kurtz, "Are Science and Religion Compatible?" *Skeptical Inquirer* 26, no. 2 (2002), http://www.csicop.org/si/show/are_science_and_religion_compatible (accessed July 17, 2011).

3. David Gates, D. Jefferson, and A. Underwood, "The Pop Prophets," *Newsweek*, May 24, 2004, pp. 44–50.

4. William Lobdell, *Losing My Religion: How I Lost My Faith Reporting on Religion in America—and Found Unexpected Peace* (New York: Collins, 2009). For more information, see "William Lobdell: Where's the Courage within Christianity?" FORA.tv video, 4:40, from a discussion at Kepler's Books in Menlo Park, CA, on March 25, 2009, posted by "Kepler's Books," http://fora.tv/2009/03/25/Losing_Religion_William_Lobdell#William _Lobdell_Wheres_the_Courage_within_Christianity (accessed July 17, 2011).

5. Brad J. Bushman et al., "When God Sanctions Killing: The Effects of Scriptural Violence on Aggression," *Psychological Science* 18, no. 3 (March 2007). 6. Sam Wang and Sandra Aamodt, "Your Brain Lies to You," *New York Times*, June 27, 2008, http://www.nytimes.com/2008/06/29/opinion/29iht-edwang.1.14069662 .html?_r=1 (accessed July 31, 2011). Also see Sam Wang and Sandra Aamodt's book titled *Welcome to Your Brain: Why You Lose Your Car Keys but Never Forget How to Drive and Other Puzzles of Everyday Life* (New York: Bloomsbury, 2008).

7. More on the "sin" of curiosity here: Stanley Fish, "Does Curiosity Kill More Than the Cat?" Opinionator, *New York Times*, September 14, 2009, http://fish.blogs. nytimes.com/2009/09/14/does-curiosity-kill-more-than-the-cat/?emc=eta1 (accessed July 31, 2011).

8. Craig Anderson, Mark Lepper, and Lee Ross, "Perseverance of Social Theories: The Role of Explanation in the Persistence of Discredited Information," *Journal of Personality and Social Psychology* 39, no. 6 (1980): 1037–49.

9. C. Daniel Batson, "Rational Processing or Rationalization? The Effect of Discontinuing Information on a Stated Religious Belief," *Journal of Personality and Social Psychology* 32, no. 1 (1975): 176–84.

10. Ibid., p. 180.

11. Ibid., p. 180.

12. Ibid., p. 184.

13. Some useful discussions of noncognitivism and religious speech acts can be found in the following: Theodore Drange, "Is 'God Exists' Cognitive?" *Philo* 8, no. 2 (2006); Malcolm Diamond and Thomas Lizenbury Jr., eds., *The Logic of God* (Indianapolis, IN: Bobbs-Merrill, 1975); Kai Nielsen, *Philosophy and Atheism* (Buffalo, NY: Prometheus Books, 1985).

14. Jonathan Haidt, "Elevation and the Positive Psychology of Morality," in *Flourishing: Positive Psychology and the Life Well-Lived*, ed. C. L. M. Keyes and J. Haidt (Washington, DC: American Psychological Association, 2003), pp. 275–89.

15. "Gaddafi 'to Mediate' in Egypt-Algeria Football Row," *Trend*, November 25, 2009, http://en.trend.az/regions/met/arabicr/1587543.html (accessed July 31, 2011).

16. Justin L. Barrett and Frank C. Keil, "Conceptualizing a Nonnatural Entity: Anthropomorphism in God Concepts," *Cognitive Psychology* 31 (1996): 219–47.

17. Daniel Dennett and Linda LaScola, "Preachers Who Are Not Believers," *Evolutionary Psychology* 8, no. 1 (March 2010): 121–50. See an online version of the article at http://newsweek.washingtonpost.com/onfaith/Non-Believing-Clergy.pdf (accessed July 31, 2011).

18. Ibid., p. 15.

19. Ibid., p. 12.

20. Ibid., p. 16.

21. Ibid., p. 21.

22. Ibid., p. 18.

23. Ibid., p. 25.

24. Ibid., p. 17.

25. Ibid.

26. Daniel Katz and Floyd Allport, *Students' Attitudes: A Report of the Syracuse University Reaction Study* (Syracuse, NY: Craftsman Press, 1931), p. 348.

CHAPTER 13. ATHEISM AND THE CASE AGAINST CHRIST

1. Jeffrey Jones, "In U.S., 3 in 10 Say They Take the Bible Literally," Gallup, July 8, 2011, http://www.gallup.com/poll/148427/Say-Bible-Literally.aspx (accessed July 30, 2011).

2. Antony Flew, "The Presumption of Atheism," in *God, Freedom, and Immortality* (Buffalo, NY: Prometheus Books, 1984), pp. 13–30.

3. A broader discussion of these distinctions and the epistemology of atheism can be found in my article on atheism in the Internet Encyclopedia of Philosophy: Matthew S. McCormick, "Atheism," Internet Encyclopedia of Philosophy, January 19, 2010, http://www.iep.utm.edu/atheism/ (accessed May 23, 2012).

4. Huston Smith, *The World's Religions* (San Francisco, CA: Harper, 1991), p. 235.

5. Emily Pronin, Daniel Y. Lin, and Lee Ross, "The Bias Blind Spot: Perceptions of Bias in Self versus Others," *Personality and Social Psychology Bulletin* 28, no. 3 (2002): 369–81.

6. Julia Duin, "Half of Americans Believe in Angels," *Washington Times*, September 19, 2008, http://www.washingtontimes.com/news/2008/sep/19/half-of -americans-believe-in-angels/ (accessed July 31, 2011).

7. J. N. Findlay, "Can God's Existence Be Disproved?" *Mind* 54 (1948): 176–83; Michael Martin, *Atheism: A Philosophical Justification* (Philadelphia: Temple University Press, 1990); Jordan Howard Sobel, *Logic and Theism, Arguments for and against Beliefs in God* (Cambridge: Cambridge University Press, 2004).

8. For some of the best modern work of this sort see: Sobel, *Logic and Theism*; William Rowe, *The Cosmological Argument* (New York: Fordham University Press, 1998); Graham Oppy, *Ontological Arguments and Belief in God* (New York: Cambridge University Press, 1995); Graham Oppy, *Arguing about Gods* (New York: Cambridge University Press, 2006); Martin, *Atheism: A Philosophical Justification*; Neil Manson, ed., *God and Design* (London: Routledge, 2003); J. L. Mackie, *The Miracle of Theism* (Oxford: Clarendon Press, 1982); Everitt Nicholas, *The Non-Existence of God* (London: Routledge, 2004).

9. PhilPapers, "The PhilPapers Surveys, Preliminary Survey Results," Institute of Philosophy, School of Advanced Study, University of London, November 2009, http://philpapers.org/surveys/ and http://philpapers.org/surveys/results.pl (accessed July 27, 2011). And for a more complete list of philosophical works on atheism, see my annotated bibliography at Oxford Bibliographies Online, s.v. "atheism," http://oxford bibliographiesonline.com/view/document/obo-9780195396577/obo-9780195396577 -0009.xml?rskey=Uy8UxN&result=1&q=atheism#firstMatch (accessed July 31, 2011).

10. Findlay, "Can God's Existence Be Disproved?" pp. 176–83.

BIBLIOGRAPHY

Adams, P., and J. K. Adams. "Confidence in the Recognition and Reproduction of Words Difficult to Spell." *American Journal of Psychology* 73: 544–52.

Aland, Kurt, and Barbara Aland. *The Text of the New Testament: An Introduction to the Critical Editions and to the Theory and Practice of Modern Textual Criticism.* Translated by Erroll F. Rhodes. Grand Rapids, MI: Wm. B. Eerdmans, 1989.

Anderson, Craig, Mark R. Lepper, and Lee Ross. "Perseverance of Social Theories: The Role of Explanation in the Persistence of Discredited Information." *Journal of Personality and Social Psychology* 39, no. 6 (1980): 1037–49.

Asch, S. E. "Effects of Group Pressure upon the Modification and Distortion of Judgments." In *Groups, Leadership, and Men*, edited by H. Guetzkow. New York: Carnegie Press, 1951.

Atran, Scott. *In Gods We Trust: The Evolutionary Landscape of Religion.* New York: Oxford University Press, 2002.

Babad, Elisha, and Yosi Katz. "Wishful Thinking—against All Odds." *Journal of Applied Social Psychology* 21 (1991): 1921–38.

Barker, Dan. *Godless: How an Evangelical Preacher Became One of American's Leading Atheists.* Berkeley, CA: Ulysses Press, 2008.

Baron, Jonathan. *Thinking and Deciding.* New York: Cambridge University Press, 2000.

Barrett, J. L. "Exploring the Natural Foundations of Religion." *Trends in Cognitive Sciences* 4, no. 1 (2000): 29–34.

Barrett, Justin, and Frank Keil. "Conceptualizing a Nonnatural Entity: Anthropomorphism in God Concepts." *Cognitive Psychology* 31 (1996): 219–47.

Basinger, David. "Miracles and Natural Explanations." *Sophia: International Journal for Philosophy of Religion, Metaphysical Theology and Ethics* 26 (1987): 22–26.

———. "Miracles as Evidence for Theism." *Sophia: International Journal for Philosophy of Religion, Metaphysical Theology and Ethics* 29 (1990): 56–59.

———. "Miracles, Evil and Justified Belief: Further Clarification." *Sophia: International*

Journal for Philosophy of Religion, Metaphysical Theology and Ethics 34, no. 2 (1995): 58–62.

Batson, C. Daniel. "Rational Processing or Rationalization? The Effect of Discontinuing Information on a Stated Religious Belief." *The Journal of Personality and Social Psychology* 32, no. 1 (1975): 176–84.

Bell, Vaughan. "Ghost Stories: Visits from the Deceased." *Scientific American*, December 2, 2008. http://www.scientificamerican.com/article.cfm?id=ghost-stories-visits-from-the-deceased.

Benson, Herbert, Jeffery A. Dusek, Jane B. Sherwood, Peter Lam, Charlse F. Bethea, William Carpenter, Sidney Levitsky, Peter C. Hill, Donald W. Clem, Manoj K. Jain, David Drumel, Stephen L. Kopecky, Paul S. Mueller, Dean Marek, Sue Rollins, Patricia L. Hibberd. "Study of the Therapeutic Effects of Intercessory Prayer (STEP) in Cardiac Bypass Patients: A Multicenter Randomized Trial of Uncertainty and Certainty of Receiving Intercessory Prayer." *American Heart Journal* 151 (2006): 934–42.

Blomberg, C. *The Historical Reliability of the Gospels*. Downers Grove, IL: InterVarsity, 1987.

Boyer, Pascal. *Religion Explained: A Cognitive Theory of Religion*. New York: Basic Books, 2001.

Boyer, Paul, and Stephen Nissenbaum, eds. *Salem-Village Witchcraft: A Documentary Record of Local Conflict in Colonial New England*. Boston: Northeastern University Press, 1972.

———. *The Salem Witchcraft Papers*. Vol. 1–3. New York: Da Capo Press, 1977.

Brenner, L. A., D. J. Koehler, and A. Tversky. "On the Evaluation of One-Sided Evidence." *Journal of Behavioral Decision Making* 9 (1996): 59–70.

Bruce, F. F. *The New Testament Documents: Are They Reliable?* Grand Rapids, MI: Wm. B. Eerdmans, 2003.

Bushman, Brad, J. Robert, D. Ridge, Enny Das, Colin W. Key, and Gregory L. Busath. "When God Sanctions Killing: The Effects of Scriptural Violence on Aggression." *Psychological Science* 18, no. 3 (2007): 204–207. http://www.psychologicalscience.org/media/releases/2007/bushman.cfm.

Byrd, Randolph C. "Positive Therapeutic Effects of Intercessory Prayer in a Coronary Care Unit Population." *Southern Medical Journal* 81, no. 7 (1988): 826–29.

Carrier, Richard. "Why the Resurrection Is Unbelievable." In *The Christian Delusion*, edited by John Loftus. Amherst, NY: Prometheus Books, 2010.

Cha, K. Y., D. P. Wirth, and R. A. Lobo. "Does Prayer Influence the Success of In Vitro Fertilization-Embryo Transfer? Report of a Masked, Randomized Trial." *Journal of Reproductive Medicine* 46, no. 9 (2001): 781–87.

Chabris, C., and D. Simons. *The Invisible Gorilla, and Other Ways Our Intuitions Deceive Us.* New York: Crown, 2010.

Clarke, Steve. "Hume's Definition of Miracles Revised." *American Philosophical Quarterly* 36, no. 1 (1999): 49–57.

———. "When to Believe in Miracles." *American Philosophical Quarterly* 34, no. 1 (1997): 95–102.

Clifford, W. K. "The Ethics of Belief." In *The Ethics of Belief and Other Essays*, pp. 70–96. Amherst, NY: Prometheus Books, 1999.

Collier, John. "Against Miracles." *Dialogue: Canadian Philosophical Review* 25 (1986): 349–52.

Cowan, J. L. "The Paradox of Omnipotence." *Analysis* 25, no. 3 (1965): 102–108.

Craig, William Lane. *Assessing the New Testament Evidence for the Historicity of the Resurrection of Jesus.* Lewiston, NY: Edwin Mellen Press, 2002.

———. "The Bodily Resurrection of Jesus." In *Gospel Perspectives I*, edited by R. T. France and D. Wenham, pp. 47–74. Sheffield, UK: JSOT Press, 1980.

———. "The Historicity of the Empty Tomb of Jesus." *New Testament Studies* 31 (1985): 39–67.

Darwin, Charles. *On the Origin of Species.* New York: Grammercy Books, 1979.

De Vries, Hent. "Of Miracles and Special Effects." *International Journal for Philosophy of Religion* 50, no. 1–3 (2001): 41–56.

Dennett, Daniel. *Breaking the Spell: Religion as a Natural Phenomenon.* New York: Viking Press, 2006.

———. *Consciousness Explained.* New York: Little, Brown, 1991.

Dennett, Daniel, and Ryan McKay. "The Evolution of Misbelief." *Behavioral and Brain Sciences* 32 (2009): 493–561.

Diamond, Malcolm L., and Thomas V. Lizenbury Jr., eds. *The Logic of God.* Indianapolis, IN: Bobbs-Merrill, 1975.

Dietl, Paul. "On Miracles." *American Philosophical Quarterly* 5 (1968): 130–34.

Ditto, Peter H., Geoffrey Munro, James Scepansky, Anne Marie Apanovitch. "Motivated Sensitivity to Preference-Inconsistent Information." *Journal of Personality and Social Psychology* 75, no. 1 (1998): 53–69.

Drange, Theodore. "The Argument from Nonbelief to Atheism." *Religious Studies: An International Journal for the Philosophy of Religion* 29 (1993): 417–32.

———. "Incompatible Properties Arguments: A Survey." *Philo: A Journal of Philosophy* 1, no. 2 (1998): 49–60.

———. "Is 'God Exists' Cognitive?" *Philo: A Journal of Philosophy* 8, no. 2 (2005).

———. *Nonbelief and Evil*. Amherst, NY: Prometheus Books, 1998.

Edgell, Penny, Joseph Gerteis, and Douglas Hartmant. "Atheists as 'Other': Moral Boundaries and Cultural Membership in American Society." *American Sociological Review* 71, no. 2 (2006): 211–34.

Ehrman, Bart, and Michael Holmes, eds. *The New Testament: A Historical Introduction to the Early Christian Writings*. New York: Oxford University Press, 2004.

———. *The Orthodox Corruption of Scripture: The Effect of Early Christological Controversies on the Text of the New Testament*. New York: Oxford University Press, 1993.

———. *The Text of the New Testament in Contemporary Research*. Grand Rapis, MI: Wm. B. Eerdmans, 1995.

Elster, J. *Sour Grapes: Studies of the Subversion of Rationality*. New York: Cambridge University Press, 1981.

———. *Ulysses and the Sirens: Studies in Rationality and Irrationality*. New York: Cambridge University Press, 1979.

Epley, N., B. A. Converse, A. Delbosc, G. A. Monteleone, and J. T. Cacioppo. "Believers Estimates of God's Beliefs Are More Egocentric Than Estimates of Other People's Beliefs." *Proceedings of National Academy of Science* 106, no. 51 (2009): 21533–38.

Evans, Stephen. "Critical Historical Judgment and Biblical Faith." *Faith and Philosophy: Journal of the Society of Christian Philosophers* 11, no. 2 (1994): 184–206.

Everitt, Nicholas. "The Impossibility of Miracles." *Religious Studies: An International Journal for the Philosophy of Religion* 23 (1987): 347–49.

———. *The Non-Existence of God*. London: Routledge, 2004.

Farmer, William, Denis M. Farkasfalvy, and O. Cist. *The Formation of the New Testament Canon: An Ecumenical Approach*. New York: Paulist Press, 1983.

Findlay, J. N. "Can God's Existence be Disproved?" *Mind* 54 (1948): 176–83.

Flew, Antony. "The Presumption of Atheism." In *God, Freedom, and Immortality*. Buffalo, NY: Prometheus Books, 1984.

Flynn, James R. "IQ Gains over Time: Toward Finding the Causes." In *The Rising*

Curve: Long Term Gains in IQ and Related Measures, edited by Ulric Neisser, pp. 25–66. Washington, DC: American Psychological Association, 1998.

Frey, D. "Recent Research on Selective Exposure to Information." Edited by L. Berkowitz, pp. 41–80. Vol. 19 of *Advances in Experimental Social Psychology*. New York: Academic Press, 1986.

Gale, Richard. *On the Nature and Existence of God*. Cambridge: Cambridge University Press, 1991.

Gardner, Martin. *Fads and Fallacies in the Name of Science*. New York: Dover, 1957.

Geisler, Norman L. "Replies to Evan Fales: On Miracles & the Modern Mind." *Philosophia Christi* 3, no. 1 (2001): 39–42.

Gilovich, Thomas. "Biased Evaluation and Persistence in Gambling." *Journal of Personality and Social Psychology* 44, no. 6 (1983): 1110–26.

———. *How We Know What Isn't So*. New York: Free Press, 1991.

Greenberg, Daniel. "President Bush's False 'Flashbulb' Memory of 9/11/01." *Applied Cognitive Psychology* 18 (2004): 363–70.

Grim, Patrick. "Against Omniscience: The Case from Essential Indexicals." *Nous*, 19 (1985): 151–80.

Grimby, A. "Bereavement among Elderly People: Grief Reactions, Post-bereavement Hallucinations and Quality of Life." *Acta Psychiatrica Scandinavica* 87, no. 1 (2007): 72–80.

Habermas, Gary. "The Case for Christ's Resurrection." In *To Everyone an Answer: A Case for the Christian World View*, edited by Francis Beckwith, William Lane Craig, and J. P. Moreland, pp. 180–98. Downers Grove, IL: InterVarsity Press, 2004.

———. *The Historical Jesus: Ancient Evidence for the Life of Christ*. Joplin, MO: College Press, 1996.

———. "Resurrection Research from 1975 to the Present: What Are Critical Scholars Saying?" *Journal for the Study of the Historical Jesus* 3, no. 2 (2005): 135–53.

Harris, Sam. *The End of Faith*. New York: W. W. Norton, 2004.

———. *Letter to a Christian Nation*. New York: Alfred A. Knopf, 2006.

———. *The Moral Landscape*. New York: Free Press, 2010.

Heard, Richard. *An Introduction to the New Testament*. New York: Harper and Brothers, 1950.

Hick, John. *An Interpretation of Religion: Human Responses to the Transcendent*. London: Macmillan, 1989.

————. *Philosophy of Religion*. Englewood Cliffs, NJ: Prentice-Hall, 1963.

————. *The Rainbow of Faiths: Critical Dialogues on Religious Pluralism*. Knoxville, TN: SCM Press, 1995.

Hitchens, Christopher. *God Is Not Great: How Religion Poisons Everything*. New York: Twelve Books, 2007.

Holland, Julie. *Weekends at Bellevue: Nine Years on the Night Shift at the Psych ER*. New York: Random House, 2009.

Holland, R. F. "The Miraculous." In *Logical Analysis and Contemporary Theism*, edited by J. Donnelly, pp. 218–35. New York: Fordham University Press, 1972.

Howard-Snyder, Daniel, and Paul K. Moser, eds. *Divine Hiddenness: New Essays*. Cambridge: Cambridge University Press, 2002.

Hubble, Edwin. "A Relation between Distance and Radial Velocity among Extra-Galactic Nebulae." *Proceedings of the National Academy of Sciences* 15, no. 3 (1929): 168–73.

Hughes, C. "Miracles, Laws of Nature and Causation." *Proceedings of the Aristotelian Society*, 66 (1992): 179–205.

Hume, David. *Dialogues concerning Natural Religion*. Edited by Norman Kemp Smith. Oxford: Clarendon Press, 1935.

————. *Enquiry concerning Human Understanding*. Edited by L. A. Selby-Bigge. 1902. Reprint, Oxford: Clarendon Press, 1975.

Keeley, Brian L. "Of Conspiracy Theories." *Journal of Philosophy* 96, no. 3 (1999): 109–26.

Kellenberger, J. "Miracles." *International Journal for Philosophy of Religion* 10, no. 3 (1979): 145–62.

Keller, James A. "A Moral Argument against Miracles." *Faith and Philosophy: Journal of the Society of Christian Philosophers* 12, no. 1 (1995): 54–78.

Koester, Helmut. *Ancient Christian Gospels: Their History and Development*. Valley Forge, PA: Trinity Press, 1992.

————. *Introduction to the New Testament*. Berlin: Walter de Gruyter, 1983.

Korff, Kal, and Michaela Kocis. "Exposing Roger Patterson's 1967 Bigfoot Film Hoax." *Skeptical Inquirer* (July/August, 2004): 35–40.

Kroeber, Theodora. *Ishi: In Two Worlds*. Berkeley: University of California Press, 1961.

Kruger, J., and D. Dunning. "Unskilled and Unaware of It: How Difficulties in Recognizing One's Own Incompetence Lead to Inflated Self-Assessments." *Journal of Personality and Social Psychology* 77 (1999): 1121–34.

Kurtz, Paul. "Are Science and Religion Compatible?" *Skeptical Inquirer* 26, no. 2 (2002). http://www.csicop.org/si/show/are_science_and_religion_compatible.

Landrum, George. "What A Miracle Is." *Religious Studies: An International Journal for the Philosophy of Religion* 12 (1976): 49–57.

Larmer, Robert. "Miracles and Overall: An Apology for Atheism?" *Dialogue: Canadian Philosophical Review* 43, no. 3 (2004): 555–68.

———. "Miracles, Evidence, and God." *Dialogue: Canadian Philosophical Review* 42, no. 1 (2003): 107–22.

Law, Stephen. *Believing Bullshit: How Not to Get Sucked into an Intellectual Black Hole.* Amherst, NY: Prometheus Books, 2011.

Lewis, C. S. *God in the Dock: Essays on Theology and Ethics.* Grand Rapids, MI: Wm. B. Eerdmans, 1994.

Lichenstein, S., and B. Fischoff. "Do Those Who Know More Also Know More about How Much They Know?" *Organizational Behavior and Human Performance* 20 (1970): 159–83.

Lichtenstein, S., B. Fischoff, and B. Phillips. "Calibration of Probabilities: The State of the Art to 1980." In *Judgment under Uncertainty: Heuristics and Biases*, edited by D. Kahneman, P. Slovic, and A. Tversky, pp. 306–34. New York: Cambridge University Press, 1982.

Loftus, Elizabeth. *Eyewitness Testimony.* Cambridge, MA: Harvard University Press, 1996.

———. *The Myth of Repressed Memory: False Memories and Allegations of Sexual Abuse.* New York: St. Martin's Griffin, 1994.

Loftus, John, ed. *The End of Christianity.* Amherst, NY: Prometheus Books, 2011.

Lowe, E. J. "Miracles and Laws of Nature." *Religious Studies: An International Journal for the Philosophy of Religion* 23 (1987): 263–78.

Lowin, A. "Approach and Avoidance: Alternative Modes of Selective Exposure to Information." *Journal of Personality and Social Psychology* 6 (1967): 1–9.

Mackie, J. L. *The Miracle of Theism: Arguments for and against the Existence of God.* Oxford: Clarendon Press, 1982.

Manson, Neil, ed. *God and Design.* London: Routledge, 2003.

Martin, Michael. *Atheism: A Philosophical Justification.* Philadelphia: Temple University Press, 1990.

———. *The Case against Christianity.* Philadelphia: Temple University Press, 1991.

———. "Why the Resurrection Is Initially Improbable." *Philo: A Journal of Philosophy* 1, no. 1 (1998): 63–73.

Martin, Michael, and Ricki Monnier, eds. *The Impossibility of God*. Amherst, NY: Prometheus Books, 2003.

———. *The Improbability of God*. Amherst, NY: Prometheus Books, 2006.

Matson, Wallace. *The Existence of God*. Ithaca, NY: Cornell University Press, 1965.

Mavrodes, George I. "David Hume and the Probability of Miracles." *International Journal for Philosophy of Religion* 43, no. 3 (1998): 167–82.

———. "Miracles and the Laws of Nature." *Faith and Philosophy* 2, no. 4 (1985): 333–46.

Mawson, T. J. "Miracles and Laws of Nature." *Religious Studies: An International Journal for the Philosophy of Religion* 37, no. 1 (2001): 33–58.

McCormick, Matthew S. "Dead as a Doornail: Souls, Brains and Survival." In *The Myth of the Afterlife*, edited by Michael Martin and Keith Augustine. Jefferson, NC: McFarland Books, forthcoming.

———. "The Paradox of Divine Agency." In *The Impossibility of God*, edited by Michael Martin and Ricki Monnier, pp. 258–73. Amherst, NY: Prometheus Books, 2003.

———. "The Salem Witch Trials and the Evidence for the Resurrection." In Loftus, *End of Christianity*, pp. 195–218.

———. "Why God Cannot Think: Kant, Omnipresence, and Consciousness." *Philo: A Journal of Philosophy* 3, no. 1 (2000): 5–19.

McGrew, Tim, and Lydia McGrew. "The Argument from Miracles: A Cumulative Case for the Resurrection of Jesus of Nazareth." In *The Blackwell Companion to Natural Theology*, edited by William Lane Craig and J. P. Moreland, pp. 593–662. Hoboken, NJ: Blackwell, 2009.

McGuire, W. J. "A Syllogistic Analysis of Cognitive Relationships." In *Attitude Organization and Change*, edited by M. J. Rosenberg, C. I. Hovland, W. J. McGuire, R. P. Abelson, and J. W. Brehm, pp. 65–111. New Haven, CT: Yale University Press, 2011.

Mencken, H. L. *A Mencken Chrestomathy: His Own Selection of His Choicest Writings*. New York: Vintage Books, 1982.

Metzger, Bruce. *The Canon of the NT: Its Origin, Development, and Significance*. Oxford: Clarendon Press, 1987.

———. *The Text of the New Testament: Its Transmission, Corruption, and Restoration*. New York: Oxford University Press, 1992.

Moreland, J. P. "Replies to Evan Fales: On Science, Miracles, Agency Theory, & the God-of-the-Gaps." *Philosophia Christi* 3, no. 1 (2001): 48–49.

Morris, Thomas, ed. *The Concept of God*. Oxford: Oxford University Press, 1987.

Neisser, Ulric, and Nicole Harsch. "Phantom Flashbulbs: False Recollections of Hearing the News about *Challenger*." In *Affect and Accuracy in Recall: Studies of "Flashbulb" Memories*, edited by Eugene Winograd and Ulric Neisser, pp. 9–31. New York: Cambridge University Press, 1992.

Nielsen, Kai. *Philosophy and Atheism*. Buffalo, NY: Prometheus Books, 1985.

Nisbett, R. E., and Timothy DeCamp Wilson. "Telling More Than We Can Know: Verbal Reports on Mental Processes." *Psychological Review* 84 (1977): 231–59.

Nisbett, Richard. *Intelligence and How to Get It: Why Schools and Cultures Count*. New York: W. W. Norton, 2009.

Nuyen, A. T. "Rationality, Religiousness, and the Belief in Miracles." *Philosophy Today* 46, no. 4 (2002): 419–28.

Nyhan, Brendan, and Jason Reifler. "When Corrections Fail: The Persistence of Political Misperceptions." *Political Behavior* 32, no. 2 (2010): 303–30.

Oppy, Graham. *Arguing about Gods*. New York: Cambridge University Press, 2006.

———. *Ontological Arguments and Belief in God*. New York: Cambridge University Press, 1995.

Overall, Christine. "Miracles and Larmer." *Dialogue: Canadian Philosophical Review* 42, no. 1 (2003): 123–35.

———. "Miracles as Evidence against the Existence of God." *Southern Journal of Philosophy* 23 (1985): 347–53.

———. "Miracles, Evidence, Evil, and God: A Twenty-Year Debate." *Dialogue: Canadian Philosophical Review* 45, no. 2 (2006): 355–66.

Owen, David. "Hume versus Price on Miracles and Prior Probabilities: Testimony and the Bayesian Calculation." *Philosophical Quarterly* 37 (1987): 187–202.

"Patterson Bigfoot Hoax." *Skeptic* 4, no. 2 (1996): 19.

Pearl, Leon. "Miracles: The Case for Theism." *American Philosophical Quarterly* 25 (1988): 331–37.

Pronin, Emily, Daniel Y. Lin, and Lee Ross. "The Bias Blind Spot: Perceptions of Bias in Self versus Others." *Personality and Social Psychology Bulletin* 28, no. 3 (2002): 369–81.

Pronin, Emily, Thomas Gilovich, and Lee Ross. "Objectivity in the Eye of the

Beholder: Divergent Perceptions of Bias in Self versus Others." *Psychological Review* 111, no. 3 (2004): 781–99.

Purtill, Richard. "Replies to Evan Fales: On Defining Miracles." *Philosophia Christi* 3, no. 1 (2001): 37–39.

Quattrone, G. A., and A. Tversky. "Causal versus Diagnostic Contingencies: On Self-Deception and the Voter's Illusion." *Journal of Personality and Social Psychology* 46 (1984): 237–48.

Randi, James. *Faith Healers*. Buffalo, NY: Prometheus Books, 1989.

———. *Flim Flam! Psychics, ESP, Unicorns and other Delusions*. Buffalo, NY: Prometheus Books, 1982.

Rees, W. Dewi. "The Hallucinations of Widowhood." *British Medical Journal* 4 (1971): 37–41.

Reppert, Victor. "Miracles and the Case for Theism." *International Journal for Philosophy of Religion* 25 (1989): 35–51.

Roberts, Oral. *The Call: Oral Roberts' Autobiography*. New York: Avon Books, 1973.

Ross, Lee, Mark Lepper, and Michael Hubbard. "Perseverance in Self-Perception and Social Perception: Biased Attributional Processes in the Debriefing Paradigm." *Journal of Personality and Social Psychology* 32 (1975): 880–92.

Rowe, William. *The Cosmological Argument*. New York: Fordham University Press, 1998.

———. "Friendly Atheism, Skeptical Theism, and the Problem of Evil." *International Journal for Philosophy of Religion* 59 (2006): 79–92.

———. "Religious Pluralism." *Religious Studies: An International Journal for the Philosophy of Religion* 35 (1999): 139–50.

Sacchi, Dario, Franca Agnoli, and Elizabeth Loftus. "Changing History: Doctored Photographs Affect Memory for Past Public Events." *Applied Cognitive Psychology* 21 (2007): 1005–1022.

Sagan, Carl. *The Demon-Haunted World: Science as a Candle in the Dark*. New York: Ballantine Books, 1996.

Salmon, Wesley. "Religion and Science: A New Look at Hume's Dialogues." Reprinted in *The Improbability of God*, edited by Michael Martin and Ricki Monnier, pp. 167–93. Amherst, NY: Prometheus Books, 2006.

Saver, Jeffrey, and John Rabin. "The Neural Substrates of Religious Experience." *Journal of Neuropsychiatry* 9, no. 3 (1997): 498–510.

Schellenberg, J. L. *Divine Hiddenness and Human Reason*. Ithaca, NY: Cornell University Press, 1993.

————. "Divine Hiddenness Justifies Atheism." In *Contemporary Debates in the Philosophy of Religion*, edied by Peterson and VanArragon, pp. 30–41 Oxford: Blackwell, 2006.

Schick, Theodore, and Lewis Vaughn. *How to Think about Weird Things: Critical Thinking for a New Age*. Boston: McGraw-Hill, 2002.

Shermer, Michael. *Why People Believe Weird Things: Pseudoscience, Superstition, and Other Confusions of Our Time*. New York: Henry Holt, 2002.

Simons, Daniel, and C. Chabris. "Gorillas in Our Midst: Sustained Inattentional Blindness for Dynamic Events." *Perception* 28 (1999): 1059–74.

Simons, Daniel, and Daniel T. Levin. "Failure to Detect Changes to People during a Real-World Interaction." *Psychonomic Bulletin and Review* 5, no. 4 (1998): 644–49.

Smith, Huston. *The World's Religions*. San Francisco: Harper, 1991.

Sobel, Jordan Howard. *Logic and Theism, Arguments for and against Beliefs in God*. New York: Cambridge University Press, 2004.

Svenson, Ola. "Are We All Less Risky and More Skillful Than Our Fellow Drivers?" *Acta Psychologica* 47 (1981): 143–48.

Swinburne, Richard. *The Concept of Miracle*. Basingstoke, UK: Macmillan, 1971.

————. *The Resurrection of God Incarnate*. New York: Oxford University Press, 2003.

Talarico, J. M., and D. C. Rubin. "Confidence, Not Consistency, Characterizes Flashbulb Memories." *Psychological Science* 14 (2003): 455–61.

Wade, K. A., M. Garry, J. D. Read, and S. Lindsay. "A Picture Is Worth a Thousand Lies: Using False Photographs to Create False Childhood Memories." *Psychonomic Bulletin and Review* 9 (2002): 597–603.

Wang, Sam, and Sandra Aamodt. *Welcome to Your Brain: Why You Lose Your Car Keys but Never Forget How to Drive and Other Puzzles of Everyday Life*. New York: Bloomsbury, 2008.

Weeks, J. C., E. F. Cook, S. J. O'Day, L. M. Peterson, N. Wenger, D. Reding, F. E. Harrell, P. Kussin, N. V. Dawson, A. F. Connors Jr., J. Lynn, and R. S. Phillips. "Relationship between Cancer Patients' Predictions of Prognosis and Their Treatment Preferences." *Journal of the American Medical Association* 279 (1998): 1709–14.

Weinstein, Neil. "Unrealistic Optimism about Future Life Events." *Journal of Personality and Social Psychology* 39 (1980): 806–20.

Weintraub, Ruth. "The Credibility of Miracles." *Philosophical Studies: An International Journal for Philosophy in the Analytic Tradition* 82, no. 3 (1996): 359–75.

Weisman, Richard. *Witchcraft, Magic, and Religion in 17th Century Massachusetts.* Amherst: University of Massachusetts Press, 1984.

Wiebe, Phillip H. "Authenticating Biblical Reports of Miracles." *Journal of Philosophical Research* 18 (1993): 309–25.

Wittgenstein, Ludwig. *Lectures and Conversations: On Aesthetics, Psychology, and Religious Belief.* Edited by Cyril Barrett. Berkeley: University of California Press, 1966.

Wolterstorff, Nicholas. *Reason within the Bounds of Religion.* Grand Rapids, MI: Wm. B. Eerdmans, 1984.

Wright, N. T. "Jesus' Resurrection and Christian Origins." *Gregorianum* 83, no. 4 (2002): 615–35.

———. *The Resurrection of the Son of God.* Minneapolis, MN: Fortress Press, 2003.

Wykstra, Stephen J. "The Humean Obstacle to Evidential Arguments from Suffering: On Avoiding the Evils of 'Appearance.'" *International Journal of Philosophy of Religion* 116 (1984): 73–93.

Zuckerman, Phil. *Atheism and Secularity.* Santa Barbara: Praeger, 2009.

INDEX